241-3 Herms = phallos!
102 arms

58 pierced bases for libations

63 boots, 211
77 eggs
90 sumptuary laws
121, 143 ; 169 ; 201

152, 161:
marriage and death

& beards 212
241 Herms

ASPECTS OF GREEK AND ROMAN LIFE

General Editor: H. H. Scullard

★ ★ ★

GREEK BURIAL CUSTOMS

Donna C. Kurtz and
John Boardman

GREEK
BURIAL
CUSTOMS

Donna C. Kurtz

and

John Boardman

CORNELL UNIVERSITY PRESS
ITHACA, NEW YORK

First published 1971

International Standard Book Number 0–8014–0643–9
Library of Congress Catalog Card Number 74–150980

PRINTED IN ENGLAND

CONTENTS

THE GREEK WORLD

LIST OF ILLUSTRATIONS

PLATES

TEXT FIGURES

MAPS

ACKNOWLEDGEMENTS

We are indebted to the scholars and museum authorities named in the Lists of Illustrations for photographs and permission to use them. We have also to thank most warmly many scholars for their advice and assistance of all kinds: Miss O. Alexandris, B. Ashmole, C. Boulter, Miss K. Braun, H. A. Cahn, N. Coldstream, Mrs P. Demolini, V. R. d'A. Desborough, O. Dickinson, P. M. Fraser, H. Giroux, R. A. Higgins, V. Kallipolitis, Mrs S. Karouzou, A. W. Lawrence, H. Lloyd-Jones, P. R. Moorey, G. Neumann, Miss B. Philippaki, C. M. Robertson, H. Robinson, B. Schmaltz, D. Skilardi, A. M. Snodgrass, Miss C. Sourvinou, Miss L. Talcott, H. A. Thompson, Mrs E. Touloupa, J. Travlos, E. Vanderpool, F. Willemsen, Miss V. Wilson. Finally, our gratitude to Marion Cox for the skilful drawings.

PREFACE

THE GREEKS' ATTITUDE to death and their views on the possibility of an after life have been understandably popular subjects with scholars of Greek civilization and religion for as long as Classical antiquity has been studied. Over the last century excavation has revealed new sources of information on these subjects, and these sources have been partially exploited—only partially, because the interests and idiom of the archaeologist and the student of religion have seldom been at one. In fact archaeology can add little to our understanding of what the Greeks *thought* about death. This is best expressed by their writers. It can tell us a very great deal about what they *did* about death. In this, as in other fields, the material evidence supplements the literary evidence without always elucidating it. But we can at least now give a fairly comprehensive account of burial practices at different periods and places in the Greek world, and we can attempt to understand the pictures of funerary rites which appear on vases and in sculpture. The value of this evidence is that it can be closely dated and located, while the remarks of ancient authors may be imprecise in these respects, or may be incomplete since their aim was generally to explain or comment on a particular point and not to describe a whole ceremony. Where late sources are used we have tried to be sure that they relate to the period we are studying. The limitation of all this evidence is that, while it tells us *what* the Greeks did, our understanding of *why* they did it has to depend on what we learn from other sources or our imagination.

The material evidence has not been ignored in the past, but it has not been systematically collected. An exhaustive account of Greek burials lies beyond the possible scope of a volume in this series and beyond the intentions of the authors. Too much that is relevant is still inadequately published and the spate of new evidence makes a definitive study impossible. We have attempted, then, to give a survey of Greek burial practices so far as they can be understood from the evidence of excavation, the study of ancient representations and of ancient authors and inscriptions. We have not gone out of our way to draw detailed deductions from this study about Greek views on the after life, but others may find it a useful source for such speculation. Nor have we dwelt upon the art history of the tomb monuments and offerings. We have, however, tried to indicate what is likely to be of service to the archaeologist or historian, and we believe that a full account of Greek burial practices will take any student of Greece as far on the way to understanding Greek views about death as a study of their poets and philosophers.

The plan we have adopted for the book is one which, we hope, presents the evidence in a way in which it can most easily be used. A major part is devoted to the burial customs of Athens and Attica. This is because the Attic cemeteries are the best known and best published in all periods, because all relevant vase representations are Athenian, and because the literary evidence is dominantly concerned with Athens. The continuity of this account would have been seriously impaired if the very diverse and less complete evidence from the rest of Greece had been considered with it. It has meant, however, that the opening chapters are rather severely archaeological in their content, and the general reader may only begin to recognize the Athens of historians, poets and familiar works of art with the chapters on the Archaic and Classical periods. In the second part of the book the evidence from Greece outside Attica is discussed, more by subject than period, and always with summary reference to Attica. Here it has been possible to take a broader view of some aspects of the subject, such as grave offerings, art, epitaphs and historical problems.

The chronological limits should perhaps be justified. The Bronze Age is omitted, not because we do not believe that the Mycenaeans were Greeks, but because Bronze Age funeral practice is a fundamentally different and wholly archaeological subject. The Bronze Age burials of Attica are, however, discussed, and the problems of the transition to the Iron Age. Roman Greece too is omitted because, although Hellenistic practices died hard, there are many new features relevant rather to Greece as a Roman province or to Christianity. Topographically we have confined ourselves to the Aegean and, selectively, to the farther flung Greek kingdoms of the Hellenistic world. Greece outside Athens is treated in less detail than Athens herself, and Greek colonies summarily and always with an eye to comparisons with homeland customs. The Notes are mainly bibliographical, supplemented by a Select Gazetteer of cemeteries outside Attica.

Dr Kurtz is mainly responsible for the first part of the book, and a more detailed account of some subjects will appear in her study of Athenian white-ground *lekythoi*. Mr Boardman is mainly responsible for the second part of the book, but there has been full collaboration in the final preparation of all chapters. The subject is a vast one, requiring now a variety of specialist studies. We hope to have indicated how illuminating it can be. We hope too that excavators will tackle cemeteries with more in view than bones, pots and jewellery: the principal obstacles in this study have been incomplete excavation and inadequate publication. We apologize for the omissions and generalizations: in such a book they are inevitable.

D. C. K.

Summer, 1970 J. B.

When the Funerall pyre was out, and the last valediction over, men took a lasting adieu of their interred Friends, little expecting the curiosity of future ages should comment upon their ashes, and having no old experience of the duration of their Reliques, held no opinion of such after-considerations.

Sir Thomas Browne: *Hydriotaphia or Urne-Buriall* (1658)

CHAPTER I

INTRODUCTION: FROM BRONZE AGE TO IRON AGE

*But who knows the fate of his bones, or
how often he is to be buried? who hath
the Oracle of his ashes, or whether they
are to be scattered?*

THE PERIOD IN AEGEAN prehistory which we have come to call
the Mycenaean Age can serve as no more than a brief introduction
to our study of Greek burial practices. The monumental tombs
and their treasures have been described many times. Nor can we
trace the lineage of the Greeks of the historical period; we can
only attempt to assess the legacy which the Mycenaeans left,
not to their way of life but to their way of death.

Although the transmission of the 'Mycenaean heritage' to
historic Greece is by no means beyond question, there is evidence
in Bronze Age Greece for cremation, for single inhumation graves,
for burial in simple and in lined pits, and for the use of grave
markers—all of them characteristic also of later practice.

Monumental *tholoi* and rock-cut chamber tombs, which have
been found throughout the Mycenaean world, sheltered the dead
and his 'family'. Vases, some of which probably once contained
offerings of food and drink, weapons, jewellery, and objects
of less certain significance like lamps and scales, could accompany
the dead, who lay on the floor of the chamber in a simple pit;
or, less frequently, on a bier or in a coffin of wood; or in a clay
sarcophagus. Despite the care with which the Mycenaeans
furnished their dead, it is clear that they were not troubled by
them. Tombs were opened, the previous burials were moved
aside, sometimes even despoiled of their offerings, and after fires of
fumigation and purification, another Mycenaean was laid to rest.

The 'cult of the dead', once a generally accepted aspect of Mycenaean religion, has become unfashionable in recent scholarship. An excavator of Mycenae concluded that 'the cult of the dead, either in honour of the common man or of the mighty princes and kings, did not exist in Mycenaean times'. The material remains of the 'cult' are not, it seems, connected with a ritual act which was repeated at prescribed intervals, but with a single rite which was executed during the act of burial. Pits in the chamber floor and niches in the *dromoi* of the tombs received the remains of children or of previous burials, not sacrifices and offerings. Fires fumigated and purified the chamber in preparation for another interment, but there were no sacrificial pyres. The material evidence from Mycenaean graves indicates the performance of rites at the time of burial, like the offering of gifts and libations, but there is no clear evidence for a 'cult of the dead' tended at regular intervals in a prescribed manner. It has been argued that 'there is definite evidence proving the existence of a cult of the dead . . . in post-Mycenaean times', but the evidence from the post-Mycenaean period has not yet received careful study.

The discovery of monumental *tholoi* and chamber tombs must have amazed the Greeks of the historic period. The standard of workmanship and the advanced knowledge of the stonemason's art which their 'ancestors' had attained were indeed remarkable. And it is not at all surprising that men stood in awe of the monuments, when they came upon them. Sometimes the tombs were reused, as in Knossos. Reuse of earlier graves was, in fact, common in cemeteries of ancient Greece in almost all periods. But often the tombs were honoured with the deposit of offerings, more votive than funerary. A similar mark of respect is the erection of enclosure walls around earlier graves—a practice attested in Greece at least as early as the Geometric period. From this period too intrusion into an earlier grave was expiated by placing an offering in it.

Before these marks of respect and piety are taken for evidence of a 'cult of the dead', we must bear in mind the lapse in time between the burial and the bringing of gifts, the uncertain character of the offerings, the irregular tendance of the grave, and the general lack of evidence that any cult act was repeated. In view of the archaeological evidence and in the light of our present knowledge of Greek burial customs, the 'cult of the dead' in the historic period, as in the Mycenaean Age, is most insecurely attested. That these impressive monuments later became associated with legendary history is, however, entirely reasonable.

By the end of the thirteenth century most of the Mycenaean palace sites had been razed. Athens and a few other areas escaped, but the bulwarks of the Mycenaean realm had fallen. An inevitable result of the fragmented political situation, and one which the archaeologist can observe, is the 'multiplicity of regional ceramic variations'. More fundamental aspects of Mycenaean civilization, like manner of dress, burial customs, and the use of terracotta figures, remained unchanged.

We do not know whether the devastation was the work of 'vassal kings' who had risen in revolt or of foreign invaders. The lack of non-Mycenaean objects at these sites suggests either that the invaders did not settle or that the devastation was not the work of foreigners. After the destruction of the palace sites there was apparently a movement of peoples to less accessible and more easily defensible areas. Although neither the precise line of destruction nor the pattern of depopulation can be determined with certainty at present, there is an influx of people in Achaia, along the Aegean-facing coasts of Attica and the Peloponnese, and in Euboea at Lefkandi. Many of these 'refuge centres' sheltered a sizeable number of people of Mycenaean culture who engaged in trade with other centres in the islands and the western coast of Asia Minor. In a period of relative stability this 'miniature Mycenaean *koine*' enjoyed a degree of prosperity, and some graves of the period are rich in characteristic Mycenaean offerings and exotic eastern imports. Trade continued and some sites flourished, but the uniformity of the Mycenaean Age was no more and the prosperity which the *koine* enjoyed was short-lived.

Some time after the middle of the twelfth century Mycenae had suffered a fatal blow. The people who continued to live on the citadel made no attempt to rebuild, and their generally low standard of living is indicated by their simple pottery—the Granary Class. The final destruction of Mycenae is generally considered the end of Mycenaean civilization. In the period which follows there is a change in the type of burial, the characteristic Mycenaean clay figurines disappear, and a ceramic style is developed which is a debased version of the Granary Class. The transition from the end of the Bronze Age to the beginning of the Iron Age is still for us a dark age, with many problems unsolved— many doubtless insoluble. Two bear directly upon the Greek rites of death—one is the use of the pit grave, the other is the rise of the Protogeometric style of pottery.

Earth-cut graves, lined and covered with slabs of stone, are often called cists because of their box-like shape. Single inhumation in a lined pit of this sort had been the standard grave type throughout the Middle Bronze Age and the lined pit is thought by some to have been a Middle Bronze Age form which was reintroduced into Greece at the very end of the Bronze Age by intrusive peoples. However, recent excavations have confirmed the use of this grave type in certain areas in the Mycenaean period, down to 1200 BC, and the number of single inhumation graves, compared with the better known Mycenaean practice of multiple burial in chamber tombs and *tholoi*, is much larger than was once thought. At Argos the number of single inhumation pit graves was sufficiently large to convince the excavators that this method of burial was far from exceptional in the Mycenaean world. Funerary practices in the pit graves appear not to have differed from those in the chamber tombs and *tholoi*.

In addition to the cist graves found in burial grounds where chamber tombs and *tholoi* predominated, there are at least two large sub-Mycenaean cemeteries which were composed almost exclusively of pit graves: on the island of Salamis and in the Athenian Kerameikos. These have no *tholoi* and no chamber tombs, no Mycenaean clay figurines and no Mycenaean dress ornaments. Both cemeteries have lined and unlined pits and grave offerings with possible northern connections. Both cemeteries have a large number of graves in which there are no offerings. The non-Mycenaean type of burial and the absence of characteristic Mycenaean offerings have suggested either an invasion of non-Mycenaeans or the emergence of a servile class. Neither can be proved, although a strong case has been made for the arrival in Greece of people from the north-west, who were characterized by their use of cist graves. In an analysis of the skeletal remains from some of the graves a northern element was recognized, but at present the question of a new people and of their origin remains open. Another possible indication that these were newcomers burying in cists is the location of cemeteries over earlier Mycenaean settlements. But north of Greece cremation and urn-fields were dominant in central Europe throughout the Late Bronze Age and the recent excavation of inhumation burials in cists in Epirus does not necessarily provide evidence for the 'origin' of the grave type or of its possible introduction into Greece.

There is a simpler explanation of the pit grave problem: the grave is perhaps not a new form introduced from outside, but a reassertion of the well-known Middle Bronze Age form which had never been totally displaced by the more elaborate *tholoi* and chamber tombs. In favour of this interpretation is the persistence of Mycenaean elements, even if debased, in the ceramic styles of Greece and of a considerable part of the Aegean world.

Argos appears to have suffered less from destruction than its neighbours at the end of the thirteenth century, and here there is continuity. At Perati on the eastern coast of Attica finds from the cemetery indicate eastern trade connections and a period of some prosperity. Perati is linked to the islands by its pottery and by the presence of cremation graves, known also at Ialysos on Rhodes, and Langada on Kos.

Cremation had been by no means unknown in Greece before this. There are a very few possible cremations from the Middle Bronze Age and scattered examples from the earlier Mycenaean period. The extensive Mycenaean cemetery at Perati has yielded both chamber tombs and cremation graves, some of which can be dated by the presence of seal stones and scarabs. Cremation was an established practice in parts of the Near East and its appearance in Greece in association with objects of Levantine

origin is not altogether surprising. The introduction of cremation to the Greek mainland seems to have been gradual. At
Argos, Perati, in the Athenian Kerameikos and on the island of
Salamis some cremation was practised concurrently with inhumation without any apparent distinction in rites. The association of cremation graves with eastern trade has been noted and
links with Troy VI have been suggested. It is, however, important
to bear in mind that at approximately the same time cremations
were replacing inhumations in barrows throughout central
Europe.

Cremation graves of the post-Mycenaean period in Athens
and on the island of Salamis, at Lefkandi in Euboea and at Argos
are secondary, that is the actual burning of the corpse did not
take place in the grave. An excavated pit accommodated the ash
urn which was covered with earth and probably marked by a
low mound. This type of cremation grave inaugurated a method
of burial which was dominant for well over a century in Attica,
but in the Argolid cremation remained relatively uncommon.
However, the chronology of the graves from Athens and Salamis
on the one hand and the Argolid on the other, and the terminology
of the ceramic styles associated with them, remain a source of
controversy.

By the middle of the eleventh century the Protogeometric
style had emerged. We do not know if the style evolved from the
'sub-Mycenaean' of the Argolid or if it was created in Attica;
whether there was one point of origin or whether similar styles
developed independently in other areas like Thessaly. Protogeometric pottery displays regional characteristics, but a uniform
technique and style—a uniformity which reflected a more stable
period when communications were restored and regional isolation
was coming to an end. There is some uniformity in burial
practices also, with only occasional examples of the continued
use of *tholoi* or chamber tombs in the Bronze Age manner—in
Crete, Thessaly, at Delphi, and in Messenia where we would have
expected a total break. Inhumation remained the preference of
much of the Greek world, but in Athens and Crete cremation
became the dominant practice, and, as the Protogeometric

period passes, we begin to discern in the Greek cities that individuality in the treatment of burials and grave construction which will occupy us much in later chapters. Greece had entered the Iron Age.

The archaeological evidence we have reviewed is the stuff of prehistory—bones, stones and pots. We have no written descriptions of a Mycenaean burial, but there is one aspect of funerary procedure common to both prehistoric and historic Greece which we can investigate from representational evidence—the lament for the dead.

Painted clay sarcophagi of the end of the Bronze Age from Tanagra in Boeotia have representations of mourners (Fig. 1).

Fig. 1 Mycenaean mourners painted on sarcophagi from Tanagra

They appear either singly or in procession, raising both hands to their heads. The rendering of the pose and gesture is schematic, but immediately recognizable as that of the mourners shown at the bier and around the grave on Geometric vases, Archaic clay plaques and vases, and on white-ground *lekythoi* of the Classical period. The scene on one sarcophagus, recently found, shows two women placing a body within a sarcophagus.

Clay figurines are characteristic Mycenaean offerings, both funerary and votive. Towards the end of the Bronze Age a variation on the well-known standing goddess figure is developed with both hands placed on the head. The clay mourners of the Geometric and Archaic periods repeat the gesture virtually unchanged. So far the Mycenaean mourners have been found in Attica at Perati, on Naxos at Kamini, and on Rhodes at Ialysos—sites which have been considered centres of the 'miniature Mycenaean *koine*'. At these sites there are chamber tombs, offerings of a similar nature and, except on Naxos, definite cremation graves. The terracottas from Perati and Ialysos stood in groups of three and four on the rims of flaring bowls—a type of vessel occurring in graves as early as the Middle Bronze Age in Crete, in clay or metal but without figure attachments. It continues to be found in mainland graves of the historic period. Some have been found with their original contents of food and this seems to have been their main use.

The lament for the dead remained an essential part of Greek funerary procedure. A more lasting embodiment of grief for a lost loved one—a painting on a sarcophagus, or on a vase, or a clay mourner figure—accompanied the dead whose family had performed the burial with the honoured funerary lament.

CHAPTER II

THE END OF
THE BRONZE AGE

TRADITIONALLY THE FOUNDER of Athens was Theseus who, on the death of his father Aegeus, settled all the residents of Attica in one city. But Athens had an earlier history which mythology alludes to and archaeology is discovering. In such a record the evidence from burials is important and, although our main interest in this section is not with the Bronze Age, but with Athens, it is necessary to review briefly the earlier evidence, since both the topography and types of burial are relevant to what comes later.

It is with the full Mycenaean period of the Late Bronze Age that we discern Athens as a city and begin that record of her cemeteries which can be traced without break into the Hellenistic period. Initially the city was the Acropolis and its slopes, eventually extending north and west beyond the *peripatos* road which followed the foot of the Acropolis. In the thirteenth century its 'Cyclopaean' walls were built. When the threat of attack came the northern entrance to the citadel, which led up from the *peripatos* in a relatively easy ascent, was no longer satisfactory. The path and the entrance were blocked and new defences were thrown up. On the site of the old ascent a few small houses were built, but growing insecurity forced the inhabitants to abandon their new homes and to move inside the Acropolis. After building an underground reservoir to ensure a supply of water during attack, the Athenians withdrew within their walls and prepared for the worst. But Athens was spared and the underground reservoir went out of use, although the people continued to occupy the citadel. There was still a feeling of insecurity.

In the lower town burials had begun in the area west of the Acropolis in the Bronze Age (Map 2). The number of Late Bronze Age graves, their situation and the continued use of the land for burials over a long period of time, suggest that this was a cemetery at least as early as the Mycenaean period for one group of Athenians. A western site for a cemetery was preferred in a number of Mycenaean towns, and in Athens the land west of the Acropolis remained a major burial ground in the historic period.

In Mycenaean Attica the chamber tomb is the commonest grave type. There are some *tholoi*, but none has been found in Athens and the soft rock of the lower slopes of the Areiopagos and Kolonos Agoraios was better suited to the construction of chamber tombs, groups of which were found throughout the Agora. Recently a chamber tomb was discovered south of the Acropolis, near the Ilissos River.

In Athens itself single inhumation in simple pits is the second principal form of burial. The grave is generally nothing more than a rectangular shaft cut into the rock or dug out of the earth, the sides of which are roughly vertical. Unlike the chamber tombs, pit graves were not regularly opened for reuse. Generally the offerings were fewer and more modest, but it does not necessarily follow that the distinction was one of class or wealth, and some pit graves are richer than chamber tomb burials. Pit graves are sometimes found very close to chamber tombs and initially some association may have been intended, but many have been found in areas where no chamber tombs are known.

Outside Athens several Mycenaean sites have been found in the Attic countryside (Map 1). It seems that the Mycenaean cemeteries on the west coast of Attica went out of use in an advanced stage of the Late Bronze Age and that subsequently the east coast enjoyed a higher level of material culture, while the west lost some of its population and may have been partly abandoned. Further excavation might, however, alter this picture.

In Attica there are *tholoi*, chamber tombs, pits, both lined and unlined, cremation burials, and pits with short *dromoi*, at present known only from Perati. The *tholoi* of Marathon, Menidi and Thorikos have yielded offerings of gold, silver, ivory and obsidian, as well as pottery. The horse burial at Marathon, where two men were buried in the *tholos* and two horses were carefully laid out in the *dromos*, is unique in Attica.

CHAPTER III

THE EARLY IRON AGE

Time, which antiquates antiquities, and
hath an art to make dust of all things,
hath yet spared these minor monuments.

SUB-MYCENAEAN (12TH–11TH CENTURIES BC)

THERE ARE TWO LARGE groups of graves whose pottery has been assigned to the sub-Mycenaean style. They have been mentioned in connection with the problem of establishing the relative date for ceramic styles of Attica and the Argolid at the end of the Bronze Age. One group is the 'Arsenal Necropolis' on the island of Salamis, the other is the 'Pompeion Cemetery' in the Athenian Kerameikos, each with more than one hundred burials. The former group has never been published in full, the latter is well-published and forms the nucleus of any study of sub-Mycenaean burials.

The 'Pompeion Cemetery' lay to the west of the Classical Agora and Acropolis, on the north bank of the Eridanos stream (Map 5). As in the Mycenaean period there were burials in the area of the later Agora, primarily on the slopes of the Areiopagos and on Kolonos Agoraios, the hill which was to mark its western boundary (Map 2). But in the area of the later Pompeion the first burials are post-Mycenaean.

In other parts of Athens there are a few burials of this date: north of the Acropolis, near the site of the later Acharnian Gate; south of the *peribolos* of the Olympieion, in the land bounded by the Ilissos River; and on Erechtheion Street, in the area of the later Haladian Gate, where a sub-Mycenaean grave lay beneath the foundation of an enclosure erected in the Classical period. The position of the grave indicates that the builders of the enclosure (*peribolos*) were aware of earlier graves, but were uncertain of the exact location. On the Acropolis itself there were fourteen graves—cists of small dimensions—one probably the grave of an adult, the others almost certainly of children.

Graves in the Pompeion and Arsenal cemeteries appear to have been laid out according to a plan. The Salamis graves lay side by side in seven rows and the Pompeion graves also lay close together in roughly parallel rows. Here, however, the original plan was not carried through and later graves on the periphery are irregular.

The sub-Mycenaean graves were roughly rectangular shafts cut into earth or bed-rock. The principle of burial—inhumation in a shaft—was the same in almost all cases and only the method of construction varied. The most carefully constructed type and the one which is most characteristic of the period is the slab-lined and covered pit—the cist. All four sides of the shaft were lined with stone slabs set vertically to support cover slabs. There were normally two or three slabs on each of the long sides and one on each end with small stones in the interstices. These sub-Mycenaean cists differ from those of the Middle Bronze Age in their larger dimensions, and while Middle Bronze Age burials were contracted, the sub-Mycenaean dead lay on their backs fully extended. Some Salamis vases appear to be stylistically earlier than the Kerameikos vases and the position of the dead in the Salamis graves also suggests an earlier date: a somewhat contracted position required by the modest dimensions of the shaft.

Sometimes the burial shaft was not lined with large slabs. Instead ledges, either cut into the sides of the shaft or built up with small stones, supported cover slabs, but the graves are the same size as the cists. Shafts cut out of the rock often lacked a stone lining. A third type of grave had neither side nor cover slabs, and the dead lay in a simple shaft which was generally shallower and smaller. These graves served adults and children. There was probably a protective cover of wood or perhaps even a wooden coffin, but all traces have disappeared.

The orderly arrangement of graves in the Pompeion and Arsenal cemeteries suggests that there was some method of marking the grave, but no markers have been found. There was a small layer of stones heaped over two graves in the Pompeion cemetery, one an inhumation, the other a cremation, and the excavators thought that these were originally part of marking mounds.

Inhumation was the standard method of burial. Cremation which had been used rarely for burials in Attica in the Mycenaean period, gradually became better established, and in the Salamis necropolis there were two cremations, in the Pompeion three. The cremations were secondary—the actual burning took place elsewhere, and the collected ashes were deposited in a vessel which stood in a roughly circular pit, its sides revetted with stone, and covered by a slab or a layer of small stones. A coarse jug was the ash urn for one of the Salamis cremations. All three of the Pompeion urns were neck-handled amphorae, standing in pits similar to the type described. The neck-handled amphora was known in the Bronze Age, but its great period of popularity as an ash urn came during the Protogeometric and Geometric periods. Recent excavations in Athens have produced more cremation burials of the sub-Mycenaean period. Cremation, then, was not introduced suddenly, nor was its appearance linked to the emergence of the Protogeometric style. The presence of sub-Mycenaean vases in cremation burials, and the existence of cremation graves among sub-Mycenaean inhumations, confirm the gradual establishment of the practice and argue against a major change in the population.

Grave offerings were neither numerous nor spectacular (Fig. 2). Some graves had none, others had a few pieces of pottery, lying in the burial shaft, around the dead, or around the ash urn. Oil-flasks, stirrup-jars and *lekythoi* were the most common, the *lekythoi* becoming dominant, especially in the Pompeion graves.

Apart from pottery there is simple jewellery in some graves, usually of bronze. Dress fastenings appear in two forms—long straight pins and curved *fibulae* or 'safety-pins'. The bronze *fibulae* continued the Mycenaean tradition, but the long straight pins are new, and a northern feature. Their appearance in pairs, one on either shoulder of the dead, who is normally a woman, has been associated with the introduction of the Doric *peplos*. Small spirals for the finger, ear, or the hair, continued the Mycenaean practice, but there are also new forms. Rings have been found in

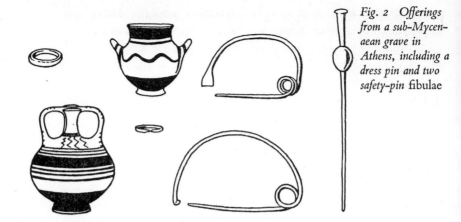

Fig. 2 *Offerings from a sub-Mycenaean grave in Athens, including a dress pin and two safety-pin fibulae*

the graves of men, women, and children, but they are most numerous in the graves of women. In one of the Pompeion graves there were twenty rings, as many as three on a finger. There is little other jewellery.

PROTOGEOMETRIC (11TH–10TH CENTURIES BC)

The Protogeometric period heralds a new style of pottery and the gradual dominance of cremation for adults. Graves which belong to the transitional stage have been found in various parts of Athens, but are most numerous in the Kerameikos area (Map 5). Here sub-Mycenaean graves had been concentrated on the north bank of the Eridanos stream, in the 'Pompeion Cemetery'. Protogeometric graves were most numerous on the south side of the stream, in an area approximately 100 m. west of the Pompeion burials. The earliest graves on the south bank lay in the easternmost part of the area, closest to the sub-Mycenaean cemetery on the opposite bank, while graves in the 'Pompeion Cemetery' which have been assigned to the transitional and Early Protogeometric period lay on the periphery to the north and west.

There are transitional graves known from other parts of Athens, generally from the same areas where sub-Mycenaean burials have been found (Map 2). Not far from the Kerameikos a large group of graves was found on Kriezi Street, the earliest burials

being inhumations in cists and cremations in urns of the sub-
Mycenaean style. The presence of cremations and objects of iron
with vases of the sub-Mycenaean style is of great importance for
the question of the introduction of cremation into Athens.

Graves with vases decorated in the full Protogeometric
style have been found over a wider area of Athens than the sub-
Mycenaean, but still the total number is small. Most are those in
the Kerameikos, mentioned already. In the Agora burials were
still made on Kolonos Agoraios and west of the Hephaisteion.
In the north-central Agora, beneath the Temple of Ares, a Protogeometric grave had been placed in the *dromos* of a Mycenaean
chamber tomb, the simple shaft grave of a five year old child
lying obliquely across it. Only one end of the shaft had cover slabs,
and around the burial a ring of small stones had been carefully
laid, as if to mark the spot of interment. In the upper fill of the
chamber tomb there were some sherds and human bones, which
the excavators identified as disturbed Protogeometric burials.
A Protogeometric grave lay in the collapsed roof of another
Mycenaean chamber tomb, beneath the Stoa of Attalos. We
mention these graves in some detail since reuse of Mycenaean
tombs in the historic period is often cited as evidence for a cult
of the dead, but the Mycenaean and Protogeometric burials
were separated in time by at least two hundred years and those
who dug the Protogeometric graves were either unaware of the
earlier burials or intentionally disregarded them. North of the
Acropolis a Protogeometric grave on Lykourgos Street is interesting, since the area was the site of a large Classical cemetery, just
outside the Acharnian Gate. Another large Classical cemetery,
outside the Diocharian Gate—the area of modern Syntagma
Square in central Athens—has yielded a few Protogeometric
sherds, but these are the only Protogeometric finds on the eastern
side of the city. Slightly west of Syntagma Square, beneath the
Metropolis Cathedral, there were two Protogeometric graves and
further excavation in the area might reveal an earlier sequence of
burials of which the Diocharian Gate cemetery was a later extension.

South of the Acropolis there were a number of groups of
Protogeometric graves. One lay on the slopes of the Acropolis,

between the Odeion of Herodes Atticus and the Avenue of Dionysos Areiopagitikos. Further south on Erechtheion Street another group lay inside an enclosure which had been erected in the Classical period, and on the Hill of the Muses a Protogeometric grave was found.

Protogeometric finds outside the city (Map 1) are not numerous and the concentration of the style in Athens itself perhaps reflects a continued feeling of insecurity and reluctance to inhabit less easily defensible areas. The conditions which had encouraged the people of the coasts and plains of Attica to seek refuge in Athens at the end of the Bronze Age were, it seems, still not sufficiently settled to favour return to the countryside. At Marathon there are a few late Protogeometric graves from an otherwise Geo-metric cemetery and at Eleusis some Protogeometric ash urns in lined and covered pits were found in an early, largely un-published excavation of the site. There are also some unpublished Protogeometric vases from Merenta which are said to have been ash urns.

At present the only cemetery known outside Athens is, in fact, scarcely outside the city, at Nea Ionia, a suburb about 7 km. from Athens on a tributary of the river Kephisos. Graves of adults and children lay inside a curved wall, probably a *peribolos*. The natural situation of the cemetery—a rocky hillside by a river, probably along a major road—has been compared with that of the Kerameikos cemeteries and the types of burials and offerings are also similar.

The standard method of burial for children was inhumation, for adults cremation. The types of grave are basically those of the preceding period, but there is a general tendency towards simpler construction. The number of carefully constructed cists is small (Pl. 1); a few had floors of small stones, but unlined and built-up pits are more common. In the latter ledges, either built up or cut out from the sides of the shaft, supported cover slabs, or wooden beams were laid over the dead.

Cremation graves have been found in large numbers in Proto-geometric cemeteries. The gradual establishment of this method of burial, the appearance of inhumation and cremation graves in the same cemetery, and the identical offerings, suggest that the method of burial chosen became largely a matter of personal preference. Where and how the body was burnt is still not clear. Protogeometric cremations were, however, almost certainly secondary. Few cremation pyres have been discovered, although traces of burning have been found around some graves. In the Nea Ionia cemetery there were two inhumation graves, three cremations, and two pyres. The pyres have been explained as 'surface pyres' or disturbed 'cremations without urns'. In both the Kerameikos and the Agora there were a few pits in which there were no urns and no urn holes, only cremated remains. It is uncertain whether these are remains of original cremation pyres or of simplified secondary cremation burials.

The standard cremation grave was a pit, square or rectangular, the largest being too small to permit the cremation of an adult in an extended position. In the floor of the pit a round hole was cut to accommodate the urn, but occasionally there were two holes or compartments in the pit, one for the urn, the other for the remains of the pyre. Sometimes the sides of the hole were revetted with slabs. Ash urns, regularly amphorae, contained the cremated remains gathered from the pyre and occasionally jewellery and other valued objects. On the basis of skeletal analysis and an examination of the offerings—neither being an infallible test—it has been suggested that neck-handled amphorae held the ashes of men and belly-handled amphorae the ashes of women. There are, however, exceptions and it seems that the choice of amphora was not too strictly observed. Also, towards the close of the Protogeometric style there is a tendency for the shoulder-handled amphora to replace the belly-handled one for female burials.

The mouth of the urn was closed by a vessel, a slab, sherd, or a metal boss; the urn hole by an additional slab, large sherd, or a packing of clay and stones. In the pit itself there was often a thin layer of ash or burnt sherds and animal bones, presumably the remains of the cremation pyre or of burnt offerings. The pyre debris was normally gathered into a heap at the end of the pit opposite the urn hole and earth was thrown in to fill.

Protogeometric graves were probably marked by a small mound of earth. There are, at present, only two graves which are known to have been marked in a different way, both of them cremation burials in the Kerameikos. Above the urn, at approximately ground level, stood an amphora which presumably had been set up as a marker. In both graves the ash urns were belly-handled amphorae as were the marking vases; their bases were intact. One of the graves was further distinguished by a small limestone slab which stood on the end of the grave opposite the marking amphora. The ash urns were late Protogeometric and some of the accessory vases were Early Geometric in style. These are the earliest post-Mycenaean grave markers known from Attica. The fragments of large vases which were found on top of cover slabs of an inhumation grave in the Agora and on top of one of the pyres at Nea Ionia may also have been markers.

The offerings found in Protogeometric graves are only slightly more varied than those of the preceding period, but they are found in graves more regularly (Fig. 3). Offerings in inhumation burials are often miniatures, suitable for children. Normally they lay around the dead in no apparent order, but two graves in the Agora had small niches cut into the sides of the pit for offerings. In cremation graves offerings lay inside the ash urn or outside around its shoulder or base. These were often complete and unburnt, whereas those in the grave pit were sherds. Only in a few

Fig. 3 Offerings from a Protogeometric grave in Athens including two dress pins

instances could the vases be restored completely and for this reason it has been suggested that some were placed around the pyre and, after the body had been cremated, gathered indiscriminately with the pyre remains.

The vases most commonly found in Protogeometric graves are *lekythoi* (they are less numerous in cremations), bowls, cups and jugs. *Kalathoi* (basket-like vases) continue into the Geometric period, and are frequently used as urn covers. Another shape which occurs in the Protogeometric style, but which has no Mycenaean antecedent, is the *pyxis*, a small globular, lidded vessel, also used as an urn cover. A distinctive coarse ware with incised decoration for bowls, beads, whorls, bell-shaped dollies with movable legs and *pyxides* with roughly anthropomorphic appearance (Fig. 3, top left) has been found in Protogeometric and Geometric graves in Attica, Corinthia, and the Argolid. Parallels have been sought in the Balkans, but the origin, development and distribution of the ware remain uncertain. Other clay figures were decorated in the vase-painter's technique, and are the earliest post-Mycenaean terracottas known from Attica. One, a stag, lay in the pyre fill of a cremation grave. The other, a small terracotta horse with wheels attached to its legs, was found in a child's grave recently discovered west of the Hephaisteion.

Very little jewellery has been found in Protogeometric graves: a few pins and *fibulae* and simple spirals, rings and bracelets, most of them from the graves of children. Pins and *fibulae*, of iron or bronze, are found in inhumation and cremation graves. In a child's grave in the Agora a long pin was found in place over each shoulder where the dress had been secured. In cremation graves the pins normally lay inside the urn and they show signs of exposure to intense heat, so the dead must have been both buried and burned in their clothes. Spirals of bronze or gold were still worn, and bronze rings and bracelets, mostly by the young.

Weapons now begin to appear in graves in some numbers for the first time since the Bronze Age. Bronze and iron spearheads have been found inside cinerary urns and outside them. Bronze bosses, generally assumed to have been shield bosses, covered the mouths of urns, sometimes the boss pointing up, sometimes down into the mouth. One closed the mouth of a belly-handled amphora, but the others neck-handled amphorae. Swords were sometimes treated in a special way: the blade was bent around the neck of the ash urn, while the hilt was placed with the cremated remains or left outside in the pyre fill.

From the excavated evidence we can be reasonably sure that offerings of food and drink were brought to the grave, and that some were subjected to fire. Animal bones have been found associated with cremations and inhumations, and other food offerings are perhaps indicated by the complete unburnt, lidded vessels found in many graves. The evidence for offerings of drink depends largely on the number of cups and jugs found in the graves and the area near by.

1, 2 Two simple grave types in Athens: an open Protogeometric cist (*left*) and a child burial in a pot, with cup offerings by its mouth (*right*).

3 Offerings from an Athenian Geometric grave including a gold band and clay models of horses, fowl, a mule carrying four jars and a pomegranate.

4, 5 Funeral scenes on Athenian grave craters showing (*above*) the *prothesis* with mourners, and (*below*) the *ekphora* with the bier placed on a cart.

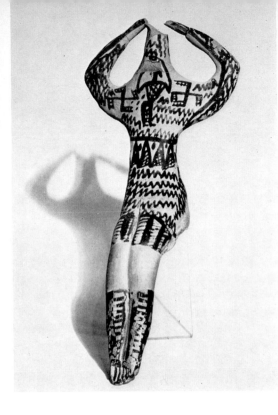

6, 7 Geometric offerings in Athens: *left*, a seated clay mourner from an offering deposit, decorated with painted Geometric patterns and a mourning figure; and (*below*) clay model 'granaries' set on a lidded chest with animal heads at each end.

8 Two pairs of model clay boots from ninth-century graves.

9, 10 Offering deposits of vases from burials of the late eighth
century (*above*) and of about 640 BC (*below*) in Athens.

11–13 Athenian funeral furniture: *top left*, a black-figure '*phormiskos*' with a scene of *prothesis* of a woman (Myrine), with mourners; *above*, a black-figure 'gaming table' with four mourners; and (*left*) a black-figure *loutrophoros*-amphora – a ritual shape showing mourners both painted and in the round on the handle.

14 Athenian funeral vases: a clay jug showing a *prothesis*, with modelled women, snakes and a flower at the lip.

15 Athenian funeral vases: a black-figure bowl with clay mourners seated on the handles.

16 A clay model of an *ekphora* (the horses missing) with attendant horseman, from Vari in Attica. Mourners stand by the bier and a child has crawled on to the shroud, beneath which the body is hidden.

17, 18a, b Funeral vases from a mid-seventh-century deposit in Athens: a sphinx *thymiaterion* (*right*) and pedestalled craters with foreparts of griffins and hens (*below*).

CHAPTER IV

THE GEOMETRIC PERIOD: 9th—8th CENTURIES BC

*How the bulk of a man should sink into
so few pounds of bones and ashes, may
seem strange unto any who considers
not its constitution, and how slender a
masse will remain upon an open and
urging fire of the carnall composition.*

THE CEMETERIES

BY THE GEOMETRIC PERIOD Athens had a developed system of
roads linking principal settlement areas with centres in the
Attic countryside—to judge from the situation of excavated
graves which lined the roadsides now as they had from the
Mycenaean period (Maps 2, 3). Significant is the concentration
of graves near known gates in the fifth-century Themistoclean
Wall, since outside these lay the cemeteries of the Classical and
Hellenistic periods.

In the Kerameikos graves were most numerous north and
south of the Eridanos Stream. The South Cemetery lay slightly
westward and diagonally across from contemporary graves in the
North Cemetery. This lay to the east, nearer the course of the
later city wall (Map 5). In the South Cemetery the oldest Geometric graves lay to the west where there were sub-Mycenaean
and Protogeometric burials, and the later Geometric graves to the
east. In the North Cemetery the early graves lay near the sub-
Mycenaean and Protogeometric burials and the later graves
spread northwards. Further to the north—the site of the Classical
Erian Gate—there were some later Geometric graves with the
so-called Dipylon vases, and graves recently excavated along
Kriezi and Piraeus streets continue to reveal the growth of the

Geometric burial grounds. The amalgamation of the North
and South cemeteries and their extension probably reflect the
growth and prosperity of Geometric Athens.

Although the well-published Kerameikos excavation is our
principal source of material, excavations in other parts of the
city have produced Geometric graves in some numbers. North of
the Erian Gate, on Sappho Street, there were a few, and further
north, near the Acharnian Gate, there were others. At present
few Geometric burials are known from the eastern side of the
city—a small group, well within the course of the Classical
wall, south-east of the Acharnian Gate. To the south Geometric
graves have been found near three Classical gates. The Olympieion area and the land to the south along the Ilissos River—
the reputed site of Kynosarges—have yielded a sizeable number.
This burial ground, which lay outside the Diomeian Gate and along
the road which led to the coast, seems to have been used for a
considerable period of time. Geometric graves recently found on
Makrygianni Street probably lay on the road which passed out of
the city through the Itonian Gate. The greatest concentration is
around the Haladian Gate, through which passed the road to
Phaleron. To the west a Geometric grave was found on the
Pnyx, and further west in the area of the Piraeus Gate several have
been excavated. The Agora graves, including those on the slopes
of the Areiopagos and on Kolonos Agoraios, are soon to be
published.

Outside Athens there are few cemeteries known in Attica from
the end of the Bronze Age to the beginning of the Geometric
period. The absence of settlements and cemeteries is possibly due
to the unsettled conditions at the close of the Bronze Age. With
the evolution of the Protogeometric style there seems to have
been a return to a more settled way of life, but apparently not
until the Geometric period did men return in numbers to the
coasts and plains of Attica. The earliest post-Bronze Age settlements in the Piraeus date from this time. Some of the Geometric
sites had been Bronze Age settlements, others were new foundations. Most of those which have been excavated lie in the southern
part of Attica, and their pottery represents a well-advanced stage

of the Geometric style, but Eleusis, Marathon and Merenta are among the few where some earlier pottery of the Protogeometric and transitional styles has been found (Map 1). The cultural, if not political, unity of Attica in the Geometric period is apparent from the similarity of grave groups and their furnishings.

CREMATION

Cremation ceased to be a preferred manner of burial in Attica at the close of the Protogeometric period. In the Geometric, as in the Archaic and Classical periods, the people of Attica both cremated and inhumed. In different cemeteries different methods were dominant and the manner of burial seems to have been a matter of personal or family preference.

The types of graves were generally those of the preceding period, although with greater variety. The cremation burials are regularly secondary, although very few pyres have been identified with certainty. As in the Protogeometric period the most common type of cremation grave was the pit in which the ash urn lay in a separate hole. The urn holes are now usually too shallow for their vases, which are closed not by a slab but by a protective packing of clay or small stones, or a few courses of dry-stone masonry (Figs. 4, 5). Some vases stood in small slab cists of their own, and these protective boxes, which also took the form of cylindrical drums, were often receptacles for metal ash urns.

Fig. 4   Two Athenian cremation graves with ash urn, marking stones and a vase in position

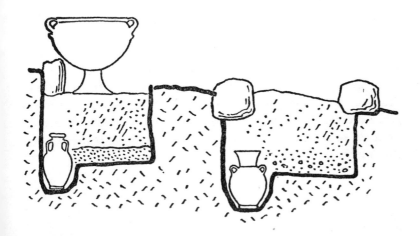

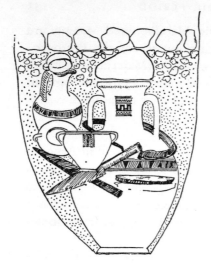

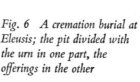

Fig. 5 *A cremation burial in the Athenian Agora. A sword has been wrapped around the neck of the urn and spear heads placed beside it*

Fig. 6 *A cremation burial at Eleusis; the pit divided with the urn in one part, the offerings in the other*

In the more common type of cremation burial, with the urn in a small hole in the pit, the material from the pyre was collected in the end of the pit opposite to the urn, or it was spread in a thin layer over the floor of the pit (Fig. 4). The composition of the pyre fill is the same as before: ash, burnt earth, carbonized wood, and vine-tendrils. Only the number of bricks increased, and these were possibly supports for the funeral pyre although they may have been laid on the floor of the cremation area to facilitate the draught. A type of cremation grave which was not very common is the divided pit. A few slabs set on end or a roughly built stone or brick wall separated the area with the pyre fill from that with the urn (Fig. 6).

The most common ash urns were clay vases—neck- and shoulder-handled amphorae, the latter having replaced the belly-handled amphora early in the Geometric period, although this continued to be made in a monumental form. The amphora with handle from shoulder to lip was not regularly employed for cremations, but vases of other shapes, such as *pyxides*, were occasionally used. Cinerary urns normally had modest proportions and often handsome decoration. Many had their own lids and for this reason there is less variety in the type of object used as covers—hemispherical bronze bowls, *kalathoi*, and *pyxides*. The bronze relief bowl in Phoenician style, which closed the mouth of an ash urn in one of the graves from the South Cemetery in the Kerameikos, is exceptional.

In the Protogeometric period the ashes of women were placed in belly- or shoulder-handled amphorae, those of men in neck-handled amphorae. In the Geometric burials weapons were usually associated with the neck-handled amphorae, and spindle whorls, and some types of jewellery, with shoulder-handled amphorae.

Metal cauldrons, normally bronze, were also used for ash urns. Their diameter is usually about 30 cm., but some were larger. They were covered by a lead or bronze lid, or by another inverted cauldron. Some have legs, either attached or as a separate stand. There are also clay stands which supported amphorae, pitchers, and jugs, as well as metal cauldrons. Some of the cinerary cauldrons lay in the grave pit without a stand, or on top of the collected pyre fill. Others rested on a stone which had been hollowed out to hold them upright. Metal urns of this type were used in Attica from the Geometric to the Hellenistic period. Inside some of them, with the cremated remains, there were traces of cloth or other material and in other graves there were traces of material on the exterior of the urn. The former are the remains of cloth in which ashes were gathered from the pyre, the latter of the covering which was laid around the urn before it was placed in the grave. Traces of cloth have also been found around the necks and bodies of the clay ash urns. Much smaller cauldron-like vessels have been found in some Geometric graves; these are not cinerary urns, rather receptacles for offerings or

themselves offerings. They lay inside cinerary urns or beside the
inhumed dead.

Cremation of a simpler type, which did not make use of an
ash urn, was occasionally practised. There is a small group on the
slopes of the Areiopagos, perhaps a family's plot, and a few have
been reported from other excavations, but this type of cremation
burial is not common before the Archaic period.

INHUMATION

When the practice of inhumation is resumed in Attica, towards
the close of the Protogeometric period, the old sub-Mycenaean
grave type reappears along with new forms. The slab-lined and
covered pits of the Geometric period resemble the sub-Mycenaean,
but their construction is simpler and their building material
different, schist replacing limestone in most cases. Small stones
filled the interstices and pebbles or stone slabs sometimes lined the
floors. The main difference between the sub-Mycenaean and the
Geometric cists is that the Geometric are relatively far fewer. At
Vari and Phaleron there are variant cists, slab-lined and covered
but open-ended.

A simpler type of cist has the walls of the burial pit lined with
field stones or rubble instead of stone slabs. These were used for
adults or children, for rich or poor. One of the richest Geometric
graves found in Attica, the 'Isis Grave' at Eleusis, was of this type.
But by far the most common type of grave was the simple shaft
cut into the earth or rock, many with ledges along the sides to
support cover slabs. Where no slabs were found in place the grave
was probably covered by wooden beams. Normally there was
an earth fill in the grave shaft and the offerings lay with the
body or outside on top of the cover slabs. Although the body
seems generally to have been placed in the grave with little more
than a shroud to cover it, in a few pit graves there are traces of
wooden biers or coffins, and sometimes of metal mountings
thought to have secured the wooden frame. In one grave at
Marathon the dead had a vase for a pillow.

There is no strict pattern of orientation, even though the
position of the body in the grave remains constant: extended

supine with both arms at the side; contracted burials are not common. Double burials are exceptional and, but for a mother and child buried together, most 'double burials' are probably examples of the reuse of graves.

One type of inhumation deserves mention, even though it is never common in Attica: the burial of an adult in a large pot. One has been found on Piraeus Street—a large coarse *pithos* with incised decoration, placed on its side, its mouth sealed by a clay slab—another has been reported from recent excavation at Thorikos.

The graves of children resemble those of adults except that they were generally constructed with less care and expense. Young children were buried in the main cemeteries, often on the periphery or in areas set aside especially for them, or in settlement areas. A well-known example of the latter is the burial of a child, his pet piglet by his side, beneath the floor of a Geometric building in the Agora. Simple pits are the most usual graves for children, although slab-lined and covered pits are not uncommon. Very small children and infants were buried in pots—*pithoi, hydriai*, amphorae, and jugs, of coarse ware with or without incised decoration, or of finer ware with simply painted patterns. The *pithoi* normally stood upright, sometimes partially sunk into the floor of the pit, while other vases lay on their sides. The mouth of the pot was closed by a smaller one, a sherd, a stone slab, or a lump of clay (*Pl. 2*). If the mouth of the pot was not large enough to permit the insertion of the body, holes were bored into the side or a piece of the wall or base was removed, the pot being reassembled after the insertion of the body. The burial of two infants in one pot in the Agora and at Eleusis is unusual. Offerings, often miniatures, lay inside or outside the burial pot, since the pit was large enough for the pot and a few offerings. The pot burials of children were sometimes placed in the graves of adults, probably to save space, but great care was taken not to disturb the primary burial. The Geometric cemetery in the Agora gives a clear picture of the economical disposition of graves, with child burials tucked in wherever there was room, but in this case not inside the graves of adults.

CEMETERY PLANS

The layout of cemeteries of the Geometric period in Attica is difficult to determine through continued use of the same land for burials over a long period of time: the Kerameikos is an excellent example. But some of the smaller cemeteries which were used for a shorter period give a better picture of cemetery planning. The graves lay close together in roughly parallel rows but the orientation within a cemetery often varied considerably, and the terrain and the road or path along which the cemetery lay dictated the disposition of individual graves and 'family plots'. These plots, or, more precisely, groups of apparently related graves, often lay within an enclosure. In the Kerameikos a group of late Geometric graves, each covered by a low earth mound, lay inside an enclosure of schist slabs set on end (the so-called *Plattenbau*). Single graves could also be set off in this way. At Eleusis a cremation pit was found beneath a *peribolos* of stone slabs and elsewhere enclosures of simpler construction have been found.

Not all enclosures, however, were erected at the time of burial. A group of graves dating from the sub-Mycenaean to the Geometric period, recently discovered in Athens, was enclosed in the Classical period, and at Eleusis in the Geometric period some prehistoric graves were enclosed. Not only were the enclosures built long after burials had been made, but they were also repaired in later periods. The respect which was shown them and the attention to their maintenance might indicate continuing family recognition of and respect for its own burial plot.

MARKERS

Enclosure of earlier graves is more than a sign of respect; it is evidence that the site of burial was remembered long after the funeral and that it had presumably been marked. The simplest method of marking a grave was the erection of a mound of earth over the burial. Markers of wood were almost certainly used, but none has survived. The most permanent marker is the slab of stone set vertically over the grave (Fig. 4). Geometric gravestones have been found in situ above cremation and inhumation graves in Athens, at Eleusis and Anavyssos. They are small, block-like, roughly hewn and undecorated. The largest is just over 1 m. high, but most are very much smaller. Stones marking inhumation graves stood at their head, while those marking cremations stood directly above the urn. Most of the urns which have been found marked in this way are neck-handled amphorae, but there is a belly-handled amphora from the Kerameikos which was marked by two stones, one at either end of the pit (Fig. 4). There is another grave at Eleusis which possibly had two gravestones.

Another type of grave marker is the clay vase (Fig. 4) and in the Geometric period these sometimes assumed a monumental form. Giant vases began to be made in Athens by about 800 BC and are most popular in the middle quarters of the eighth century. Amphorae of the neck-handled and shoulder-handled types, pedestalled craters, pitchers and jugs were produced in monumental form, but only the belly-handled amphorae and pedestalled craters are known to have been used as grave markers. Large vases were also placed inside the grave, some with food offerings, others as ash urns.

The number of marker vases found in situ above graves is small. Many were excavated in the last century and no record was kept of their provenance. Almost all of those from supervised excavations have come from Athens, primarily the western part of the city along Piraeus and Kriezi streets, the area of Plateia Eleutherias and the Kerameikos. There are very few marker vases from cemeteries outside Athens but for some small and simply decorated examples from Eleusis.

Monumental vases were expensive to produce and rather impermanent as markers. They were exposed to the elements, and easily toppled or shattered. There were various solutions to the problem of holding the large vases in place. Sometimes the grave shaft was not filled to ground level, but left open to a depth of more than half a metre, and a marker vase standing in such a depression was considerably protected. Other methods of securing vases included setting the base over a post, probably of wood, which had been driven vertically into the ground. For this purpose an opening was made in the base before the vase was fired;

at other times the base was broken off when the vase was set up. Some have thought that these pierced bases were intended for libations or for the drainage of rain water. The feet of some craters have a series of small holes bored into their vertical faces, probably also for some form of anchorage.

The choice of the type of vase which stood above the grave may, as before, have been determined by the sex of the dead. Of the giant vases which marked cremation burials amphorae stood above shoulder- or belly-handled amphorae, while pedestalled craters stood above neck-handled amphorae, but there are, of course, exceptions. When the vases have been found in place above inhumations the graves of men were most often marked by pedestalled craters and those of women by amphorae.

VASE SCENES

The elaborate figure scenes on many of the marker vases might be expected to furnish criteria for determining the sex of the body whose grave they marked. Unfortunately this is not usually so. Scenes of combat and naval engagements are common on craters and not on amphorae, and so may support the association of craters with the burials of men. Chariot processions are found on amphorae and craters. Two of the scenes which occur on the vases are especially relevant to a study of burial customs and the question of the sex of the deceased: the *prothesis*, the formal lying-in-state of the dead, and the *ekphora*, the carrying out of the body to the grave. In these scenes the dead is represented, but because the figure is heavily geometricized, his sex generally cannot be determined. Even when anatomical details are added for attendant mourners, they are rare on the figure of the dead.

The *prothesis* in Geometric vase-painting shows the dead lying in state upon a high bier (*Pl. 4*). He may be shown with his legs either together or somewhat apart. It is unlikely that the former represents a woman and the latter a man, since both types were painted, apparently indiscriminately, on different types of vases. Beneath the head there is often a cushion which lifted it and kept the jaws from gaping in an unsightly manner. A pall sometimes covers the body, but more often it is represented as a roughly rectangular area suspended above the bier or held clear of the body by attendant mourners. Normally the *prothesis* scene is simple and details are kept to a minimum. Exceptionally a warrior lies in state with his weapons. Two vases with this scene are neck-handled amphorae and the dead lies with legs together.

There are two basic types of mourning figures: those who raise both hands to the head and those who raise only one. The former is the traditional female gesture of lament which is found in the art of the Late Bronze Age in Greece and continues virtually unchanged into Hellenistic art. The latter gesture is the male expression of grief and figures who mourn in this way are further distinguished as men by their weapons. Men stand to mourn; women stand, kneel, or sit on small stools. Geometric vase-paintings and later representational and literary evidence agree in giving women the major role in the preparation of the corpse for burial, in attendance at the *prothesis*, and in the performance of the lament.

Geometric vase-painters represent depth by arranging their figures in registers. Those who appear kneeling beneath the bier are kneeling in front of it; those who sit above the bier or pall are sitting behind it (*Pl. 4*). The small figures who stand or sit on the bier itself are not necessarily children, nor need their position be interpreted literally. When children come to the *prothesis*, they stand beside their mother and grasp her hand, or they sit on her lap.

In some of the *prothesis* scenes a woman stands at the head of the bier, on a slight elevation which enables her to reach it more easily. She adjusts the drapery or offers a flower or the sprays which are a frequent attribute of mourners, who lay them on the bier or raise them in the air. One of their functions may have been as fans to discourage flies and other insects which must have plagued the ceremony in the hot summer months.

A detail which occurs in a few scenes are cauldrons beneath the bier or associated with the *prothesis*. They are perhaps prized possessions of the dead, but they were suitable for heating water to bathe the dead and also for offerings of food. Food offerings are probably indicated by the strings of animals which men hold approaching the bier in one scene, and the dead animals shown elsewhere. Other animals might be offerings or courtyard creatures.

The *prothesis* scenes are very common on amphorae, less so on craters, and infrequent on pitchers and *oinochoai*, although one pitcher carries four *prothesis* scenes.

The *ekphora* is not common on Geometric vases, but then it is also rare in the visual arts of the Archaic and Classical periods. Although the number of representations known is small, there is the same regularity of detail which we noted in the scenes of *prothesis*. The bier stands on a horse-drawn cart; men with weapons lead the procession, women follow (*Pl. 5*). Unlike the *ekphora* of epic, pall-bearers seem not to have been used.

The *prothesis*, *ekphora* and lament are the scenes in which funerary rites are unquestionably represented, but there are a few other scenes on Geometric vases which may also have a funerary significance—dances and chariot processions. A chain dance of men, sometimes holding weapons, and of women, regularly holding sprays, occurs on many late Geometric vases, sometimes in association with a *prothesis* scene. The dance may be funerary, but we cannot be certain. Chariot processions are found on large amphorae and craters, in association with scenes of *prothesis* and *ekphora*, as well as with scenes of no obvious funerary significance. Preparation for the funeral games has always been a popular interpretation, and some chariot teams are racing, but we do not know that funerary games were a customary rite in Attica at this time. Some chariot groups may be no more than a procession of mourners to the grave—a child appears on one chariot—or they may in some contexts have no funerary significance.

Fig. 7   A funeral rite shown on an Athenian Geometric vase, with 'musicians', shields and a table

There is another problematic scene, occurring on a small number of vases related in shape and style of decoration. Two figures sit beside a block-like structure, shields, or vessels (Fig. 7). One or both of them holds a pair of objects variously identified as clappers, rattles, cymbals, sprinklers or pomegranates. They are likely to be noise-making, and the lyre-players on some of the scenes suggest the enactment of a ceremony accompanied by music. But the interpretation of the scene depends on the certain identification of the centrepiece.

One further point about these vase-paintings should be made. The scenes which we have been describing, especially those of the *prothesis* and *ekphora*, are important to our knowledge not only of burial practices among the Greeks, but of the development of their narrative art. For although they have been considered representative of funeral ceremonies in honour of heroes of myth and legend, many details of iconography reflect contemporary practice. Apparently scenes of everyday life held more appeal for Geometric vase-painters than the exploits of heroes and myth.

OFFERINGS

Scenes on vases give a general picture of some aspects of burial procedure; for details we must look to the contents of the graves themselves. Jewellery and other personal ornaments were not standard furnishings, but enough have been found to give some idea of what the funeral dress of the wealthy included. There is, in Attic graves for the first time since the Bronze Age, gold jewellery of high quality. Among the most numerous, and least well understood, pieces are bands of thin gold foil: narrow, outlined strips with one or two holes in each end, approximately 30 cm. long (*Pl. 3*, bottom left). Attic gold bands vary in decoration, but not in other basic details. They were impressed on matrices with orientalizing animal friezes and, later, with Geometric figures like those on the vases. They have been found in the graves of men, women, and children, with inhumations and cremations. In cremation burials they lay rolled inside the urn or in a vessel outside the urn, and they were placed inside vessels in inhumation graves. More relevant to the question of their use is their position in undisturbed inhumations, where they have been found near the head and some almost certainly worn on the forehead. But the position in which they are most often found in Attic burials is on the arm of the body, either the upper arm or the wrist. The matrices which produced the gold bands were also used to make somewhat larger sheets of gold foil, which were coverings for wooden chests. Pieces of ivory inlay found in a few graves probably also decorated luxury chests.

Other pieces of gold jewellery show more variety. A group of jewellery—earrings, necklaces, and a pectoral—from graves at Eleusis, Spata and Anavyssos (and a votive deposit at Brauron) appear to be products of a workshop of eastern craftsmen who settled in Attica. Of a different style, and possibly Cypriot, is the fine pair of gold earrings found not long ago in a rich ninth-century grave in the Agora. Different again is the gold brooch from Anavyssos: a spectacle-spiral which resembles a well-known Mycenaean type. Less exotic, but far more numerous, are the gold finger-rings, earrings, and hair-spirals, which are most often simple hoops or bands, with occasional relief decoration.

Richly furnished graves are not numerous: a few scattered in Attica at Eleusis, Spata, Anavyssos; rare in Athens itself, in the Agora and Kerameikos, and only slightly more common in the newly discovered graves south of the Acropolis, west of the Agora, and north of the Kerameikos.

The pins and *fibulae* found in position in a few inhumation graves show that the body was dressed, and burnt *fibulae* inside cinerary urns indicate that the dead were also dressed for cremation. *Fibulae* were sometimes joined together to form a chain before they were placed in the grave.

The weapons which have been found in Geometric graves are spearheads, swords and knives. Spearheads have been found in pairs in Attic graves, lying beside the dead, with the cremated remains, in vessels or in offering places. Iron swords have been found beside the inhumed dead, and in cremation burials swords lay against the cinerary urn, on top of it, or their blades were coiled around the neck of the urn and their hilts placed inside with the ashes (Fig. 5). In one grave the blade was not coiled, but folded. Short daggers or knives have been found in many graves and not only those of men. Some of the small, delicate knives were probably toilet articles, not weapons, and small knives even occur in the graves of children. The 'shield bosses' which were found in some Protogeometric graves are known from one Geometric grave from the Kynosarges excavation, and a pair of bronze greaves was recently discovered in a grave on the slopes of the Acropolis.

There are a few other grave furnishings known from only a small number of graves which deserve mention: clay boots, 'granaries' and figurines. Clay boots (*Pl. 8*), miniature replicas of those worn in life, have been found in two inhumation graves (that of a youth and of a woman) and one cremation. Two of the graves had two pairs, the third had only one. The boots, painted black or decorated with Geometric patterns, are thought to have served the same purpose as those found in graves outside Greece: provision for the dead's long journey to another world. 'Granaries', roughly ovoid clay objects, with flat base and an opening near the apex, sometimes with a flap projecting above, are found more often, but their significance is not clear. There is considerable variety in their shape, size, and style of decoration; most are small, under 10 cm., but one is almost 30 cm. high; one has a lid, another has a bird's head over the flap. Decoration varies from simple slip or painted stripes to fine Geometric patterns and on some of the later pieces there are horses and birds. They have been found singly in graves and in groups: in one grave five were mounted on a clay chest, handsomely decorated with fine Geometric patterns (*Pl. 7*); the other known example of a group differs from all those we have mentioned both in clay and in style of decoration: two small 'granaries' joined together, but now lacking their base, in the distinctive coarse ware with incised decoration. This group arrangement prompted the suggestion that the objects were granaries and, like the clay horses on *pyxis* lids, symbols of wealth—a theory somewhat more plausible for the small number of fine examples and those combined in groups, than for the rather larger number of less distinguished pieces found singly. Other suggestions that the objects are rattles or whistles are equally difficult to support. They are found primarily in women's graves, spanning more than a century, and since they are regularly found only in graves they may have a particular significance in Attic funerary rites as yet unknown to us. Their resemblance to house urns in Chalcolithic and Bronze Age cemeteries of the Near East and in the Iron Age cemeteries of central Europe is striking, but probably coincidental.

Although clay figures are not numerous in Geometric graves, they are by no means limited to the horses on *pyxis* lids. There are animals (*Pl. 3*), centaurs, chariot groups and female figures. The last, with the exception of one who is equipped with her own 'throne', look like successors to the Mycenaean mourner figures and precursors of the Archaic, who sit on the rims of vases, performing the traditional gesture of lament (*Pl. 6*). There is another group of female figures whose importance lies not in their number, for there are only five of them, nor in gesture, since they stand rigid with both hands at their sides, but in their material—ivory. Other Geometric graves have yielded ivory inlay, already mentioned, and ivory seals. In the same grave with the ivory girls there were faience lions, and faience seals have been found in other graves in Athens: in the so-called Isis Grave at Eleusis there was a faience Isis and three Egyptian scarabs.

The graves themselves sometimes offer evidence for rites of burial, although we may be sure that there were many rites enacted at different times which have left no trace. Offerings of food and drink, as well as gifts of vases, jewellery, weapons and other objects, were made to the dead. How, why or by whom they were presented, we may never know, but some of the offerings were presented in a special way. Burnt offerings were acceptable whether the dead was male or female, cremated or inhumed. Burnt deposits occur in so many different forms that it is unlikely that they were all intended to serve the same purpose. Some are rectangular, others circular or irregular in outline. Some are shallow, others are deep; some are small, others large. The composition is equally varied: burnt earth, ashes, vine-tendrils and animal bones. Human remains are not regularly found in these deposits and the problem of where and how the bodies were cremated remains largely unsolved. The burnt deposits lie in, on top of, or beside places of burial and are especially easy to detect in association with inhumation graves. Burnt layers, often with burnt pottery and animal bones, have been found directly beneath or just above the cover slabs, and occasionally even the cover slabs show signs of burning. In simple inhumation pits there is often a layer of burnt stones, animal bones, and pottery over the clean fill which blanketed the dead. Burnt deposits are associated with cremation graves, but they are not large enough to have been places of cremation. Furthermore the burnt layer regularly lies above the burial. It is not uncommon for a cinerary urn to be covered by a clean earth fill, then by a burnt layer, and sometimes by yet another layer of burnt stones.

At the end of the eighth century burnt deposits of a type which is prominent in the Archaic period begin to appear. They are distinctive in their construction and composition. A long, narrow and shallow ditch was cut into the earth near the place of burial and the sides of the ditch were lined with mud bricks set on end. Inside the ditch there were ashes, burnt earth and burnt sherds of the Late Geometric style. Since the vases are closely related stylistically, it is generally assumed that the ditches were used only once and were then covered over. The two Geometric examples of these ditches—the German *Opferrinne*—are both in the South Cemetery of the Kerameikos. Since the ditches were independent of the graves, it is not easy to determine which burial they served, but one was possibly associated with the inhumation of a child, the other with the inhumation of an adult. The same types of vases were found in both: small cauldron-like vessels with open-work stands and ring handles, on the handles modelled birds and on the rims modelled snakes; cups and bowls of various types and some open-work stands which may have supported ribbon-handled bowls and plates. The vases are small and their decoration is rather simple, but there are a few pieces—jugs and an amphora—which are larger and decorated with *prothesis* scenes and processions of chariots and mourners.

The pottery from the ditches is paralleled in the burnt deposits of irregular shape found in the South Cemetery and in the Agora (*Pl. 9*). These either lay over graves of all types or were quite independent of the burial place. Their contents resemble those from the ditches in shape, style of decoration and date. The only difference is the presence of terracotta figurines in the Agora deposits: birds, horses, chariot groups, as well as human figures, some of whom were seated on chairs, others probably attached to vases.

We should probably also include here the very early Geometric 'grave 3' in the South Cemetery in which no skeletal matter was found. The small pit, wider above than below, had a ledge 0·50 m. wide just over 0·50 m. above the floor, under which were eighteen miniature vases, five clay balls and burnt matter. The excavators considered it a child's grave, largely because of the miniature vessels, while others have suggested that it was actually a cenotaph furnished with objects made especially for the grave. In this respect we note that the vases characteristic of the later Geometric deposits are lacking; here there are only cups, jugs, *kalathoi*, *pyxides*, a plate and an amphora.

Animal bones in many Geometric graves indicate the custom of animal offerings to the dead. In the few graves in which there is a complete skeleton the animal, a dog or a piglet, was probably a pet, not an offering. Analysis of skeletal remains has revealed that birds, hares, goats, lambs, pigs, and probably cattle, but not necessarily whole beasts, were offered at the grave. The bones were sometimes scattered, but often they were carefully collected in a heap in one part of the grave or placed inside a vessel, under its foot, or beneath it, inverted. Cups and bowls are the most common receptacles. A large pitcher and jug, containing animal remains, stood beside the head of a man, and at the foot of another stood two amphorae of modest size: one of them, which was lidded, contained the unbroken bones of small animals and some carbonized matter. There were probably other offerings of food, but they have rarely left traces: a few burnt figs, grapes and olive stones, and egg-shells. Complete unburnt vases, often equipped with lids, probably also contained food.

Offerings of drink were presented more regularly than offerings of animals or of other foodstuffs, to judge from the number of cups, bowls, and jugs found in most furnished Geometric graves. In inhumations the vessels lay on the floor of the shaft, inside or outside the coffin, in the fill, on the cover slabs, or scattered near by. In cremation burials cups and bowls were placed in the mouths of the cinerary urns or they were set around the outside. It is not uncommon for one grave to have many cups, but jugs are less numerous, often only one to a grave, standing upright. In inhumation graves they often stood beside the head or foot of the dead, where large pitchers and jugs have also been found. Sometimes the jug and a few cups lie in a small compartment cut into the side of the shaft. In cremation burials jugs stand beside the cinerary urn, and even beside pot burials of infants there is often a jug, upright and with small cups placed around it.

CHAPTER V

THE ARCHAIC PERIOD

Some bones make best Skeletons, some
bodies quick and speediest ashes: Who
would expect a quick flame from
Hydropicall Heraclitus?

THE CEMETERIES

THE ARCHAIC PERIOD in Attica is well defined. Its beginning is
marked by some degree of recession just after the Geometric
period and by the newly accepted 'orientalizing' styles in art;
its end by the Persian Wars, which also mark a change in the
appearance of Attic grave monuments. In contrast to the preceding periods, the Archaic is well represented by finds from
provincial sites and from the city of Athens. The movement to
the coasts and plains which began towards the end of the Geometric period had created prosperous centres in the Attic countryside and a propertied class whose wealth attracted the finest artists
of the time. Many provincial sites have been excavated, but few
have been published. Most were on or near the coast—Vari,
Anavyssos, Thorikos, Vourva, Petreza, and Marathon (Map 1).
In the port area of Athens isolated burials have been found in
many places and sizeable cemeteries have been excavated at
Palaion Phaleron and Palaia Kokkinia. Inland in the fertile
Mesogaia, Liopesi, Spata, Koropi, Lambraka, Markopoulo,
and Keratea have produced fine sepulchral monuments, but no
undisturbed burials, with the exception of the cemetery excavated at Kalyvia Kouvara, in the district of Volomandra.
In western Attica a group of burials was found near the site of the
later Academy, and further west coastal Eleusis has produced
many graves of children, but as yet no cemetery for adults.

The site which has been systematically excavated and published
in detail is the Athenian Kerameikos. Although graves lined

Piraeus Street and extended north-east beyond Plateia Eleutherias, the greatest concentration was in the Eridanos basin, over the twelfth- to eighth-century graves (Map 5). On the south bank Archaic graves extended from the Tritopatreion to Piraeus Street, in the area between the Sacred Way and West Road, while the north bank graves are nearer the city wall, east of the north-south road which linked the Sacred Way and the Academy Road, and west of the north-south road near Piraeus Street. In the Archaic period, and probably much earlier, avenues and smaller thoroughfares connected the burial grounds of the Kerameikos, separated the burial plots and provided the axes for their disposition. At present the finds from the south bank are more impressive and more numerous, but this is probably because the north bank was deprived of its monuments during the construction of the Themistoclean Wall: the fine 'Dipylon Head' from the north bank may give some idea of the lost monuments and their high quality. The Themistoclean Wall is the first city circuit of which we have detailed knowledge. It was thrown up hurriedly after the Persian Wars and Thucydides (i 93) describes how grave monuments were built into it. We shall see (pp. 84ff.) that it remains a rich quarry for the finest Archaic gravestones and bases.

Archaic burials in the Agora have not yet been fully published. Our knowledge of the site depends largely on a group of forty-eight graves which lay inside a walled enclosure on the lower slopes of the Areiopagos at the junction of two important roads (Map 3). This 'Archaic Cemetery' (to distinguish it from the 'Geometric Cemetery' south of the Tholos) and a small group of nearby graves have been published in some detail and provide comparative material for the Kerameikos series.

Most of the Archaic graves elsewhere in Athens have been chance finds or products of small rescue excavations necessitated by construction work in the modern city centre. Details of these are almost entirely lacking. Recent excavations in the Kerameikos area, on Piraeus and Kriezi streets, have produced Archaic burials. To the north, the area of the later Acharnian Gate, a cemetery with Archaic burials was discovered early in the nineteenth century. There were almost fifty graves, among them the well-known 'Burgon Amphora' (which contained cremated remains), but unfortunately there is no record of the excavation and much of the pottery was destroyed. Recent excavation in the same area has revealed Late Geometric and Classical graves, foundations of the city wall and traces of the Acharnian Gate. On the eastern side of the city the earliest graves known are Late Archaic. South of the Acropolis graves have been found in a number of places where Geometric burials had been made—along Kavalotti, Parthenos, and Erechtheion streets. The 'Olympieion Cemetery', which was also used in the Geometric period, has pottery of the type often associated with Archaic graves, but no undisturbed burials have yet been found.

The location of Archaic burials in areas where there were earlier graves and their general absence in the centre of the city after the sixth century have been considered evidence for reconstructing the course of roads and outlining the circuit of a wall around the Archaic city. Although the earliest walls and gates which have been discovered are Classical, there is reason to think that the Themistoclean Wall had a predecessor, built when the Peisistratids were undertaking a programme of public works. Both Herodotus (ix 13) and Thucydides (i 89.3; vi 57) allude to a pre-Themistoclean wall. But the only literary evidence of an Athenian practice of burying the dead outside the city's walls comes from a letter of Cicero (*ad Fam.* iv 12.3): 'I was not able to arrange with the Athenians for a grant of a burial place within the city, because they said they were forbidden on grounds of religion.' On the basis of these words, it has been assumed that there was in Athens a ban on burials within the city, which was probably introduced about 500 BC—the time when other aspects of Athenian funerary procedure show noticeable changes. It is true that burials in central parts of the city—for example in the Agora—appear to end by about 500, but there are intra-mural burials of the Classical period—mostly of children, and children are a well-known exception to funerary legislation. The few graves of adults are, however, less easily dismissed. The relevance of Cicero's words to burials of Late Archaic and Classical Athens remains obscure.

INHUMATION

Inhumation burials of adults are less numerous than cremations, but the magnificence of some of the graves and their furnishings indicate that this method of burial was not always a result of economic necessity. The simplest inhumation grave was a pit or shaft cut into the earth or rock, or dug out of the sand. The dimensions were determined by the height of the dead. Many of the pits were probably never covered by more than a layer of sand or earth. Some pits had ledges along the sides which supported wooden beams or stone cover slabs; others had bricks set on end. Traces of wooden coffins have been found in many graves, but metal mountings are rare. One coffin from the Kerameikos was painted red inside; others lay in shafts whose walls had been plastered. Some of the graves in which wood has been preserved have bits of cord or leather straps which probably bound the beams of wooden biers (*klinai*), whose cross-beams were occasionally found in position. In a few Late Archaic graves in the Kerameikos not only were beams and planks preserved, but also bits of ivory with amber inlay, which had once faced the wooden frames of *klinai*.

The stone slab-lined and covered pit—the ordinary cist—is no longer common. Most of the examples known are Late Geometric or Early Archaic. Slabs of schist or poros were set on all four sides or along the two long sides of the pit.

Inhumation of adults in large coarse-ware *pithoi* continued to be an exceptional form of burial. Apart from these, the body was regularly extended supine in the grave, except in the case of children, whose bodies were sometimes contracted. Orientation of the graves varies considerably, apparently determined by the terrain and by the course of the road along which the cemetery lay. In inhumation graves the offerings are normally inside the burial pit, along the sides of the body or clustered around the head or feet, in no apparent order. Some offerings lay outside the grave in special ditches or shallow pits.

Inhumation burials of children are very numerous—a testimony to the high infant mortality rate in antiquity. Children were buried near adults, or laid together in one area; infant cemeteries have been found on many Attic sites—Eleusis, Anavyssos, Thorikos, Phaleron. Inhumation was the standard method of burial and the types of graves were similar to those of adults. Wooden coffins were sometimes used and towards the end of the Archaic period 'vats' or 'tubs' made from terracotta were adapted for funerary use (cf. Fig. 17), although simple shafts remained more common. For infants and small children the most common type of grave was a pot. Sometimes even older children were buried in this way, an excellent example being the mid-seventh-century 'Polyphemos Amphora' (1·42 m. high) from Eleusis. Burial pots lay on their sides or stood upright in modest pits, and a few stones or sherds were set around the vases for protection. A sherd, slab or small vase covered the mouth of the vessel, or it was left open. A burial *pithos* in the Kerameikos had a wooden lid, held in place by a plaster sealing. Amphorae—often the 'SOS' type—and *pithoi* were the standard burial pots. Some were simple 'household ware', coarse and undecorated, others were beautifully potted and handsomely decorated. Among the Kriezi Street graves a burial amphora, of a type used for children, had the letters *MNE* inscribed on the shoulder, presumably an abbreviation for *MNEMA*, 'tomb' (Fig. 8; cf. p. 215). Offerings— often miniatures—were placed inside or outside the burial pots. Some vessels which looked like infant burials were found filled with small vases and since there was scarcely room even for an infant these were possibly offerings.

Fig. 8   An amphora from Athens inscribed mne(ma)

CREMATION

In the Archaic period a distinctive type of cremation grave was evolved in Attica. From the Protogeometric period onwards secondary cremation had been the standard practice. Now, in the late eighth or early seventh century, primary cremation predominates: the dead was cremated in the grave itself, not on a nearby pyre and sometimes the charred logs are found in situ, lying across the pit.

Primary cremation graves are simple pits with dimensions somewhat larger than those of inhumation shafts. The depth varies: 2 m. is not exceptional. The problem of kindling and sustaining a fire which was sufficiently strong to effect a complete cremation was met by ventilation channels in the pits: single longitudinal furrows or more complex ventilation systems with lateral arms, cut into the floor of the grave shaft, through which air circulated around the mass of logs, branches, vine-trimmings and resinous wood with which the cremation shafts were regularly filled (Fig. 9). After the combustible material had been piled into

Fig. 9 *Plan and sections of a cremation burial with mound, marker and offering ditch*

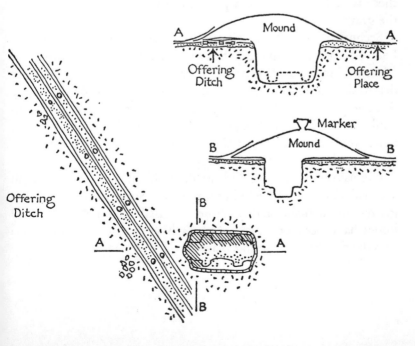

the shaft, the plank-like bier was set in place. Projecting handles, which fitted into cuttings on the sides of the shaft, secured some of the biers, and bits of twisted and burnt cord found in other graves probably served a similar purpose. At least some of the biers had legs: small circular holes containing bits of carbonized wood have been found in the floor of the grave shafts.

The heavily burnt floors and walls of primary cremation pits testify to the intensity of the blaze and size of the pyre. Over the floor, which was occasionally plastered, there was regularly a burnt layer, approximately 0·25 m. thick, with burnt wood and some-times sherds and animal bones. Over this blackened layer was a thin layer of white ash—the ashes of the dead. In most cases the cremation had been so complete that it was impossible to deter-mine the original position of the corpse in the grave. The ash layer was normally free of any other material, although some graves contained animal bones, astragals, and pieces of cloth. Over the ash deposit there was often another burnt layer, which was probably formed when the bier collapsed. Layers of earth, either clean or mixed with stone, rubble, or sherds, filled the remainder of the pit. The sherds from these upper layers of fill showed signs of intense burning—so vases may have been placed around the bier during the process of cremation. Offerings, if there were any, were often placed in special pits or ditches near the grave.

Secondary cremations are not numerous. Most of them are Late Geometric; some are, however, Archaic, for example the 'Burgon Amphora'. Bronze cinerary urns sealed in stone boxes or drums have been dated to the end of the Geometric or very early Archaic period, but three lying together in one cist on the north bank of the Eridanos were Archaic. Both the type of grave, apparently a triple cremation, and the associated offerings, decorated bronze bowls, are exceptional.

Cremation of infants and small children was, it seems, an acceptable, but not a customary, practice. Some of the cremation graves are unquestionably those of small children; the small bones have been preserved. Others have no human bones and may be remains of offering places.

POSITION OF OFFERINGS

In the Archaic period, when vast sums were spent on the outward appearance of the grave—the erection of monumental earth mounds, built tombs, and fine funerary sculpture—the actual grave was often unfurnished or very modestly furnished. Apart from the contents of the 'offering places' and 'offering ditches' (*Pl. 10*) most of the furnished graves in Athens and elsewhere in Attica had little more than a cup, bowl or a pouring vessel, occasionally an oil bottle. Weapons, jewellery, and other metal objects are virtually unknown. The disposition of offerings in special areas is a distinctive feature of Archaic burials in Attica. These offering deposits have been found apart from graves or closely associated with them. Their preserved contents are almost exclusively pottery, although some have animal bones and remains of other food offerings.

'Offering places' (German *Opfergrube, Opferplatz*) are irregularly shaped, shallow deposits of variable composition: an alternation of burnt and clean earth layers, with or without animal bones and sherds, is most common. The deposits have been found in many locations: near the grave or some distance from it (Fig. 9), in the grave (for example, on top of the slabs covering the burial) or on top of the mound which marked its site. Not infrequently graves with offering ditches also have offering places, but the fine pottery is normally found in the former. Most of the rich offering places are associated with graves which lack offering ditches.

'Offering ditches' (German *Opferrinne*), unlike the offering places, were apparently first used towards the end of the eighth century. Although they continued to be constructed in the Classical period, most of the richest known are Archaic. These ditches were optional, undoubtedly expensive adjuncts to the standard funerary outlay. Fine pottery, elaborate tombs, and impressive sepulchral monuments are often associated with them. Long shallow furrows were cut into the ground near the grave, beside or beneath earth mounds, under, beside or a short distance from built tombs (Figs. 9, 10). Their length varies from an impressive 12 m. to a more modest 2 to 3 m., their width from 20

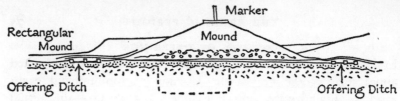

Fig. 10   The section of a cremation burial with mound and marker, and of a rectangular mound, with offering ditches for other graves

to 30 cm. Mud bricks, approximately 20 cm. square and 10 cm. thick, were set on end along the sides of the shallow ditch. Sometimes an additional median row of bricks divided it into two equal sections. Very rarely the ditches were built of stones laid on end. The heavily burnt earth floor of the ditch was covered with burnt wood, ash, and burnt sherds, sometimes with a few animal bones and shells. Above this was another layer of burnt earth, then a sealing layer of mud or lime plaster. In a few of the longer ditches there were small round holes at regular intervals on each side of the median strip. Inside were bits of carbonized wood—the remains of posts which probably once supported a wooden plank or table-like structure. Around some of the holes were bones of small birds and mussel shells. Additional evidence that offerings were set on a table comes from the orderly arrangement of the broken pottery in the ditch.

After the offerings had been made, and the flames had died down, the ditch was closed and was apparently never used again. The position of some offering ditches beneath mounds or built tombs seems to indicate that the ceremony during which they were used was the climax of the service of burial.

OFFERINGS

We have already mentioned the typical offerings in Archaic graves, but there are some special types which deserve separate treatment.

A bottle-shaped clay object, with holes in the neck for suspension, has been found in and associated with graves in Attica, Boeotia, Rhodes, Sicily, South Italy, on the Black Sea, at Olbia, and in the Hellenistic period at Taman in South Russia. The iconography of some of the Attic pieces suggests a funerary purpose: scenes of *prothesis* and the lament (*Pl. 11*). Similar bottle-shaped vessels, equipped with stoppers and suspension holes, were produced in Corinth in the Archaic period, but unlike them our objects were clearly not designed as ordinary bottles since they cannot be filled or emptied; the only apertures are the suspension holes. Therefore previous suggestions that they are ritual sprinklers (*ardania*) or sack-like vessels (*phormiskoi*) seem unlikely. A possible clue to their use comes from their provenances: graves, especially those of children, and sanctuaries of chthonic deities. The shape and manner of construction are suitable for rattles, and rattles are appropriate gifts for children, as well as instruments of cult. Moreover, real clay rattles of this shape have been found in a child's grave of about 500 BC at Olbia, and Geometric rattle-like objects have also been found in graves. One example of these objects, from Thebes, has a 'door' in its side exposing four astragals, which are themselves commonly found in graves, and we may recall the scenes on Geometric vases of the 'Rattle Group' (p. 61).

Funerary offerings of eggs, either real or imitations in stone or clay, were common in Greece. We have already noted the presence of egg-shells in Attic graves and burnt deposits. Our concern here is with the painted clay ovoid or spherical objects which first appear in Geometric graves, are numerous in the Archaic, and continue into the Classical. The Geometric examples are in fact ovoid vessels equipped with lid and holes for suspension. Some later examples retain the lid and ovoid shape while others are spherical, pierced only with a small hole in one end or both; a few lack apertures. It seems unlikely that all of these objects were designed for the same purpose. The decoration also varies: coloured patterns painted on a white ground, white decoration on a dark ground, and scenes in black- or red-figure, occasionally funerary—the *prothesis* or lament.

An offering place in the Kerameikos and one at Vari had clay 'tables'. The Vari table (0·18×0·24 m. and 0·18 m. high) has floral and abstract patterns in the Protoattic style on its sides and five furrows on its top. The Kerameikos table is somewhat later with lions in the full black-figure style on its sides (*Pl. 12*).

Both were found with a small clay die and for this reason are thought to be 'gaming tables'. But unlike other known gaming tables, these have modelled female mourners, their cheeks streaked with red paint for blood, at each corner. The effect is that of a *prothesis* bier with attendant mourners. Clay mourners like those on the tables were also attached to vases, to the rims or shoulders of jugs, *loutrophoroi* (*Pl. 13*), tankards, ribbon-handled bowls (*Pl. 15*) and pedestalled craters. Some are covered with white slip and decorated with matt paint, others are painted black except for their faces and hands. Many of them have traces of red paint preserved on their faces and breasts. The vases themselves are either covered with a white slip or decorated with matt painted scenes, not infrequently of the *prothesis* or lament (*Pl. 14*). Occasionally modelled snakes, familiar from the Geometric period, appear on the handle, neck or rim. Most of the vases have been found in offering places or in offering ditches, but in at least one instance in situ above a grave monument; a built tomb in the Kerameikos was marked by two pedestalled cauldrons with clay mourners sitting on the rim. There can be little doubt that these vases were designed especially for the grave.

The most elaborate example of a clay model designed for the grave was found during early excavations at Vari: a four-wheeled cart led by a man carries the bier which is covered with a cloth and attended by four mourning women (*Pl. 16*). The cloth is a lid, which when lifted reveals a clay figure of the dead. The model which is dated before the middle of the seventh century, and is therefore one of the earliest post-Geometric terracottas, is covered with white paint and details are added in matt. A clay horse mounted on wheels and another wheel in the same technique and style of decoration were found in an offering place in the Kerameikos. The excavator is perhaps correct in considering the fragments part of another 'death cart'.

Another terracotta type deserves mention: the mid-seventh-century *thymiateria* or 'incense burners'. An offering ditch in the Kerameikos yielded two different types of support, one a sphinx (*Pl. 17*), the other a woman. Both have bases and carry shallow bowls on their heads. On the woman's cheeks there are streaks of red paint. Sphinx-supports similar to these, but of stone and considerably later in date, have been found on Cyprus. Both the form and the style of the Kerameikos pieces have parallels in the east, and other objects from the ditch also display orientalizing features, notably the clay cauldrons on high pedestals. Unlike the Geometric pedestalled cauldrons, the Archaic have a high conical foot and clay modelled foreparts of hens or griffins, or clay lotus blossoms (*Pl. 18*). The animal foreparts and the open-work feet of the vases betray their metal prototypes. Another group of pedestalled cauldrons—five reasonably well-preserved pieces from Vari, now in Mainz, and a fragment from Athens—retain the ring handles of the Geometric. They are also earlier than the Kerameikos vases, larger and even more elaborately decorated, with applied clay florals and 'snakes' in addition to friezes painted on a slipped surface (Fig. 11).

MOUNDS AND BUILT TOMBS

In Archaic Attica several of the earth mounds which stood above graves were distinguished from their predecessors by greater size and more substantial construction. Earth mounds stood above cremation and inhumation graves of adults and children. The mound, composed of earth, either clean or mixed with sherds,

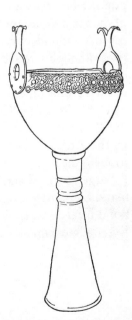

Fig. 11 A pedestalled crater from Vari in Attica with clay floral attachments at the handles and rim

was raised directly over the burial shaft, or over a simple foundation layer of stones or pebbles (Figs. 9, 10). The round mound built of stone at Vourva is exceptional. Layers of mud and lime plaster which covered the surface from apex to base offered protection from the elements while helping to retain the roughly conical shape of the mound. In the Kerameikos mounds are concentrated on the south bank of the Eridanos, probably by reason of space. Here they most often covered single graves, but some of the large mounds were in use for more than one generation and later burials were made on the periphery or in the upper fill. In the countryside—at Anavyssos, Vari, Velanideza, Vourva, and Petreza—modest mounds covered single burials, large ones grave groups.

'Modest' mounds with a diameter of 4 to 6 m. and a height of 0.50 m. were surpassed by grander monuments 6 to 10 m. in diameter and over 1 m. high. Around 600 BC the problem of space became acute in the Kerameikos and the solution was the superimposition of funerary monuments. The 'life span' of many mounds was very short, probably less than a generation. Some merely encroached on neighbours, others completely covered their predecessors. Occasionally they were so close together that they formed one large impressive structure.

In the Kerameikos the earth mound appears to have been most popular before the end of the seventh century and the majority of the great round mounds date before 600 BC. After the turn of the century mounds were fewer in number and generally smaller in size, although a few retained the old grandeur. Indeed, the largest known, a gigantic 30 m. in diameter and over 5 m. high, was erected around the middle of the sixth century over many earlier monuments. But even this great mound was soon covered, and in the Kerameikos the day of the large round mound had passed. In the Attic countryside, where space was presumably less restricted, they may still have been built for some time.

Large plastered earth mounds often had some sort of crowning marker. Fragments of craters decorated with centaurs, water birds, floral bands, and sphinxes were found above four mounds in the Kerameikos (Fig. 9). Three mounds, 6 to 10 m. in diameter, which

lay close to each other on the south bank, had crowning *stelai*
(Fig. 10). The earliest of the three, of about 650 BC, was a thin
slab with sides tapering downwards to a limestone base, into
which it was leaded. The bottom of the base was left rough for
insertion into the ground. The second *stele*, of about 625–600
BC, was a limestone shaft with parallel sides and a rectangular
limestone base into which it was leaded. The third, a slate slab,
leaded into a limestone base, was found in the fill of a mound
which it probably crowned.

Among the Archaic *stelai* found in situ in the Kerameikos one,
a limestone slab without a base, covered with stucco on three sides,
stood over a grave which was not covered by an earth mound,
and no doubt many *stelai* were set up in this manner.

Contemporary with the great round mounds were rectangular
mounds, apparently a slightly less grand funerary monument.
This seems to be indicated by the number and quality of the grave
furnishings, but the rectangular mound was still an expensive
affair. The earliest example known, of about 700–650 BC, owes its
preservation to its size and manner of construction. Clean earth
had been firmly packed over a primary cremation burial to form
a 4·4 by 2 m. structure with a flat roof and sloping walls, which
were covered with plaster. Rectangular mounds of the second
half of the century, whose dimensions vary from 2 to 4 m. by
2 to 3 m. and were roughly 0·50 m. high, were more substantially
built. The earth core was mixed with sand and stone; layers of
mud and lime plaster covered the surface.

Around 600 BC the type of construction changed and with it the
form of the monument. Vertical walls built of mud bricks
(roughly 7 × 10 cm. before 600 BC, 6 × 8 cm. after) laid in regular
courses, began to replace the sloping walls of the earth mounds
(Fig. 12). These brick walls held the composite earth core firmly in
place. The change in construction permitted large, impressive
structures—built tombs—which required less space than the
great round earth mounds. In the Kerameikos almost all of the
built tombs had brick walls. In the countryside built tombs had
brick walls, stone walls in ashlar or polygonal masonry, or were
constructed in a combination of materials. Plain earth mounds

Built Tomb

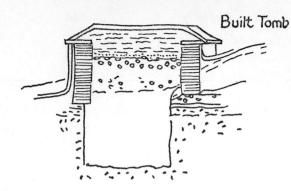

Fig. 12 A built tomb of brick covered with mud and plaster, over a cremation grave

did, however, continue to be built in the sixth century and they differed from the built tomb in material and manner of construction only. The principle of burial remained the same: a single grave deep in the ground, beneath the structure.

Built tombs in the first half of the sixth century were generally larger and more impressive than those of the second half. Like the round mounds, they too were restricted by space. In the Kerameikos almost none of the built tombs was free-standing; each encroached on another, earlier structure. And just as the round mounds sometimes joined together to form one large mound, so did built tombs. In the Attic countryside, where space was less scarce, a number of built tombs were free-standing.

The construction of the sixth-century built tomb was similar to that of contemporary domestic architecture, but the analogy is misleading. The monument was not a house for the dead, since the dead lay beneath it, not inside. Built tombs stood directly over the filled burial shaft or on a foundation of brick or stone. The walls, made of brick or stone, stood vertically or at a slight inclination. If the superstructure was earth, not brick or stone, normally it has disappeared leaving only the foundation courses. Since even the built walls are rarely preserved to any height, it is difficult to determine what type of roof they originally supported, but the roofs which have been preserved are flat with slightly sloping sides, and it seems unlikely that any of the Archaic built tombs had high pitched roofs. Bricks, stone slabs, or irregularly broken stones were found on the tops of some and were probably put there to protect the surface from the elements. The roof was not the only part of the structure which required protection and the upper faces of the mud-brick walls were especially vulnerable. Many tombs had brick or stone cornices which protected their walls from driving rain. An additional protection for the entire structure was provided by sealing layers of clay and lime plaster which occasionally bore painted decoration.

Since the discovery of the built tombs, a group of painted clay plaques with scenes of the laying out of the dead (*prothesis*) and lamentation have been connected with them. The plaques may be divided into two groups—those which were complete in themselves ('single plaques': *Pl. 33*) and those which formed part of a larger series. The series plaques, which have a roughly uniform shape and size, are known from just before the end of the seventh century to about 530 BC. It is generally thought that these plaques, which have no apparent means of attachment, were set into the plaster walls of the built tomb or were arranged on projecting ledges. None of the plaques have been found in situ, nor have any built tombs shown marks of such attachment, but there are no other tomb monuments known to which they might have been fitted, and one is inscribed as a *sema*.

The plaque series were painted by leading artists of the day— Sophilos, Lydos, Exekias—and have been found in Athens, Kalyvia Kouvara, and Spata. From the most fully preserved series, by Exekias, we can see that the centre plaques, perhaps at the narrow ends of the tomb, showed mourning within the house, *prothesis*, and the cart for the *ekphora*. The many other plaques showed a procession of mourners. Each measures about 37 by 43 cm. The single plaques were much smaller, and pierced for nailing or suspension. Most are of the end of the sixth century. The change from series to single plaques is not accompanied by any observed differences in the construction of the built tombs, which continue into the Classical period.

Also of uncertain use are three large marble slabs of the late Archaic period decorated in low relief, with figures identified as Hermes Psychopompos and the deceased. But the iconography is obscure owing to the damaged condition of the slabs, which had been built into the Themistoclean Wall, and it is generally thought that they decorated the façade of a large funerary monument. We cannot be certain, and there are other relief slabs whose purpose also remains obscure, among them the 'Marathon Runner'.

Decoration of the built tombs leads us to discuss the vases and sculpture which have been found associated with them. Although many built tombs have only a few courses of their original height preserved, the contemporary practice of crowning round earth mounds with vases and sculpture, and the find spots of the pottery and sculptural fragments beside or immediately on top of built tombs, suggest that they too had crowning members.

In the Kerameikos crowning vases were found above two built tombs and one rectangular earth mound. A spouted bowl marked one built tomb and a crater the earth mound. The second of the built tombs had two vases—high-footed cauldrons covered with white slip. The smaller of the two had modelled female mourners seated on the rim and fragments of similar, but larger, figures may have adorned the other.

Very little sculpture in the round has been found above graves, although a few lions and sphinxes have been found associated with them, both at Vari and in the Kerameikos. In the latter a lion of modest size was found in situ above a built tomb and it may be that some of the lions and sphinxes of unknown provenance were set up in a similar way.

We have described the types of monuments—built tombs, round and rectangular mounds—and the vases, sculpture and *stelai* which have been found with them. The remainder of this chapter will be devoted to gravestones with relief decoration, whose exceptional quality merits more attention.

GRAVESTONES

There are two basic types of gravestone known in Archaic Attica—the narrow slab of dressed stone (*stele*) and sculpture in the round. Almost none of the monuments has been found in situ. In Athens, many were broken, retooled, and incorporated into the Themistoclean Wall. Many sites in the Attic countryside have yielded gravestones of very high quality—another indication of the

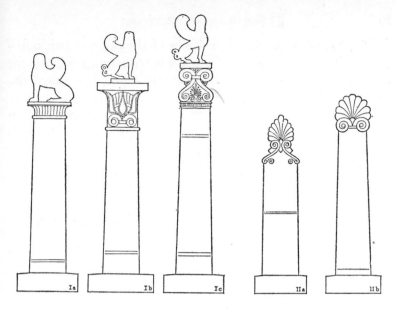

Fig. 13   Types of Attic sixth-century stelai. *The transition between Types I and II comes about 530 BC*

wealth of the landed nobility at this time—but they too have rarely been found in situ.

The *stele* of the first three-quarters of the sixth century had a separate base and finial, or crowning member. The *stele* of the last quarter retained the separate base, but its simplified finial was carved in one piece with the shaft and the total height was less (Fig. 13). The shape of the *stelai* was well suited to reuse and for this reason few have survived intact. Reconstruction of the 'monolithic' *stele* presents little difficulty, that of the 'composite' *stele* is less easy. Attractive reconstructions have been offered by Miss Richter in *The Archaic Gravestones of Attica*—the major study of the monuments—but we cannot always be sure of the form of the originals.

The earliest inscribed and decorated *stelai* were of limestone. The surface was covered with stucco, the decoration rendered in low relief, light incision, or paint. Marble *stelai* were similarly carved or painted, but the stucco coat was omitted. On both stones additional paint was applied to broad surfaces and to minor

details, but unfortunately few traces of the original rich polychromy survive. The shape of the slab restricted the composition,
and a profile view of a single, standing figure best suited the
narrow field (*Pl. 19*; Fig. 14). Athletes and warriors, men with
their dogs, and elders leaning on staves are the most common
subjects; women were never represented on their own. Beneath
the principal composition there was often a small, roughly
square field or predella, carved in low relief or painted.

Sphinxes seated on cavetto capitals seem to have crowned the
earliest *stelai*, but not all early sphinxes from cemeteries were
necessarily mounted thus. The cavetto capital is once, at Lamptrai,
decorated in low relief with mourners and a horseman (Fig. 15).
In the third quarter of the century the cavetto beneath the sphinx
is replaced by a lyre-shaped scroll. From about 530 BC the
sphinxes disappear, the decoration is often simpler, and the finial
is a carved palmette in the East Greek manner.

Inscriptions on Attic gravestones are normally short, giving
only essential details: the name of the dead, those who mourn
him, those who erected the monument in his honour. Inscriptions do appear on the finial, but are more often on the shaft or
base. It is not uncommon for the shaft to bear one inscription,
the base another. Alternatively, the shaft or base bears the only
inscription. On a few gravestones two figures are represented
and both are named. Such monuments probably did not stand
over the grave of one person or a double burial, but rather over
a family plot, commemorating persons whose deaths may have
been, but need not have been, separated by a number of years.
In the Classical period grave monuments were similarly used.

In the Archaic period shorter, broader slabs with relief decoration were used for votive and sepulchral monuments. One of the
earliest examples of the former is the so-called 'Hermes and the
Graces' from the Athenian Acropolis. Of the latter, Attic gravestones provide a few examples: bases with exceptionally wide
cuttings and fragmentary relief slabs of unusual breadth and
thickness. Women's names are inscribed on two, possibly three,
of the bases, and on one of the reliefs there is a seated woman
cradling a small child. These compositions—a seated woman with

Fig. 15   The capital (see Fig. 13, Ib) of a stele from Lamptrai in Attica, with a horseman on the front, male and female mourners on the sides

Fig. 14   An incised and painted stele from Athens showing a youth holding a flower (no longer visible)

Fig. 16   A painted marble disc, inscribed as the sema of the doctor Aineas

a child or with some domestic attribute, and a seated woman confronted by another—are very common on Classical funerary monuments in Attica, and outside Attica they have been noted on gravestones dated to the first half of the fifth century (see p. 222). Possible evidence that the graves of men were sometimes marked by a broad relief comes from a fragmentary relief found in the Attic countryside at Velanideza.

DISCS

There are at least five thin marble discs which have been included in collections of Attic funerary monuments (Fig. 16). Their provenances are largely uncertain, although all are said to have come from Attica. Their function is entirely uncertain, although their similar shape and size (about 28 cm. in diameter) suggest a common purpose. Two bear inscriptions like those on contemporary gravestones—'I am the monument (*mnema, sema*) of', and the name follows. The other three have obscure inscriptions employing the phrase—'from the *erion*'. Depending on whether *erion* is translated 'funeral games' or 'grave mound', the disc is considered either a 'genuine' discus from an athletic victory or funerary games, or a disc-like cover for a cinerary urn. Although the dimensions are suitable for the latter and the translation of *erion* as mound is preferable, there are similar objects, both stone and metal, found in and associated with graves outside Attica, which render both interpretations uncertain.

STATUARY

Marble statues of youths (*kouroi*) and maidens (*korai*) are the most numerous representatives of early large-scale sculpture in the round in Attica. Like *stelai*, the figures stood on a separate base, often inscribed with the name of the youth or maiden, the name of the dedicator, and sometimes the sculptor who fashioned it. *Kouroi* and *korai* have rarely been found complete or in situ, but a few are known to have been funerary monuments (*Pl. 20*). They have been found in cemeteries in Athens and in the countryside. The *korai* were far more rare, it seems; only two graves, one in Athens and the other at Vourva, are known definitely to have been marked by them, but the head of a *kore* from Merenta is said to have come from a grave monument.

Although few seated figures cut in the round are known from the Archaic period in Attica, there is good reason to believe that they too were sometimes funerary. The most famous, the so-called Dionysos, was found in the area of the Erian Gate, a known cemetery site. A very similar statue was found in the Kerameikos, as were two fragments of two other figures, one of them generally considered female. In addition to these sculptures, all from known cemeteries, there are bases with cuttings which seem too large for a single standing figure and some of these may have accommodated seated figures; the base from the Kerameikos with reliefs of warriors and 'hockey players' is an example; another, also from the Kerameikos, bears a funerary inscription on its principal side. There can be little doubt that seated figures were sometimes grave monuments, even though none has been found in situ. Some graves may have been thus distinguished in recognition of age, rank or social position.

Horsemen carved in the round were favourite dedications in the Archaic period, but they were also grave monuments. The Vari and Kerameikos cemeteries have each produced one, and some of unknown provenance may have been funerary. In addition there are a few bases whose cuttings seem appropriate to equestrian statues and one of them, from the Kerameikos, is inscribed. Horsemen were also painted or rendered in relief in the lower panel of *stelai* and the Lamptrai capital, which bears a horseman in relief on its principal face (Fig. 15), is thought by at least one scholar to have supported a small equestrian group.

CONCLUSION

During the Archaic period funerary art and architecture flourished in Attica. The monuments which have survived are high-quality works by some of the best artists of the time. But before the end of the sixth century this grandeur appears to have declined. The later monuments which survive are fewer in number and generally somewhat inferior in quality. Whether natural causes, such as lack of space, or contemporary political, social and economic conditions determined this development, we do not know. The Athenian funerary legislation mentioned by Cicero in the *de Legibus* (ii 26.64) is regularly discussed in this context:

> Some time later [i.e., after Solon] on account of the size of the tombs which we see in the Kerameikos, it was decreed that no one should make a tomb which required the work of more than ten men in three days, and that no tomb should be decorated with plaster (*opus tectorium*) or have the so-called 'herms' set on it.

But Cicero's chronology is uncertain and his terminology ambiguous. In short, his account offers more problems than solutions. He does, however, seem to be describing impressive monuments adorned with painted and plastered decoration and crowned with fine sculpture. The temptation to connect his words with the funerary monuments of Archaic Attica is very great. Both the change to the simpler palmette *stele* and the change from plaque series to single plaques have been associated with hypothetical legislation of about 530 BC.

Other funerary legislation of the Archaic period and evidence for pre-burial rites are discussed in the following two chapters.

CHAPTER VI

THE CLASSICAL PERIOD

> *But these are sad and sepulchral Pitchers,*
> *which have no joyful voices; silently*
> *expressing old mortality, the ruines of*
> *forgotten times, and can only speak with*
> *life, how long in this corruptible frame,*
> *some parts may be uncorrupted; yet able*
> *to out-last bones long unborn, and*
> *noblest pyle among us.*

THE CEMETERIES

THE NUMBER OF EXCAVATED Classical burial grounds in Athens
and throughout Attica is considerable. Scattered burials have been
found in many parts of Attica, and cemeteries of various sizes
have been excavated at Draphi, on the slopes of Mt Pendeli, at
Vari, Merenta, St John Rente, Eleusis, Thorikos, and at sites on
the south coast between Athens and Sounion (Map 1). Unfortunately, few excavations have been published in any detail and
the provincial sites must therefore be largely ignored in this study.
Reference will be made to non-Athenian sites only when the
finds are in some respect exceptional.

In Athens itself the problem is much the same: although many
Classical burials have been found, and more are discovered each
year, information about them remains incomplete. Furthermore,
excavation in Athens is difficult since the heart of the city covers
the extent of its Classical predecessor. Most of the excavations
have been small, hastily done, and inadequately published. Often
the occasion for the excavation was urgent—demolition, construction, or maintenance work in the modern city centre. Brief
reports, sometimes with photographs and plans, have appeared
in Greek periodicals, but much remains unpublished. Only the

Greek archaeologists are equipped to write the topography of Athens; we attempt no more than a summary, based on the available information.

As a result of recent excavation the topography of the ancient city is becoming more clear. The theory proposed in the last century, that graves lined the major roads and that their positions could be used to reconstruct the course of the city wall and its gates, has now been substantially confirmed (Map 4). In the previous chapter we mentioned the problem of the 'pre-Themistoclean' wall, possible funerary legislation passed in the Archaic period, and Cicero's ambiguous account of a ban on burials in the city. Little more can be said. At present there are a few Classical burials known within the city walls. They are recent finds and have received only brief preliminary publication: two groups, one with eleven graves on Leokorion Street, the other with two graves on nearby Karaïskake Street—the area on the north side of the Agora, through which passed a major ancient road. In the first group there are pots, which were apparently infant burials, and pits, also thought to have been graves, although there is no mention of human skeletal matter. The associated pottery dated from the late Classical period to the Hellenistic. Among the other finds in the area were sherds from the Archaic through the Hellenistic periods, and a small *Totenmahl* relief. The Karaïskake Street graves have been dated to the end of the fifth century: two pits with traces of burning and accompanying vases, identified as ash urns. Both pits are, however, shallow and one is exceptionally large (over 4 m. square). Further information is necessary before we can determine whether these two groups are, in fact, intra-mural burials. Outside Athens, at Thorikos, there is another probable example of burial within the settlement: children's graves and at least one of an adult were found near the theatre.

After the construction of the Themistoclean Wall, existing cemeteries extended outside some of the gates and new ones grew up outside others. This siting of cemeteries is easily understood, when we remember that burial grounds had to be reasonably accessible. In the topographical summary which follows we shall describe cemeteries in relation to their positions outside the gates of the Classical wall, and, where more precision is necessary, in terms of modern street names.

In the western part of the city the Kerameikos continued to be an important burial ground. The two major roads which traversed the area—the Sacred Way and the Academy Road—were marked by gates. The Sacred Gate, which stood at the point where the Sacred Way to the sanctuary at Eleusis left the city of Athens, incorporated the channel of the Eridanos Stream on its north flank. The land south of the Sacred Way, which had been a cemetery at least as early as the Protogeometric period, continued to be used throughout the Classical. But some time in the late fifth or very early fourth century, the terrain was transformed. 'West Street', also known as the 'Street of the Tombs', and 'South Way', sometimes called 'Lateral Way', were laid out in a grand manner, and impressive plots were thrown up on the sloping hillsides (Map 5). From the magnificence of the preserved funerary architecture and sculpture, we may assume that this area—often called the 'Eridanos Cemetery' (somewhat incorrectly since the Eridanos lay on the other side of the Sacred Way)—became a burial ground for notable Athenians. The land east of 'South Way', nearer the gate, was at different times a cemetery for children, state officials, and ordinary citizens, but after the terraced plots were thrown up to the west, this land seems to have fallen into disuse. Not until the Hellenistic period were there again burials in any number. The north side of the Sacred Way, near the gate—the site of the sub-Mycenaean 'Pompeion Cemetery'—was apparently not used for burials in the Classical period. The area to the west, towards Piraeus Street, has produced mounds, built tombs, and terraced plots, similar in size and magnificence to those on the south bank. On Piraeus Street and farther along the course of the Sacred Way Classical and later burials have been found.

North of the Sacred Way there was a larger gate whose strategic purpose is apparent from its manner of construction. This gate, built into the Themistoclean Wall, was called the Thriasian Gate, because the road which passed through it led to Thria in the Eleusinian plain. After the Peloponnesian War the course of the road was widened to accommodate better such state occasions as the Panathenaic Procession, torch races, and state funerals. In the fourth century further alterations were made; this time for defence purposes. The resultant double bulwark was called the 'Dipylon' or 'Double Gate'. The name has become familiar to us through its misuse to describe the Geometric graves and their contents—especially the giant 'Dipylon vases'—which were excavated in the last century along Piraeus Street, around Plateia Eleutherias. The earliest known use of the name is a third-century inscription. Unlike the land around the Sacred Gate, where burials had been made from the early Iron Age, this area, just outside the Thriasian Gate, seems not to have been envisaged as a major burial ground until much later. Indeed, the cemetery does not gain prominence until the Classical period, when the state graves, described by Pausanias, and traditionally set out by Kimon, were laid along the Academy Road.

There was a large cemetery north-east of the Kerameikos, around Plateia Eleutherias, on land which had been used for burials from the end of the Bronze Age; mention has already been made of the sub-Mycenaean and early Iron Age graves. Classical graves were especially numerous west of Plateia Eleutherias, along Piraeus Street, and recent excavations here continue to increase their number. Formerly these graves were considered an extension of the Kerameikos cemeteries, but now they are known to comprise a large cemetery which grew up outside the so-called Erian Gate—or 'Gates of the Dead'. The name has been derived from an oblique reference in Theophrastos (*Characters* xiv 13) to 'the gates through which the dead were carried out'. Traces have been found of both the gate and the ancient road whose course followed roughly that of modern Leokorion Street. It began in the Agora, left the city through the Erian Gate, and, at some distance (roughly 800 m.) from the walls, branched in two directions: north of Hippios Kolonos, perhaps on the line of modern Ioanninon Street, and south, possibly along the course of modern Lenormant Street, where Classical graves have been found as well as foundation courses of a large mound (9 m. in diameter) covering a number of graves, and part of an enclosure wall.

At some time during the Classical period, if not earlier, the cemeteries of the Kerameikos and the Erian Gate were joined by cross-roads, running roughly east-west. A series of Classical graves, lining such a road, was recently discovered on the north side of modern Achilles Street (Map 4).

On the northern side of the city the Acharnian Gate was the point of exit for a principal road north to Acharnai. Remains of the wall and gate have been found along Sophokles Street, between Aiolou and Pesmazoglou streets. The land south of the wall, which lay closer to the Agora and Acropolis, had burials as early as the sub-Mycenaean period. As the city grew the burial grounds extended and during the Classical period they covered a large area between Aiolou, Sophokles, and Lykourgos streets. These graves have not yet been published.

On the eastern side of the city remains of the Themistoclean Wall and gate—the Diocharian Gate—have been found near modern Syntagma Square, between Nike and Boule streets. Unlike the cemeteries which we have described already, here no graves have been found which are earlier than the late Archaic period. The excavated cemetery extends north-east of Syntagma, along Stadiou and Panepistemiou streets. Excavation beneath Syntagma will probably reveal an even larger cemetery. The Diocharian Gate cemetery is especially important to our study of Classical burials, since it comprises a large group of roughly contemporary graves arranged in plots, whose physical features and contents have been published in detail.

The southern circuit of the Themistoclean Wall which extended south of the Acropolis, from the Olympieion in the east to the Piraeus Gate in the west, was marked by a number of gates, but we shall treat the area more summarily for the following reasons: the course of the wall is more difficult to plot and the terrain is less regular; modern topographers cannot agree on the names of the gates; almost none of the excavated material has been published. Modern topographers locate the Diomeian Gate on Dikaios Street, between the Olympieion and the Ilissos River,

through which passed the road to Kynosarges on its way to the
coast. Ancient literary references to a Classical cemetery here are
being substantiated by excavation. Early work on the Kynosarges
site, just north of the intersection of Vourbache and Vouliagmeni
streets, yielded, in addition to the Geometric graves already mentioned, a large number of Classical and later burials. Recent
excavations in the area continue to reveal the extent of the
cemetery in the Classical period.

A second gate, the Itonian, lay farther west on Makrygianni
Street, and many Classical graves, unpublished, have recently
been found here. The road passing through the Itonian Gate ran
south to Phaleron and, judging from the number of Classical
graves excavated on Dimitracopoulos Street, this modern road
may overlie the Classical. Further west, near the Long Wall and
along the bank of the Ilissos, there were Classical burials which
may have lined an ancient road skirting Philopappos Hill, and
leaving the city through the Haladian Gate. As a result of recent
work the site of this gate on Erechtheion Street has been localized.
On the other side of the Long Wall, south of the Sacred Gate,
there was one gate, very possibly two. Although gravestones have
been found built into walls in this area, excavation has not yet
revealed a Classical cemetery.

INHUMATION

In the Classical period the people of Attica practised cremation
and inhumation, and, as in the preceding periods, the choice of
burial remains a matter of personal or family preference. There is
no apparent difference in either the rites or offerings which have
been found associated with the graves, and the predominance of
one method over the other varies from place to place. We should,
however, point out that the excavators of the two largest Classical
cemeteries in Athens—in the Kerameikos and outside the Diocharian Gate—noted a marked decrease in the number of cremation burials in the course of the fourth century.

The simplest inhumation grave was a shaft or pit cut into the
ground. Sometimes the walls had a plaster or fine stucco facing
and the natural floor a covering of pebbles or stones, but most

pits had neither. Remains of coffins or of some other protective device, such as cover slabs, were sometimes found. Offerings, if there were any, lay inside the shaft or in the nearby area; usually their quality was not high. Pit graves were single burials, as were virtually all other graves. The few examples of mass burials were the result of extreme circumstances, such as the epidemic in the Peloponnesian War (Thucydides iii 87).

Tile graves, first found in the Late Archaic period, become common in the Classical. Large flat roof tiles, of fired clay and sometimes painted, were balanced against each other to form a protective tent over the body. The ends were closed by additional tiles or were left open. The body lay on the natural floor, less often on tiles or some other form of paving. The offerings, neither numerous nor outstanding in quality, lay inside the grave or in the area immediately outside. In a few tile graves only part, almost always the upper part, of the body was covered. Not infrequently these 'half-graves' cover ashes and disturbed skeletal remains which show signs of burning: perhaps remains of incomplete cremations, caused by improper ventilation, insufficient fuel, or some other reason, which were covered by a few hastily placed tiles. Since one of the basic purposes of the practice of cremation is the total destruction of the physical body, a partial cremation was particularly unacceptable. In these cases the body seems to have been treated as an inhumation burial, and, if possible, given some form of protection.

Slab-lined and covered pits are found, as are sarcophagi. Both were made of limestone or of marble. Sarcophagi for adults were either monolithic or composite, with a horizontal or slightly gabled lid. Often the walls and lid had plaster or stucco facings, sometimes even painted decoration.

Children were buried in stone sarcophagi, but more frequently they were placed in a smaller, cheaper version of the adult sarcophagus: clay tubs (Fig. 17), one being inverted over another to enclose the small body (rarely used for an adult). Although the tubs, which were either rectangular or oval, were made of clay, this type of burial differs from the tile grave in its sealed burial compartment. Some tubs were brightly painted, both inside and

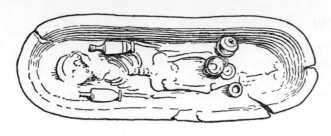

Fig. 17 A clay tub with the burial of a child

out, and richly furnished. The offerings associated with them and with sarcophagus burials are especially important, since their sealed contents provide a clear picture of the types of offerings and sometimes even of their original positions.

Children were also buried in pits covered with flat clay roof tiles or with round clay pipes, like those used for water ducts. Pot burials are numerous, frequently clustering in special infant cemeteries. As in the preceding periods there is great variety in the type of pot used. On the shoulder of a Chian amphora—a type of vase which is frequently used for child burials at this time—containing the burial of a small child at Thorikos, the letters *ERIAS* (see above, on the Erian Gate) are inscribed, perhaps an allusion to its sepulchral use. Similarly, a cup found in a cremation grave at Vari was inscribed *PYRES* ('of the pyre').

CREMATION

Primary cremation graves, familiar from the Archaic period, continue into the Classical virtually unchanged, except for a noticeable tendency towards simplification: thus, ventilation channels are now much less common. Secondary cremations are more numerous than they had been in the preceding period and there is now a greater variety in the types of ash urn. The clay urns were either coarse and unslipped, discreetly painted in the manner of some household pots, or they were more elaborately painted with red-figure scenes. It would seem that on the whole these vases were not made specifically for the grave and some have obviously served a domestic purpose. The vase was either set directly in the ground and marked by a gravestone, or it was placed inside a protective box. Metal ash urns—bronze cauldrons and *hydriai* are most common, less often clay urns—were placed in lidded stone boxes. On some have been preserved traces of cloth in which the cremated remains were wrapped, and with which the vase itself was sometimes covered. An exceptionally well-preserved grave in the Kerameikos shows how carefully the ashes were sometimes treated: they were gathered from the pyre into a purple cloth, placed in a bronze cauldron, which was itself wrapped in cloth (*Pl. 23*). The urn lay in a wooden chest inside a stone box, which was buried beneath a built tomb.

In the Classical period, as in the Archaic, the cremation of infants was an accepted, but apparently limited, practice. The bones of children have been identified in a small number of burnt deposits, but in most cases the soft skeletal remains were probably reduced to imperceptible bits by the fire. For this reason it is difficult to determine whether small burnt deposits, found in cemeteries and in domestic quarters, were infant cremations or the remains of burnt offerings. A group of deposits from the Agora, Classical and Hellenistic, have been considered infant cremations, even though the small amount of bone matter defies analysis. The small, shallow, irregularly-shaped deposits, similar to the 'offering places' of the Archaic period, contained ash, burnt wood, unidentifiable bone (some bones of animals have been identified) and burnt vases. The vases represent types which are not regularly found in domestic deposits, specifically the solid 'dummy' *alabastra*, ribbon-handled banded plates, black-painted *pyxides*, and unslipped miniature cooking pots (*Pl. 22*). This ware, apart from some common plates, saucers, and cups, which were found associated with them, has been considered funerary. The vases are distinctive and similar types have been found in contemporary graves, but they are perhaps more characteristic of 'cult ware' than they are of funerary use: the dummy *alabastra* and the miniature cooking pots were certainly never designed for normal household use. The accessory vases were perhaps used by those who participated in rites involving burnt sacrifices. These sacrifices need not, but could have been, funerary.

CENOTAPHS

In addition to inhumation and cremation graves there are empty graves. The cenotaph was most often used for those who lost their lives far from home or those whose bones were for some reason irrecoverable, as in loss at sea. Cenotaphs formed part of the state burial complex on the Academy Road, but they were also required for private burials. They received the same offerings and respectful treatment as other graves. In some cenotaphs the body of the dead was supplied by a large stone around which offerings were placed.

OFFERINGS

Offerings have been found lying around the dead in no apparent order, in the fill of the grave shaft, and in special 'offering places' and 'offering ditches'. Some of the ditches closely resemble the Archaic type: long, narrow, brick-lined furrows (rarely stone-lined) filled with ashes, sherds and animal bones, beneath or beside the funerary monument. Others, cut out of the rock or constructed from stones or bricks, lay beside the grave or parallel to the enclosure wall. Often broken pots have been found in an orderly arrangement in the ditches and it seems likely that they were originally arranged in a row on a low platform.

Offering places are more numerous than ditches and, as in the Archaic period, there is great variety in their size, shape, and composition. Among the pottery there are large numbers of cups, bowls, and ribbon-handled banded plates, as well as *chytrai, lekythoi, hydriai,* and *lebetes gamikoi* (Pl. 21). The more elaborate vases of the Archaic period with their modelled snakes, griffin and hen heads, blossoms, and mourners are no longer found. There are some free-standing clay mourners—one offering ditch in the Kerameikos yielded several rather large ones (Pl. 24)—but the type is represented more fully now in Boeotia.

Allowing for the disappearance of perishable goods, the standard grave furnishings are *lekythoi*, cups, bowls, jugs, and lidded containers of various types. Ribbon-handled banded plates are found, but not in any number. Two other types of vases, worthy of note, are associated with the burials of children: the 'feeder' and the *chous* juglet. The former is black-painted and regularly shows signs of use; the latter usually has scenes in red-figure of children at play.

The cups, bowls, jugs and containers represent types which appear in non-funerary contexts, such as wells and domestic deposits. The most common type of decoration is black paint, with or without stamped patterns. Undecorated, unslipped household ware and fine red-figure vases are also found.

There are stone vases of various shapes in graves and in offering deposits: lidded containers—*pyxides*—of marble with painted decoration; *plemochoai*, such as we see carried by women on white-ground *lekythoi*, made of stone and often quite large; *alabastra* of alabaster, marble or limestone. There are also clay *alabastra*, covered with white slip, probably in imitation of the more expensive stone vases, a few of which were perhaps imported. Some of the stone *alabastra* were very large, and although they were not all designed exclusively for the grave, the solid, or 'dummy' almost certainly were, since they could serve no practical purpose.

Apart from the vases, most of the offerings look like cherished possessions of the dead: strigils, mirrors, and toys. At present, jewellery is not well represented in Classical burials in Attica, but this picture may change with further excavation. Metal jewellery —bronze and gold—consists of rings for the fingers and ears, and floral sprays and wreaths. There is also imitation jewellery in clay in the form of earrings and decorative rosettes painted polychrome and gilt. The clay figurines found in Classical graves represent well-known types: seated female figures and armless busts, both of uncertain identity, seated women holding infants (frequently from children's graves) and toys, dolls and animals.

In Classical burials, as in those of the Archaic period, there are a few objects which, although they do not occur in number, are important because of their possible significance in funerary rite. Miniature arms (approximately 10 cm. long) have been found in a few graves of adults and children. They are cut off at the elbow: some with flat bases, presumably to stand upright, with all four fingers and thumb extended, but held closely together in what has been called an apotropaic gesture (*Pl. 25*). The resemblance of the gesture to that of men honouring the dead may be deceptive. One sarcophagus burial of a woman had four of these clay arms, covered with a white slip, and one with a bracelet painted on it. Another group of four, white-slipped and wearing bracelets, now in the British Museum, is also said to have come from a single grave, and a similar white-slipped arm was found in a child's grave. In these graves there were clay figurines, among them busts of women and dollies, but the arms showed no signs of ever being attached. A grave recently discovered on Piraeus Street produced a clay arm and another of ivory. The latter differed from the others in the position of the fingers which appear to hold a *phiale*. The purpose of the arms is not clear. Other objects associated with some graves are lead 'coffins' and curse tablets (see p. 217). A crescent-shaped tablet was found in the pot burial of a child. These objects, however, are not immediately relevant to the burials they accompany.

WHITE-GROUND LEKYTHOI

The offering which is most characteristic of Classical burials is the *lekythos*—a generic name for oil vessel. Since oil was widely used—in the bath and boudoir, at the *palaistra*, in the preparation and consumption of food, and in the performance of funerary rites—the vessels which contained it were produced in different shapes and sizes and were decorated in different ways. In the Classical period the *lekythoi* most frequently found in graves are tall, slender vessels with the shoulder set off from the body, and short, squat vessels with a broad base and no distinct shoulder. The former are regularly covered with a white slip, although some are decorated in red-figure; the latter are black-painted with red-figure decoration, of which the simple palmette *anthemion* is the most popular, and this type continued to be supplied to graves in the fourth century, when the production of the slender form had apparently ceased. Our interest here is in the white-ground *lekythoi* whose figure decoration, whether rendered in black-figure, glaze or matt outline, contributes to our understanding of contemporary burial practices. We must remember, however, that not all white-ground *lekythoi* had figure decoration and those which do are not always funerary in their iconography. There are mythological and domestic scenes, such as one finds on black- and red-figure vases, and, most important, there is a large group decorated with patterns: lattice work, diamonds, palmettes, ivy-berry clusters, laurels, etc. These so-called 'pattern *lekythoi*' are common in graves of the Classical period and, like white-ground *lekythoi* with figure decoration, sometimes had false interior chambers which held a fraction of the oil necessary to fill a complete vase, thereby enabling the mourner to economize in his presentation of precious oil at the grave.

If the regular occurrence of oil vessels in graves is not sufficient evidence for the importance of the substance in funerary rites, scenes on white-ground *lekythoi* are. We see *lekythoi* standing around the gravestone or hanging from it; mourners bring *lekythoi* to the tomb or prepare baskets of them for presentation at the grave (*Pl. 26*). In the *prothesis* scenes the vases stand about the bier, for after the body was washed it was anointed and then dressed for the formal lying-in-state. It has been suggested that *lekythoi* also held perfumed essences whose scent freshened the air during the funeral. There are, however, shallow, wide-mouthed vessels equipped with lids (*plemochoai*) which would have served the purpose better, and they are often represented in tomb scenes, but are less often found in graves. The number of *lekythoi* placed in graves and the regularity with which they were offered suggest that the contents were as necessary to the dead as to the living.

Apart from the mythological and domestic scenes which are common on early white-ground *lekythoi*, there are two general categories into which the scenes can be divided: those on which Death is represented allegorically in the persons of Charon, Hermes, Thanatos and Hypnos, and those on which people are seen executing the rites of burial practised in Classical Athens. There are, of course, scenes which fall outside these major groups, but their number is small.

The mythological ministers of Death were familiar motifs which the painters of white-ground *lekythoi* found ready to hand in the literary, graphic, and plastic arts of the time. Charon, the most frequently represented of the mythological figures, is seen guiding his boat in much the same manner as he must have done in the famous painting of the *Nekyia* by Polygnotos in the Delphian *Lesche* (Pausanias x 28.1). Sometimes Charon confronts the dead by himself; at other times Hermes escorts the dead to the waiting boat. Hermes is more often represented in this role of *psychopompos* intervening between the dead and the minister of Death than he is by himself. Just as he conducts the dead to Charon, he often looks on while Thanatos and Hypnos perform their duty. These brothers, Sleep and Death, known to us best in the epic tradition from the burial of Sarpedon (*Iliad* xvi 671-5) are most often seen bearing the body of a warrior in full panoply, although the painters of white-ground *lekythoi* felt free to alter the composition.

There is also a non-mythological scene in which the vase-painters represent the dead—the *prothesis*. The dead lies on his bier, in funeral dress, adorned with fillets and wreaths. Attending the bier are mourners who tear their hair, lacerate their cheeks, and strike their heads and breasts in performance of the ritual lament.

By far the greatest proportion of the *lekythoi* with funerary iconography show visits to the tomb. Men, women and children come to the grave bearing tokens of remembrance—vases, garlands, and fillets with which they decorate the tomb (*Pl. 27*). Some sit by the grave, mourning their loss, some fall to the ground and express their grief more openly, and others stand by quietly, occasionally covering their faces to conceal their sorrow.

An interpretation of the iconography of the funerary scenes on white-ground *lekythoi* is often combined with that of the grave reliefs and it is commonly held that the dead is shown beside the gravestone witnessing offerings being made at it. However, we cannot certainly distinguish the dead by any criterion of dress, pose, or gesture, and arguments from the scenes on relief gravestones are irrelevant, since the compositions, not to mention the purposes for which the compositions were designed, are significantly different. The most common scene on the vases, the visit to the tomb, appears, as we shall see, on a very small number of gravestones—on marble *lekythoi* whose disposition in the cemetery and whose style of decoration correspond to that of the large clay *lekythoi* whose form they almost certainly imitated. Secondly, we note an absence on the grave reliefs of gestures openly expressive of intense grief. On white-ground *lekythoi* mourners perform the lament at both the bier and the grave. Thirdly, the handclasp, or *dexiosis*, which is so often used on grave reliefs is virtually unknown on white-ground *lekythoi*. In the circumstances it might be better to exercise caution in identifying both the dead and the living together in single scenes.

MOUNDS AND BUILT TOMBS

For the Classical period in Attica we have not only funerary monuments, but also descriptions of them in the words of ancient, often contemporary, writers. Historians, orators, geographers, tragedians, and comedians mentioned the monuments which they saw lining the roads from their cities. The references are casual. No explanation was given because none was necessary; everyone knew the monuments well. Indeed, 'monument' is what they were called—*mnema* and *sema*. The more precise terminology which modern scholars have developed is often neither authentic nor accurate.

Round earth mounds of the Classical period resembled their Archaic predecessors: some are large, covering more than one grave, others are smaller, covering a single grave. A few mounds were clearly used for more than one generation, presumably by members of the same family, since considerable care was taken not to disturb earlier graves and there was sometimes only one monument, bearing inscriptions of different date. A mound in the Kerameikos, Eukoline's mound, just under 10 m. in diameter, was crowned by a relief monument bearing the names of five persons, not all carved at the same time; beneath the mound, and on its periphery, were five graves of adults and children (Fig. 18). In addition to the excavated mounds, we have descriptions and pictures of them in contemporary literature and art: a platform or base of encircling stones supported an earth mound, covered with light-coloured plaster and crowned by a gravestone, sculpture or vase. In vase-paintings mounds are most often covered with loops and swags of coloured ribbons and this was probably

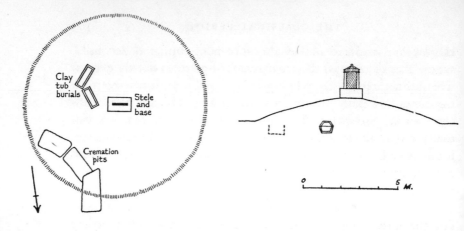

Fig. 18 Plan and section of the burial mound of Eukoline in Athens, surmounted by a relief gravestone but covering various tub and cremation burials

their commonest form of ornament. In Greek religion ribbons were widely used to set off the object which they adorned as something special, something sacred.

The rectangular mounds and built tombs of the Archaic period continued into the Classical, and since they seem to have remained virtually unchanged they require little comment. Some of the built tombs were constructed entirely of brick, others had brick side walls and an ashlar masonry façade. They were crowned by low cornices and these, in a few examples, still retain traces of their original rich polychromy. Offering ditches have been found inside built tombs and outside, along the wall. Frequently boundary stones (*horoi*) marked one or more of the corners. Towards the end of the fifth century a grander type of built tomb appeared. During the following century its popularity and magnificence increased until, in the last quarter of the century, the legislation of Demetrios of Phaleron brought its development to an end. In principle the *peribolos* tomb is no more than a group of graves in an enclosed area (Fig. 19). The dead may have been of one family, but we cannot be certain.

The *peribolos* tomb differs from an enclosed plot in its general plan and manner of construction, and these it shares with the built tombs. Like them, *peribolos* tombs were free-standing or, more often, enclosed on one or more sides. In the Kerameikos, where the terrain was irregular, many were set out on terraces. The side and rear walls were executed in various materials but the front walls, which lined the road, were regularly rendered with care, and at great expense, in fine ashlar masonry (Fig. 20). But ashlar blocks were ideal building material and were often later removed for reuse elsewhere. In the Kerameikos many of the *peribolos* tombs suffered serious damage towards the end of the third quarter of the fourth century. When they were rebuilt, shortly thereafter, fine ashlar masonry was no longer the rule. Contemporary literature records the use of 'tombs' for the defence against Philip of Macedon in 338 BC and the excavators of the Kerameikos are no doubt correct in giving this explanation for the damage to the monuments.

The graves of *peribolos* tombs were not inside the monument, but beneath it, just as they were beneath built tombs, but beneath

Fig. 19   A tomb enclosure, 16 m. wide, at St John Rente in Attica, including several sarcophagus burials of the first half of the fourth century BC

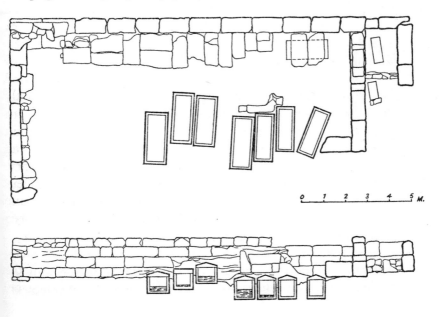

the latter there was one grave, beneath the former several (Fig. 19). Most of the *peribolos* tombs were, however, used for some time and the later graves are in the superstructure. Again, like built tombs, gravestones were erected above the walls of *peribolos* tombs. Normally there is more than one monument, as one would expect with several burials in the area, and these cluster along the front wall (Fig. 20). Such a disposition of the gravestones accords well with the showy effect of the monumental tomb, but it often meant that the exact site of the grave, within the enclosure, was not marked.

Perhaps the best known example of the *peribolos* tomb, although in several respects not a canonical example, is the tomb of Dexileos, who died fighting in Corinth in 394 BC, on 'West Road' in the Kerameikos (Fig. 20, left). Most *peribolos* tombs in Athens and elsewhere in Attica were roughly rectangular in plan; the quadrant shape of Dexileos' is probably due to the location of the tomb at the junction of two roads. Just as plots had *horoi* to mark their boundaries, so did *peribolos* tombs—either simple slabs or more elaborate sculpture. Shrubbery and potted plants completed the adornment.

STATE GRAVES

The Academy Road which left the city of Athens through the Thriasian/Dipylon Gate had 'sanctuaries of the gods and graves of heroes and men' along its course (Pausanias i 29.2). The area immediately outside the city gate was a state burial ground. For the Athenians, unlike other Greeks, did not regularly bury their dead on the field of battle (Demosthenes xx 141) but brought the bones home for burial in a public grave. According to Thucydides (ii 34.1) this was their ancestral custom, *patrios nomos*. We do not know when the custom began or if, after its institution, it was followed without exception, but we do know at least two occasions in the fifth century—Marathon and Plataea—when the Athenians buried their war dead in the traditional Greek manner (see pp. 198f.).

Pausanias, writing in the second century after Christ, described the state graves in what appears to be a roughly topographical

Fig. 20 Grave plots along the West Road of the Kerameikos in Athens. That on the left is of Dexileos and behind are two Hellenistic 'mensae'

order (i 29). His account is the only one which we have. It is not accurate, nor could it be. Even if he used the reliable fourth-century topographer Diodoros Periegetes, the terrain of the Kerameikos had already, by the time of Diodoros, suffered alterations by human and natural means. By the middle of the fourth century the *horoi* along the Academy Road were raised to compensate for the rising ground level, and little more than a decade later the land and its tombs were sacrificed for the defence against Philip (Aeschines *Ktesiphon* 236); a layer of rubble and brick bears witness to the destruction. Further evidence that the graves were soon covered is the series of Hellenistic graves laid in the area of the state graves which were also oriented along the Academy Road. Finally, before Pausanias came to the cemetery, the land suffered devastation at the hands of Philip V in 200 BC and Sulla in 86 BC.

The earliest state graves which have been so far discovered lie parallel to the Themistoclean Wall, from which they were divided by the so-called Ring Road (Map 5). An early date for the complex is indicated by the eastern boundary—a Themistoclean retaining wall. In the second half of the fifth century a parapet was erected which ran parallel to the Themistoclean Wall and was separated from it by the Ring Road. By the end of the Peloponnesian War, when Athens was forced to capitulate, these state graves were covered. Soon after, however, the entire area was transformed: construction of the Classical Pompeion began, fortifications were strengthened, new water lines were laid, the Ring Road was lengthened and the Academy Road was widened to its greatest extent (37 m.). State graves were now laid out on the north and south sides of the parapet wall, on both flanks of the city gate. Further down the Academy Road, between *horoi* 2 and 3, state graves were also set out. Although Pausanias describes approximately twenty monuments to men who died in battle during the fifth century—monuments which the author of the original 'guide book' must have known, since he describes the sculpture which adorned some of them—the earliest grave known to us from excavation and whose identity is beyond question is the grave of the Lacedaimonians (404/3 BC)—an impressive ashlar masonry structure more than 11 m. long, crowned by an inscribed cornice block recording the names of the polemarchs and the battle in which they and their forces fell. The monument was, in fact, a *peribolos* tomb, which differed from those of private burials in its internal division into three chambers. The burials were beneath the somewhat irregularly laid foundations, as they were in *peribolos* tombs. Thirteen men were buried here, some with points of spears and arrows still lodged in their bodies. In the centre chamber three men had been laid out with greater care, and they were perhaps the three whom the inscription named. On the west side of the tomb of the Lacedaimonians there was a series of warriors' graves, also enclosed within *peribolos* tombs, some of which had interior chambers, and they were separated from each other by a narrow passageway. Although each had its own rear wall, they all shared a common façade on the Academy Road. As in the Lacedaimonians' tomb the burials were beneath the monument. There were communal graves, single graves and cenotaphs. The single burials were in marble sarcophagi, lined or unlined pits. Some had stone *alabastra* and bronze strigils, but most were unfurnished. There were, however, traces of offering places with 'ritual' vases resembling those found in other offering places—cups, bowls, and jugs, both painted and unpainted. There were also ashes and some animal bones.

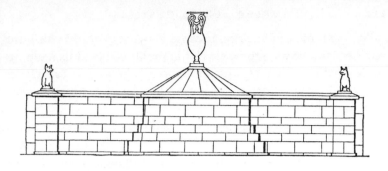

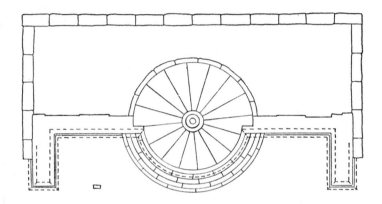

Fig. 21   The 'Tomb at horos *3' in the Kerameikos, 15 m. wide. A state grave for an unknown occasion of the mid-fourth century BC*

At *horos* 3, on the south side of the Academy Road, a magnificent tomb was built around the middle of the fourth century whose remarkable style of architecture is, so far as we know, unique (Fig. 21). The large ashlar monument combined the two basic types of funerary architecture—the round and rectangular mounds. In the centre of the rectangle was a circular structure which supported a large marble *loutrophoros* (2 m. high) richly painted and adorned with bronze. Two guardian stone dogs, well over life-size and flashing eyes of inlaid glass, marked the corners of the façade. Although this 'Tomb at *horos* 3' lies in the area of the state graves, it is not certainly one of them. It is sometimes called the tomb of Chabrias, because Pausanias says that his tomb was here and because the style of the monument and its sculpture accord with the date at which Chabrias is known to have fallen in battle (357 BC), but no inscription has yet been found to confirm the identification.

Along the Academy Road excavation has revealed a series of post holes of at least two different sizes. Since the holes appear to have been made at regular intervals, it is thought that they supported tribunes during the state funerals, but other explanations are possible.

The State honoured its war dead in two types of ceremonies. One took place on the day of the funeral and corresponds to *ta trita* of private burials. The other was an annual celebration. Both were apparently performed at the grave. The best-known example of the first occurs in Thucydides' account of Perikles' Funeral Oration (ii 34). There was the *prothesis*, followed by the *ekphora* with the women performing the lament. The state funeral differed from private funerals in being financed by the State and in the delivery of the Funeral Oration, which was not originally part of the public funeral (Thucydides ii 35.1). Although the earliest *epitaphios logos* of which we have record is that delivered by Perikles for the men who fell in 439 BC against the Samians (Plutarch *Perikles* 28.4), according to later ancient sources the custom began soon after the Persian Wars (Dionysios Halikarnassos *Ant. Rom.* v 17.4; Diodorus xi 33). Probably around the same time inscribed monuments, the so-called Casualty Lists, were set up in honour of the year's war dead. There are more than thirty of these monuments known and the earliest dates to 464 BC. Initially there seem to have been ten *stelai* set up over the grave, one for each tribe, on which the names of its fallen were inscribed. Although later monuments were not physically separate units, some maintained sunken vertical channels in imitation of the original ten *stelai*. There was only one monument set up each year and if there were years of peace there were no monuments, just as there was no Funeral Oration, for these were special honours which Athens bestowed on her fallen 'whenever the occasion arose' (Thucydides ii 34.8).

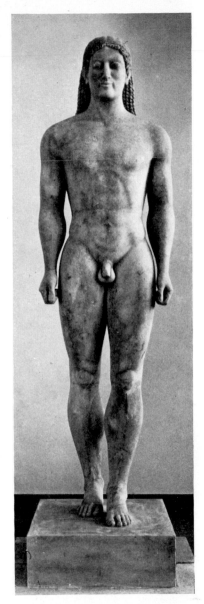

19, 20 Sixth-century monumental grave markers from Attica: *left*, the *stele* of Aristion by the sculptor Aristokles; and (*right*) the *kouros* marking the grave of Kroisos.

21, 22 Vase offerings from Athenian graves of about 420 BC (*above*) including two *lebetes gamikoi* and several squat *lekythoi*, and of about the mid-fourth century (*below*).

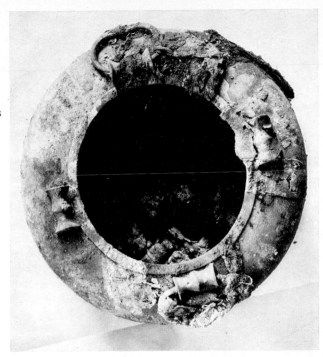

23 A bronze cauldron used as an ash urn with traces of the cloth it was wrapped in.

24, 25 *Below, left:* a clay mourner from a Classical Athenian grave.
Below, right: a clay bust and arms from a Classical Athenian grave.

26, 27 Two Athenian white-ground *lekythoi*: the one on the left shows
women taking ribbons and *lekythoi* from a chest; the other shows a
stele bound with a ribbon and with *lekythoi* hanging at either side,
approached by women, one weeping and carrying a ribbon, the other
with a box of ribbons and fruit. The circles on the *stele* base are not
explained.

28–30 Three Classical Athenian grave markers: *left*, a marble *lekythos* on a drum base; *below, left*, a marble griffin cauldron on the capital of an acanthus column; and (*below*) the gravestone of Eupheros, shown holding a strigil.

ΕΥΦΗΡΟΣ

31 The gravestone of Ampharete, holding her grandchild. For the epitaph see p. 262.

32   The gravestone from the Ilissos. This would have been set in an architectural frame.

33 A black-figure funeral plaque by the Sappho Painter showing a *prothesis*. The plaque was probably fastened to a grave monument.

34, 35 Black-figure vases showing funeral processions, with the bier being carried on a mule cart, towards a rectangular tomb, and by men.

Some of the tombs of men who fell in battle were adorned with inscribed and elaborately decorated cornices, while others bore sculptured reliefs, most often of horsemen and warriors. The production of these reliefs was not affected by the funerary legislation which otherwise severely limited the number of sculptured reliefs during the Early Classical period. Pausanias describes the relief monument of Melanopos and Makartatos who fell at Tanagra in 457 BC (i 29.6).

The annual celebration in honour of the dead corresponds to *ta nomizomena* which the family performed annually on behalf of its own departed members. The public ceremony differed from the private in being financed by the State and being celebrated on a grander scale. Plato mentions musical competitions, athletic and horse events (*Menexenos* 249B), Lysias tells of contests of 'strength, wisdom and wealth' (ii 80). Evidence for torch races at state celebrations is late—second-century ephebic inscriptions. Responsibility for the execution of the rites rested with the Polemarch (*Athenaion Politeia* 58.1) and even in the time of Plutarch the Polemarch was presiding over the annual ceremony in honour of the Plataean war dead (*Aristeides* 21.2).

GRAVESTONES

At the end of the sixth century in Athens the production of gravestones with figure decoration rendered in relief came to an end, presumably as a result of the legislation recorded by Cicero in the *Laws* (see p. 90). The continued absence of relief gravestones in Athens until the end of the third quarter of the fifth century need not be related to any decision of the Athenians (the 'Oath of Plataea') to suspend all sacred building until all Greece was free, and we shall see that in Athens during these years there were grave markers of other types.

According to Cicero funerary legislation was passed at least three times in Athens: (1) during the period of Solon; (2) sometime thereafter—*post aliquando*; (3) under the rule of Demetrios of Phaleron. The monumental size which grave mounds and built tombs attained during the sixth century and the magnificence of their sculpture were open invitations to sumptuary laws. Athenians were apparently prone to extravagance in their funerary art and architecture to judge from the frequency with which legislation was levelled against it. Only one of the recorded legislations, that of Demetrios of Phaleron, expressly limits the type of monument and its size. The *post aliquando* legislation stipulates that the work on the grave (*sepulcrum*) must not exceed that required of ten men in three days: Plato suggests five men in five days in the *Laws* (xii 958). Within this limitation it was possible to build tombs of some magnificence and recent excavation on the Sacred Way has revealed a series of plastered earth mounds and built tombs from about 500 to 450 BC. The *post aliquando* legislation also bans the ornamentation of tombs with *opus tectorium*, some sort of decoration more extravagant than the plaster layers with which all the Kerameikos structures were covered, and the erection of crowning *hermai*. None of the structures found along the Sacred Way from the first half of the fifth century, so far as we know, had crowning *stelai*. The legislation recorded by Cicero does not forbid marking graves and from this period we not only have gravestones, we also have representations of them on vases. They are, however, on the whole modest and undecorated markers suitable to a period during which the sumptuary laws were still effective.

Apart from a few reliefs of disputed place of manufacture, such as the relief of a seated woman found in the Piraeus (Conze no. 36) and the reliefs which adorned state burials, gravestones with figure decoration rendered in relief begin to reappear in Athens only when work on the Parthenon was drawing to a close. The many sculptors who had been recruited for that great programme found themselves in need of work; some must have turned their talents to the production of grave reliefs. As we have noted, the effectiveness of funerary legislation is short-lived. Just as Solon's restrictions were soon evaded and extravagances set in, so in the course of the fifth century the production of funerary art and architecture regained prominence. It soon flourished to such an extent that Demetrios of Phaleron found it necessary to pass more stringent legislation even before the fourth century came to an end.

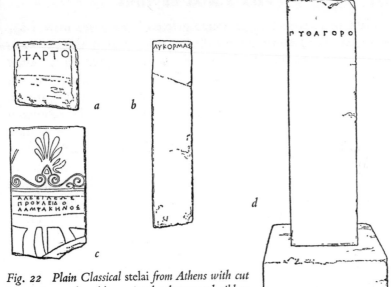

Fig. 22 *Plain Classical* stelai *from Athens with cut inscriptions and on (c) a painted palmette and ribbon*

SLAB STELAI

Small stone markers were a common and economical means of designating the place of burial and many of them were well under 1 m. in height. They resemble *horoi* in their often irregular shape and in the lack of a base, the lower part being left largely untooled, for insertion into the ground. The name of the dead was inscribed on the upper part of the shaft (Fig. 22a, b). The use of modest markers of stone is, as we have seen, attested at least as early as the beginning of the Iron Age in Attica. These small slabs continued to be produced throughout the Classical period, even when impressive relief monuments reappeared, and some of them were painted in imitation of the sculpture. They have been found in situ over graves and along *peribolos* walls. One, with the name of the dead inscribed on the upper shaft, which measured in all 46 cm., was found in place over a red-figure *pelike* by the Peleus Painter (about 440–430 BC) which contained cremated remains (Fig. 23). Not all small stone markers were undecorated. Painted ornament, especially bright coloured ribbons, was common and sometimes details of *anthemia* were painted (Fig. 22c).

Slabs of greater height, ranging from 1 to more than 2 m., were produced apparently without break during the fifth and fourth centuries. The Early Classical *stelai* resemble the Archaic in shape and manner of composition—a slender slab, with or without finial, attached to a stepped base—but unlike them, there was normally no figure decoration. Simple crowning mouldings or palmette finials, painted non-figure decoration such as ribbons, and short inscriptions completed these unpretentious gravestones. Many of those with low pediment or terminal mouldings resemble record and decree *stelai* of the same period, and on white-ground *lekythoi* similar austere monuments are represented. The *stele* of Pythagoras, *proxenos* of Selymbria (Conze no. 1440a), which stands on the Sacred Way, is perhaps the best example we have of an early Classical *stele* of some importance. It is an undecorated marble shaft, without finial, on a stepped base; the total height is 3·16 m. (Fig. 22d). Similar *stelai*, some with painted decoration, have been found in Attica, and they too have been dated within the first half of the century. Unfortunately the tall slender shafts were easily broken and frequently reused in antiquity; therefore few have survived complete. Nevertheless, with the aid of representations on *lekythoi* we can trace the development of the Classical *stele*.

During the third quarter of the fifth century the acanthus plant, which had recently appeared in architectural decoration, was introduced into the *anthemia* of gravestones. Initially the acanthus played a discreet supporting role, but soon its luxuriant foliage came to predominate and at the peak of this 'florid' style birds, other animals, sirens and mourning women made their way into the acanthus *anthemia*. Generally two tendencies can be observed in the sculptural decoration of the *anthemia*: (1) they become more three dimensional; some leaves are almost cut free of the stone, and there is a conscious effort to exploit the light and shade of the forms for artistic effect; (2) the style of decoration is equally ornate, but it remains essentially linear and calligraphic (Fig. 24a).

Some types of *stelai* are not regularly represented on the *lekythoi*, and these are probably forms which became fashionable in

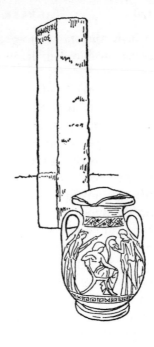

Fig. 23 *A cremation burial in a red-figure vase marked by a plain* stele

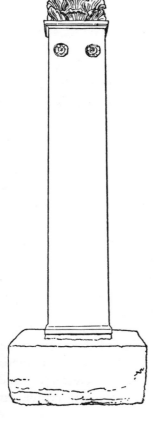

Fig. 24 Anthemion stelai *from Athens and the Piraeus:* (a) *with two rosettes on the shaft, and* (b) *with a relief scene*

a

b

Athens after the white-ground *lekythoi* with funerary scenes ceased to be produced in large numbers: rosette *stelai* and *stelai* with relief panels.

The presence of rosettes or rosette-like ornaments on grave monuments in Greece and elsewhere over a considerable period of time perhaps strengthens the theory that they have a symbolic importance in funerary art. Rosettes had decorated Attic grave-stones as early as the Archaic period, but the rosette *stele* seems to have been a creation of the fourth century. The basic form of the monument—a slender shaft with a pair of rosettes in relief on the upper part of the principal face (Fig. 24a)—remains uniform, although the treatment of the rosettes varies: some are no more than a series of concentric circles of different sizes, others are elaborate systems of overlapping petals. The latter, both in size and form, resemble very closely the plaster rosette, painted red and blue with gilt, which was found on the left breast of a woman, Hipparete, buried in the Kerameikos. Most *stelai* have only the pair of rosettes; some have two more, one on each of the small sides—an arrangement found on an Archaic limestone *stele* from the Themistoclean Wall—and rarely there is only one central rosette on the upper principal face. Therefore the suggestion that the position of the rosettes on the shaft is in any way anthropomorphic becomes difficult to support.

The rosette *stele* of Eutychos and Eirene (Conze no. 1615) is one of the earliest: its sculptural ornament—a doubled acanthus supporting a sprung palmette—is closely paralleled on the *stele* of Euphanes and his brother, dated epigraphically to the end of the fifth century, and on *stelai* painted on vases by the Quadrate Painter. Inscriptions on rosette *stelai* appear above or below the rosettes and sometimes there is, in addition, a relief panel. The finial is either a simple moulding or a more elaborate *anthemion* like that of Eutychos' and Eirene's monument.

Stelai with small panels of relief decoration on the upper part of the shaft (Fig. 24b) appear not to have been fashionable in the fifth century although a white-ground *lekythos* by the Tymbos Painter represents such a monument. We may, therefore, assume that the *stele* with relief panel was known in the fifth century, if not widely used. Often the panel has an architectural frame and small antae are indicated in low relief. The frame and the iconography of the panel relate these *stelai* to the broader relief monuments to which we shall soon turn.

VASES

On some of the *stelai* the frame is omitted and the decoration is either painted or in relief on the face of the shaft—scenes similar to those framed within antae, and representations of vases used in various aspects of funerary rite—*lekythoi, loutrophoroi, hydriai* and *chytrai*. Vases are also sometimes seen on more modest slabs, but on these they are the only form of decoration (Fig. 25); one such slab is an amphiglyph—a *lekythos* appears on one side, a *loutrophoros* on the other. Vases carved in the round—*lekythoi* and the two types of *loutrophoros*, the amphora and *hydria*—seem to come into fashion in Athenian cemeteries when white-ground *lekythoi* are on the decline, towards the end of the fifth century. Perhaps transitional between the two are the small group of very large clay *lekythoi* whose form and style of decoration are unlike other white-ground *lekythoi*, and an equally small number of stone *lekythoi* related to the clay types in either iconography or manner of decoration. The former—the 'Group of the Huge Lekythoi' (0·68–1·10 m. high)—are completely covered with white slip, perhaps in imitation of stone, the mouth being detachable. The subsidiary decoration is extremely ornate; the primary picture panel, executed in polychrome with some shading and use of perspective, almost certainly reflects contemporary free-painting.

Fig. 25   A stele with a lekythos shown in relief

Although most of the decorated stone vases have relief scenes similar to those of other grave monuments, a few are painted like clay *lekythoi*, only somewhat more elaborately: horizontal bands of decoration framing the picture panel completely circle the body of the vase, and its neck, mouth and foot, instead of being painted black, have intricate pattern work in polychrome. The primary decoration borrows from the repertoire of the clay vases. One of these stone *lekythoi* was even found buried with the dead—the usual practice for clay white-ground *lekythoi*. A small number of stone vases with relief decoration also borrow themes from white-ground *lekythoi*—tomb scenes, preparation of offerings, decoration of the grave. This similarity in iconography and in style of decoration is entirely reasonable when we remember that both clay and stone vases were displayed in the same way in cemeteries—on top of grave monuments or in front of them, or at each end of a plot, marking its boundary. Bases of the vases have been found in situ in these positions and a few of the stone ones are inscribed *horos mnematos*. Some vases, instead of being set into other larger monuments, had their own bases, either round (*Pl. 28*) or square, which could bear an inscription or relief decoration.

Apart from the few scenes mentioned above, reliefs on stone vases regularly reproduce those of larger grave monuments, multi-figure groups linked by the *dexiosis* or handclasp being especially common. Some of the reliefs have a large number of figures, not infrequently all named (occasional small figures, presumably

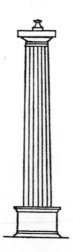

Fig. 26   A grave marking column which supported a stone vase (only the base preserved) in the Athens cemetery

servants, remain anonymous), and this suggests that the vases were sometimes family gravestones. On one *loutrophoros* from the Kerameikos two women hand over an infant while a girl stands holding a box. On another two groups of figures, some standing, others seated, are linked by handclasps. Battle scenes are not uncommon; an extremely fine example was recently found during excavation around Syntagma Square. Also from the Diocharian Gate cemetery comes the large marble *lekythos* of Myrrhine, notable for its iconography: Hermes leading the dead by the hand. Reliefs alluding to the manner of death are as rare on these vases as they are on *stelai* and other grave monuments, death in childbirth occasionally being represented.

Finally there are stone vases whose decoration recalls metalwork: on the body ribbing, on the shoulder ornate bands of pattern in relief. A few of these also have relief panels with figure decoration.

COLUMNS

Columns were sometimes used to mark graves instead of *stelai*. They bore the name of the dead on the capital or base and were decorated with ribbons or garlands just like *stelai*. In both Attic and South Italian vase-paintings, graves are sometimes marked this way. Columns were apparently designed to support other objects, especially vases in the Classical cemeteries. In a plot on the Sacred Way a column supporting a vase bore the oldest inscription and was given pride of place in the enclosure (Fig. 26). A fine marble acanthus column, dated about 350 BC on the basis of its sculptural decoration, supported a marble cauldron with griffin foreparts (*Pl. 29*). Other marble cauldrons with cuttings for foreparts, similar capitals and griffin heads, found in Athens, the Piraeus, and reported from elsewhere, were probably assembled in a similar manner. Additional evidence for the use of columns in cemeteries is supplied by bases with circular cuttings of appropriate size.

BASES

Cemeteries have yielded bases of different sizes and shapes—

circular, square or rectangular, with cuttings on their tops, or otherwise suitably worked to receive free-standing sculpture. But the object originally set in the base and the purpose for which the complete monument was designed are not always clear. The following few examples are cited not because they are representative, but for their unusual form or type of decoration. A square base, with simple moulding framing a relief panel on three sides, the fourth being only roughly tooled, was found in a burial plot near the Academy. The scene recalls Dexileos: a horseman riding down a foe. Although a marble grave vase was found at the same time, the rather large rectangular cutting is more suitable for a gravestone. Another base with simple mouldings framing reliefs on three sides was recently found in Athens. It shows Hermes, a priest, and a scene of apple-picking. It is not certain what its purpose was, nor what was set into its circular cutting. It may have been a vase, but the base does not have the proportions (0·83 × 0·50 m.) of most other vase-monuments, and, unlike them, it has beneath a roughly worked tenon for insertion. Different again—and these may not be bases for grave monuments but rather decorative revetments for large tombs— are two sets of joined slabs with low relief decoration from Salamis and the Piraeus. The dimensions of each set, as preserved (0·48 × 0·66–0·77 m. and 0·41 × 0·94 m.), are roughly similar and both have simple mouldings framing reliefs of coursing greyhounds. They date from the second half of the fourth century, when the monumental tomb plots were especially favoured.

GRAVESTONES WITH FIGURE DECORATION

There is a series of grave reliefs, shorter and broader than the old Archaic type, which are decorated in the style of the Parthenon sculptures. The more old-fashioned style, a taller more slender shaft with a single figure standing in profile, was also produced at this time and we have an excellent example in the *stele* of Eupheros (*Pl. 30*). The boy stands holding a strigil in his hand, his name carefully inscribed on the broad cornice of the crowning pediment. The pose of the boy and the hang of his drapery find a close parallel on an Athenian decree relief of

430/29 BC. Another example of a single figure in relief on a slender slab, the gravestone of Namenes (Conze no. 914), is almost certainly earlier. In all probability this is one of the few examples we possess of an Athenian *stele* with relief figure decoration from the first half of the fifth century.

By the beginning of the last quarter of the century grave reliefs were being produced whose style reflected that of well-known sculptors of the day. The lovely 'Salamis Relief' (Conze no. 1032) which has been associated by some with the work of Agorakritos, has sculptural decoration similar to that on the Eupheros relief, but in no way old-fashioned. It is a broader slab (1·09 × 0·80 m.) and only the head of the youth is in profile. The broader surface of the stone is covered by the almost frontal body of the youth and by his extended hand. A small boy leaning against a pillar completes the relief. The exquisitely carved finial is paralleled by only one other relief, a gravestone with the representation of a seated woman which was found in the Piraeus (Conze no. 103). Although the relief of Mnesagora and her little brother (Conze no. 887) now lacks its finial, in style it is closely related to the gravestone of Eupheros. The inscription above the relief tells us that the dead sister and brother were given this memorial by their parents. Another relief, that of Chairedemos and Lykeas, can be dated to this period on the strength of the pose of one of the figures which betrays the influence of the sculptor Polykleitos.

Architectural frames enclosed 'votive' reliefs at least as early as the Late Archaic period and they were often applied to decree reliefs of the fifth and fourth centuries. Presumably it was from this type of relief sculpture that the architectural frame came to be used on Attic gravestones. We have already mentioned the *stelai* with relief panels framed by antae. Broader relief monuments, with one, two or more figures, were frequently enclosed within an architectural frame and crowned by a pediment (*Pl. 31*). It was convenient in these multi-figure compositions to employ the seated position for one, rarely two, figures, thereby creating more space for the others. Initially the frames were indicated in low relief and details of the architectural members were picked out in paint. But even in this early phase figures sometimes overlap the frame; the relief of Hegeso is a well-known example (Conze no. 68).

During the fourth century the architectural frame became more pronounced and the figures were rendered in higher relief: one development obviously necessitating the other. The architectural frame had a practical advantage also, and this may explain its continued popularity in fourth-century sepulchral art, since the anta capitals occupied the top corners of the slab, which were otherwise difficult to fill. Furthermore, figures which overlapped the architectural frame could be rendered more summarily in low relief. Lastly, the frame itself provided protection from the elements. Some scholars have attached iconographical significance to the relative depth of relief of the figures, but this is better explained as a basic technical necessity. Figures in very high relief either stand in front of a rather shallow frame or they are enclosed within a deeper one. Accentuation of the architectural frame culminated in a series of monuments whose frames were made from separate slabs. Sometimes the high-relief figures were carved from simple rectangular slabs to which separate frames were added. At other times the figures were virtually free-standing sculpture displayed within an independent architectural frame, heads, arms, and legs being sometimes added separately. There were also additions in metal, such as wreaths around the heads, or weapons. The monument of Aristonautes (Conze no. 1151) exemplifies this accentuation of the architectural frame. Five separate pieces—base, pediment, side walls and relief—made up the gravestone. Some of these composite monuments used more than one type of stone, Pentelic and Hymettan being the most common, and some of them had additional figures carved in low relief on the side walls.

SCULPTURE IN THE ROUND

Two innovations in Attic funerary art—very high relief and separate architectural frames—at times make it difficult for us to distinguish free-standing sculpture from high-relief sculpture, originally framed. Unworked surfaces on some pieces indicate that they must be included among the latter, but others are carved fully in the round, and although found in cemeteries, they may copy well-known non-funerary sculpture of the period.

The seated figure familiar in the round from the Archaic period and in relief from the Classical, takes a new form in the early Classical period: a seated woman, legs crossed, head on hand in a position of mourning. Although she appears in relief sculpture, painting and the minor arts, the original is generally thought to have been a major sculptural creation of the second quarter of the fifth century. She is often called Penelope, but the type could serve more than one purpose and identity. In the course of the fifth century it was adopted in funerary art, appearing in high relief on a Boeotian gravestone and in Cypriot terracottas from a tomb at Marion, which include large figures (over 0·70 m. high) and small figures standing on the back of a chair occupied by a seated woman—a type also seen on a Cypriot grave relief.

In addition to the terracottas, 'Penelope', or, more generally, seated women in an attitude of mourning, occur in relief decoration, as in the *anthemion* of a *stele* in Berlin (two sitting on the volutes of the acanthus, between which stands a grieving siren), on the metope of a Doric frieze, found in Athens and generally, but perhaps incorrectly, considered funerary, and on a small pediment in Zürich, said to be from an Attic grave monument.

We should also include here the 'servant girls', roughly life-size, who sit, legs crossed, head on hand, in a pose not unlike 'Penelope's'. Two were found at Acharnai, north of Athens, and are said to have come from one large tomb, presumably set up as pendants. Another was found in the Diocharian Gate cemetery, possibly one of a pair. We have also a pair of male figures—Scythian bowmen—from the Kerameikos, which are thought to have been similarly displayed at the corners of a large tomb.

Among the types of standing figures known to have been funerary is a woman, heavily draped, extant in two forms, one larger and more matronly, the other smaller and more youthful— the so-called Herculaneum Maidens. There are Hellenistic and Roman copies of both. The originals were probably created under the influence of Praxiteles, to judge from the style of the drapery.

But at least as early as the last quarter of the fourth century they were included among funerary sculptures: the side panel of a large framed grave monument found in the Kerameikos bears the heavily draped matron in high relief. The same type in the round was found in the Diocharian Gate cemetery. It has been suggested that the free-standing figures were grave monuments, the larger for married women, the smaller for young girls, but for this we have no evidence.

Two other figures deserve mention—sphinxes and sirens: our interest is their role in Attic funerary art, not the problems of their origin, identity and function. Little needs to be said about sphinxes, since they are not prominent in the funerary art of the Classical period, and there are very few examples carved in the round. Sphinxes now appear most often in relief, as subsidiary decoration on shafts of *stelai*, flanking or supporting *lekythoi* or *loutrophoroi* or as acroteria. Silenis' gravestone in Berlin differs in having a sphinx as only one of the side acroteria, the other being a *loutrophoros*. A sphinx, also in Berlin and said to come from Attica, is larger than most acroteria and for this reason has been thought by some an independent grave monument. At present our evidence for such in the Classical period depends on vase-painting: on a white-ground *lekythos* in Athens a sphinx stands on a stepped base, but this representation is not unquestionably funerary.

Sirens, unlike sphinxes, do not become prominent in Attic funerary art until the Classical period, indeed not before the fourth century, when they appear in relief and in the round. The Classical siren retains the vestiges of an animal form—the feet, wings and tail of a bird; sometimes a feathered torso, but not infrequently fully human. Her head is that of a beautiful woman; her face reflects only sorrow. No longer does she threaten or enchant; she laments for the dead and offers consolation:

Feathered maidens, virgin daughters of Earth, would that you might come bearing Libyan flute or pipes or lyres to accompany my lament, with tears to match my cries of grief, sorrow answering sorrow, strain answering strain: O that Persephone would send me your music to chime with my lament, songs of blood, so that down in her chambers of night she may receive from me as thank-offering a paean accompanied by tears for the dead and gone (Euripides *Helen* 167–78; trans. Dale).

And these are the two types of funerary sirens: the mourners, often tearing their hair and beating their breasts like mortal women (on some grave monuments the mourning siren is even accompanied by mourning women); and the musicians, with the lyre or double pipes. Both types of sirens occur in relief, being especially common on the *anthemia* of gravestones, and in the round, as acroteria, or, in some cases, as independent statues, originally one of a pair set up on the corners of the tomb or family plot: Dexileos' tomb had a pair of sirens.

We have no clear material evidence for the funerary use of free-standing statues of men. There is, however, reason to believe that there were such memorials; indeed Pausanias describes them. But they are, it seems, statues over graves of illustrious men of state or of letters, this being one of the primary purposes of the Greek portrait statue. Evidence for statues of less distinguished men is lacking. Equally scant is the evidence for funerary statues of children. An appealing group, found in Athens near the Ilissos River, is Hellenistic, and although considered funerary by some, is more probably votive.

Animals carved in the round had been placed over graves before the Classical period, but they are not numerous in Attic cemeteries until the fourth century. There are lions, panthers, bulls, rams, goats, dogs, swans, doves, cocks and partridges, but most are known only in relief, in the *anthemia* or, less frequently, on the shafts of gravestones. Lions, dogs and bulls are, however, represented by examples in the round. In Attica during the later Classical period lions and panthers were set up in pairs, one at either end of a large tomb façade. Monuments with this sculptural arrangement have been found in Athens, along the Academy Road and outside the Sacred Gate, and are reported from Kallithea and Piraeus. Others of uncertain provenance were perhaps similarly displayed. Sepulchral lions were functional as well as decorative: they marked the extent of the burial plot.

Dogs too were placed at the corners of tomb façades. Great mastiffs stood on the corners of the monumental 'Tomb at *horos* 3' (Fig. 21), and south of the Sacred Way, along West Road, another plot was bounded by dogs; lions were similarly displayed in the adjoining plot. A more docile dog, in an attitude of repose, is said to have come from a child's grave in the Piraeus. Other dogs identified as greyhounds, carved in the round and provided with plinths for insertion into larger bases, may also have been funerary.

There is one fine example of a bull, from the Kerameikos. Originally he was not displayed on the framed grave monument which stood in the centre of the plot, each end of which was marked by a lion, but on a separate support built behind it (*Pl. 28*, left). The closest parallel for such an arrangement is found on a white-ground *lekythos* in Athens on which a lion-crowned monument is represented.

REUSE AND REPRODUCTION OF GRAVE MONUMENTS

Before turning to the iconography of Attic grave reliefs two other aspects deserve mention: their use in Attic cemeteries and reproduction elsewhere. Gravestones were frequently reused in cemeteries, most easily by the addition of inscriptions, for example the names of sons being added beneath that of their father. Monuments belonging to other families were relieved of original inscriptions and new ones were added. Not infrequently, however, monuments underwent more drastic changes—figures were chiselled away or altered to suit. A different form of reuse involves the adaptation of a non-funerary monument; *stelai* inscribed with records or decrees were especially susceptible, since they were often an appropriate shape and size. Either a new inscription was cut or a relief panel was superimposed. Reuse of gravestones for building material, as in the Themistoclean Wall, is a different and non-funerary matter.

Attic gravestones were widely copied in the later Classical period, as they had been in the Archaic. Some of the Atticizing reliefs are successful—the Thespiae group comes to mind (see p. 224). Others fail to achieve the form of the original, often by fault of proportion or misunderstood iconography, rather than material or workmanship. A gravestone found in Crete, near Heraklion, will serve as example. The form is Attic, a relief slab framed by antae and crowned by a low pediment, as are the figure types: a maid servant with a chest, a small boy with an *aryballos* on his arm, and a bearded man. Apart from their unbalanced proportions and arrangement, their combination on a single monument is quite un-Attic: the maid servant lacks her mistress (cf. Hegeso's relief), the boy lacks his master (cf. the Ilissos Relief) and the man lacks any exact Attic counterpart, especially in his dress. The eclectic result is sufficient proof that the monument was not imported, but executed on the island for local use—perhaps for a family of means who especially wished to honour their dead in an Attic manner.

THE ICONOGRAPHY OF GRAVE RELIEFS

Attic grave reliefs display conservatism in iconography and in technique—a characteristic feature of non-secular art. The compositions continued to be produced in virtually the same format with monotonous regularity. The monolithic gravestones were almost certainly roughed out in the quarry and then brought to the workshops where prospective clients were expected to choose from stock. The regularity of the compositions, the use of the same stock figures in only slightly different arrangements and occasionally the later addition of more 'personal' features, such as a beard, suggest that the client was given a pattern book from which to select his monument. Presumably many of the reliefs were not made to order. Only if the client could afford it and if the sculptor was adventuresome, was a 'new' composition attempted; the 'Salamis youth' looks like one of these special pieces.

As the demand for grave reliefs increased during the course of the fourth century, sculptors were forced to save time by leaving less conspicuous areas, such as the bottoms of chairs and tops of heads, unfinished. The number of later fourth-century monuments left in an unfinished state is quite large.

Grave reliefs have been divided into broad groups on the basis of the number and position of the figures represented. The single, standing figure is a composition with which we are familiar from the Archaic period. Unlike the Archaic, the Classical figures are often seen frontally, and perhaps it is for this reason that the slabs are generally broader. Another feature not found in the Archaic period is that women as well as men are commemorated. The standing woman lifts her cloak, a gesture familiar from the Hera on the east frieze of the Parthenon, or she holds a mirror or vase. Standing males are often shown as youths with athletic gear or as warriors with shield and spears. At some time in the fourth century the standing figure type was varied by the introduction of a pillar or large vase, against which the figure leans. The seated position is used for both men and women, although it is more common for the latter. Women sit beside baskets, holding mirrors, spindles, or other household objects. Seated men hold staves, less frequently an attribute which is perhaps indicative of their profession. Males shown seated are draped and often bearded. We may therefore assume that the seated position was more regularly used for men of mature years.

With two figures the following combinations were possible: both stand, one sits and one stands, or, rarely, both sit. Unlike the Archaic reliefs on which two figures were shown in profile, one often overlapping the other, the Classical two-figure reliefs preferred an antithetic composition. Children are often introduced into these, although they sometimes had their own reliefs. The adult and child composition presents little problem of unity. However, when two adults are represented, there is usually some attempt to join them together either by the 'presentation' of a vase, bird or box, or, more directly, by the gesture of clasping the hands. This *dexiosis* motif is extremely common on Attic gravestones. It is used to link two standing figures, or a seated figure with a standing one, and it is virtually unknown on white-ground *lekythoi*, a group of vases whose iconography is often considered in conjunction with the grave reliefs.

Compositions with more than two persons are often called 'family groups', presumably because the monuments were erected over 'family plots', more than one figure is often named, and children are not infrequently represented. In these more complex compositions, often enclosed within pronounced architectural frames, the *dexiosis* motif regularly links the foreground figures, while those in the background look out from their frames, resting their heads in their hands or observing the action of the figures before them. The problem of creating a unified composition with so many figures and within the space available was great. Apart from these sedentary group compositions, the standard repertoire of relief scenes includes horsemen and warriors, and some of these monuments are known to have commemorated those who fell in battle.

Although relief monuments adorned the grave, the actual manner of death is almost never shown or even alluded to. There are a few reliefs which seem to represent women who died in childbirth (Conze no. 155), but this was apparently an acceptable variation. The relief of Demokleides (Conze no. 623), who seems to have died at sea, is exceptional. There is, so far as we know, one relief on which a *prothesis* is represented (Conze no. 1179). Figures reclining on couches, in the company of others and with the addition of objects for food and drink (Conze no. 1173) form a distinct group, the so-called *Totenmahl* reliefs (see p. 234). In Attica the series is not well represented until the later fourth century.

The greatest problem in any study of Attic grave reliefs of the Classical period is the interpretation of their iconography. The reliefs have been the occasion for much study, but little agreement. Those who find it necessary to distinguish the living from the dead are thwarted by the overall similarity of the figures, one not being distinguished from another in any regularly predictable manner. Nor are inscriptions of much use, since often more than one figure is named. Furthermore, inscriptions were cut on the stones at different times and later inscriptions were also added to some of the tall slender *stelai*. There are a few monuments on which two figures are represented and which also bear inscriptions stating that both are dead. Ampharete sits holding a small child in her arms; the inscription tells us that in death she holds the dead child of her daughter as she did when they were both alive (*Pl. 31*, and p. 262). Mnesagora and Nikochares play with a pet bird; above the relief the inscription records the dedication of the monument by the grieving parents to the memory of their two dead children. Another relief, that of Timarete (Conze no. 888), which used the same compositional motif, has only one figure named. Reliefs with more than two figures may have the names of all figures inscribed or those of only some of the figures.

Gestures are equally difficult to interpret. There are those who see in the *dexiosis* motif the uniting of the world of the living with that of the dead, but sometimes both figures are named and are, therefore, presumably dead: the reliefs of Demetria and Pamphile (Conze no. 97) and that of Hippomachos and Kallias are familiar examples. Then there are reliefs on which both figures independently perform essentially the same gesture, for example both women lift their cloaks. After around 350 BC, when architectural frames became more pronounced and multi-figure compositions more common, there is a tendency to render emotion more explicitly. And yet, on these later reliefs we still find no open gesture of grief such as we see on white-ground *lekythoi*: no one tears his hair, lashes his cheeks, or strikes his head or chest. Only the sirens in the *anthemia* and flanking the great monuments express their sorrow openly.

We could find no better example of the problems which confront an interpretation of the iconography of the reliefs than the so-called Ilissos Relief (*Pl. 32*). A youth, his hunting stick at his side and dog at his feet, looks out from the (now missing) architectural frame. An old man raises his hand to his beard and a small boy, tucked into the corner at the foot of the pillar against which the youth leans, rests his head on his arm. The motif of the accessory figure, a small boy or girl accompanying a youth or maiden, is found on a number of grave reliefs, and is generally assumed to be little more than an attribute. The youth is said to be the dead because of his outward gaze, which we have already noted on a number of low-relief background figures, and his 'heroic nudity'. But compare the very similar reliefs (Conze nos. 1054, 1056-7) on which the 'heroic nude' youth lowers his head, apparently wrapped in sorrow, while an old man looks on and the same small boy huddles in the corner at the youth's feet, holding his oil pot and strigil. On the Ilissos Relief, it is the old man who looks sorrowful, or at least he draws his hand to his beard, a gesture which, on this relief, and a somewhat later one from Rhamnous, is considered the feature which distinguishes the 'grieving survivor'. But the gesture is not common on Attic grave reliefs, nor is its significance entirely clear. Furthermore, the second figure on the Rhamnous relief, a woman, is not distinguished for us in any obvious way. Lastly, the problem of the identity of the figures in the Ilissos Relief is obscured by the metal fillets or wreaths which both the youth and the old man wore, as we can see from the small holes beside their heads indicating the points of attachment.

Since the grave reliefs were often set up in plots, along the side of the enclosure, not over specific graves, and since they were an expensive type of memorial, it is reasonable to regard them as communal monuments and to consider those whom we see represented as members of the family who died at different times. But we must also remember that many of the reliefs were not made up specially, but were chosen from stock; consequently some monuments were perhaps more appropriate to the deceased members of some families than they were to others. This qualification is probably most valid for the multi-figure 'family group' reliefs. With these limitations in mind, we shall probably not err if we consider Classical grave reliefs in the same light as the Archaic: monuments set up to the memory of the people whom we see united in death as they were in life.

CHAPTER VII

FUNERAL RITES

*The Solemnities, Ceremonies, Rites of
their Cremation or enterrment, so
solemnly delivered by Authours, we shall
not disparage our Reader to repeat.*

IN THE FOLLOWING PAGES we offer an account of burial procedure
and rites of death, based on the available archaeological evidence
and supplemented by contemporary art and literature. Its validity
for parts of Greece outside Attica during the Archaic and Classical
periods is questionable, but man's attitude towards death is one
of his most conservative and the rites known to have been practised in Attica are the standard socio-religious rites of veneration
and purification observable in societies widely separated by time
and space: the living respect and honour the dead, but because of
the *miasma* of death they must purify themselves. The period of
mourning during which the family has been set off from the
society is concluded by rites of 'solidification'—the *rites de passage*—which enable the mourners to resume normal life in the
community.

We have already examined the archaeological evidence in
detail and considered the iconography of the vases and sculptured
reliefs. It remains to review the literary evidence. Contemporary
literature is not, unfortunately, so helpful as one might expect,
since funerary rites were so familiar that ancient authors, for
example historians, mention them only indirectly, rarely offering
explanation. Tragedians concern themselves with death and
funerary practice, but we cannot always be certain whether the
poet is describing contemporary practices or whether he is
elevating them to heroic status. Comedians are somewhat more
reliable, but the orators are by far the most informative: cases
involving adoption and inheritance frequently require the

defendant to describe the rites of burial which he performed on behalf of his 'family'.

Apart from contemporary literature of this type, there are also the records of Athenian funerary legislation preserved by writers of later antiquity: Cicero, in Book Two of the *Laws*, excerpts from the *peri tes Athenesin Nomothesias* of Demetrios of Phaleron, Plutarch's *Life of Solon*, and Pseudo-Demosthenes' *Oration against Makartatos*. There is also Plato's description of funerary procedure in Book Twelve of the *Laws*. For the Hellenistic period, see p. 162.

IMPORTANCE OF BURIAL

For the people of Attica burial in their native land was greatly prized, and perhaps for this reason denial of burial in Attica was considered one of the greatest penalties which the State could impose. We have already observed the Athenians' concern to bring home their war dead.

It was essential that the dead receive the customary rites of burial, but it was equally important that he receive them from the proper hands. Responsibility fell on the immediate family, and under normal circumstances it was considered improper for the dead to receive burial at the hands of one to whom he was not related. If, however, the dead had no family, or if his family could not bear the expense, the responsibility fell to a close friend or to the demarch. It seems to have been a particular duty of the son to bury his parents, especially his father, in a fitting manner. There are numerous references in literature of the Classical period to the great expense of burial, and when Plato restricts the amount which his highest class can spend on funerals, he allows the quite considerable sum of five *minae*. It is, moreover, important to remember that expense was not incurred in the furnishing of graves, for many were unfurnished and very few were rich in offerings, but in the preparation for and execution of burial and funerary rites.

PROTHESIS

It was the duty of the women of the family to prepare the body for burial. According to Demosthenes only those women who were over the age of sixty or very closely related to the dead could take part. They bathed the body, anointed it with oil, dressed and adorned it with flowers, wreaths, ribbons and jewellery. The *prothesis* took place on the day after death at the home of the dead. The significance attached to the house at which the *prothesis* took place and from which the *ekphora* began is clear from accounts, preserved by the orators, of men attempting to remove corpses from the house of death to their own homes to demonstrate that they, not the 'family', were the legitimate heirs.

The *prothesis* normally lasted one day; Plato recommended that it last only long enough to confirm death. The body was displayed on a plank-like structure with high legs—a dining couch, bed, or *kline*. The body, wrapped in a shroud, *endyma*, lay on a thick carpet-like *stroma* and was covered with *epiblemata*. Pillows—*proskephalaia*—elevated the head, and, as an added precaution against the unsightly gaping of the jaws, chin straps, *othonai*, were sometimes fitted around the head and lower jaw (*Pl. 33*).

The purpose of the *prothesis* was not only to confirm death, but also to provide an opportunity for the performance of the traditional lament and for the friends and family to pay their last respects. Representations of the *prothesis* on vases and painted plaques show remarkable uniformity. The dead lies on the bier with his feet pointing towards the left, presumably towards the door, since it is from this direction that the men come in procession, raising their right hands, palm outwards—a gesture which men perform on foot and on horse, at the bier and at the grave. Women lament, tearing their hair, striking their head and breasts. Restricting the *prothesis* to the home discouraged such displays of intense grief and turned a potentially public ceremony into a private one.

THE THIRD DAY

On the third day, before sunrise, the dead was borne out to the grave in a procession which was required by law to pass quietly through side streets. Restricting the *ekphora* to the early morning

hours and banning the performance of the lament outside the
house likewise encouraged a simple family procession, not a
sumptuous public cortège. But on a black-figure *kyathos* an
ekphora is being accompanied by the lament; this vase and another
like it are among the very few representations we have of the
ekphora (Pls. *34, 35*). Vase-paintings show us the body, completely covered except for the head, being carried by pall-bearers
or drawn by a cart (cf. *Pl. 16*). Men lead the procession and
women follow. As at the *prothesis* the attendance of women was
limited by age and family relation; even their dress was prescribed by law. When women went to the tomb, they could not
travel by night unless they rode in a cart with a lamp, and they
could not carry more than one obol's worth of food and drink
or a basket exceeding a cubit in length. Further, they were not
permitted to visit the tombs of those to whom they were not
related except at the time of interment.

When the funeral cortège arrived at the grave, the body was
lowered into the ground (*Pl. 36*) without great ceremony, and
Solon expressly forbade the sacrifice of oxen at the grave. But
according to Cicero it was customary, from the time of Cecrops,
to perform a simple ceremony over the filled grave shaft: to
sow the earth with the fruits of its bounty (*frugibus obserebatur*),
assuring the dead a quiet repose, and, at the same time, purifying
the land, thereby returning it to the use of the living. We know
that there was a ceremony of some sort conducted at the grave on
the day of burial—*ta trita*—and this traditional sowing of the
land may have been part of it. There is, however, frequent mention in Greek literature of drink offerings (*choai*) made at the
grave and cups and pouring vessels found outside graves may be
mute testimony to this last libation. We have already described
the offering places and offering ditches found in association with
some graves of the Archaic and Classical periods and have
pointed out that they were used only once, possibly during *ta
trita*.

The traditional interpretation of *ta trita* as an independent
celebration performed three days after the burial is not supported
by contemporary literature, where *ta trita* and burial of the dead

are regularly mentioned together. That the ceremony connected with the burial, which took place on the third day after death, should be called 'the third-day celebration' is entirely reasonable.

After the burial the mourners apparently returned to the home of the dead, which, during the period of mourning, was marked by a vessel standing outside the door—a notification of death and a warning of the *miasma* which affected the house. It contained water brought from outside with which the mourners purified themselves on leaving. For the Classical period in Athens there is no evidence for the later practice of hanging a lock of hair or a branch of cypress on the door.

PERIDEIPNON

Whenever I turn my talents to the *perideipnon*, as soon as they come back from the *ekphora*, all in black, I take the lid off the pot and make the mourners smile; such a tickle runs through their tums—it's just like being at a wedding (Hegesippos *Adelphoi* 11–16).

These lines from a fragmentary play of the New Comedy, in which a cook boasts of his culinary skills, and a passage from Menander's *Aspis*, describing the plight of a cook out of work because of his master's 'death', who stays on in the house waiting for a commission for the *perideipnon*, are surely sufficient to disprove the traditional interpretation of the *perideipnon* as a meal taken at the grave. There are burnt deposits—ashes, bones of animals, and sherds of cups, bowls and plates—associated with some graves, and these are probably remains of food offerings made at the grave. Literary sources, apart from the comic passages cited, allude to the importance of the meal, but do not describe it. Most imply that it was taken at the home of the dead, and this is in keeping with the elaborate purification of the house and the restrictions placed on those permitted entrance. Of the *perideipnon* itself we know nothing except that it was an occasion for relatives to gather, wreathe themselves and speak of the dead. The suggestion that the meal marked the end of mourning, thereby serving the important function of a *rite de passage*, seems unlikely in the light of the words of Hegesippos and Menander.

THE NINTH DAY

On the ninth day after the burial, family and friends again gathered at the tomb to perform the customary rites—*ta enata*. We know nothing about the rites except that they were well enough known to be mentioned in law courts without any explanation and sufficiently formalized that one could perform them properly or improperly.

END OF MOURNING

The end of mourning was marked by additional ceremony. Although there is mention in later sources of a thirtieth-day rite concluding mourning, in Athens during the Archaic and Classical periods the length of time is not specified. According to contemporary literature the family resumed normal life in the community after they had done the customary things—*ta nomizomena*.

ANNUAL CELEBRATIONS

The end of mourning did not, however, mark the end of the family's responsibility to its departed. The annual commemorative rites, if we may judge from the number of times they are mentioned in Classical literature, were even more important than *ta trita* and *ta enata*. Assurance of proper performance of annual rites was reason enough for a man to adopt a son. Scholars of later antiquity were aware of the importance of annual rites, but, unfortunately, they knew very little about them. Perhaps it is for this reason that we have records of many different celebrations purporting to be annual: *Genesia, Nemesia, Nekysia, Epitaphia, Allatheades, Horaia, Apophrades, Miarai Hemerai, Anthesteria, Eniausia,* and, more simply, *kath' eniauton*. Although we cannot here pursue the problems presented by each of these names, the *Genesia* deserves mention, since it is named in a fifth-century source: when Herodotus describes an annual celebration which the Issedones performed on behalf of their deceased fathers, he refers to the *Genesia* celebrated by the Greeks (iv 26). Since he offers no explanation, the *Genesia* must have been known to his audience. The *Genesia* is also named in the excerpted second-century AD *Antiatticista*: a public festival held in Athens on 5

Boedromion mentioned by Philochorus and by Solon on the *Axones*. The nature of the festival is, however, not specified. Since we know that there was an annual celebration in honour of the dead, it is not impossible that at some time it was called the *Genesia*, and this name may have some connection with the *gene*. For although the *gene* by the Classical period had lost their political and military powers, they remained important social and religious bodies in whose care rested recognition of adoption, performance of funerary rites and, in particular cases, even burial in a communal tomb.

Because the annual rites were so familiar, Classical sources say no more than 'the customary things were done each year'. There were probably visits to the tomb, offerings of flowers, garlands and ribbons—traditional signs of respect and reverence. Plato's description of a funeral conducted in the best taste stipulates that the annual rites must not be disregarded in the interest of economy. Not all rites were, however, performed at the grave. Each year one also did the customary things at home on behalf of the 'ancestral objects'—the *hiera patroa* and the *theoi patrioi*. Plato alludes to a *nomos* governing the setting up of the 'ancestral objects', but precisely what they were is not clear. They were apparently handed down from generation to generation and were a necessary qualification for some public offices. Although they were portable, they were not to be uprooted, since removal or maltreatment of them not only brought censure upon the perpetrator of the offence, but also, in some way, deprived the ancestral dead of their due rites, for these 'ancestral objects' were associated with the annual offerings, *ta nomizomena*, on behalf of the dead.

REPRESENTATIONS OF BURIAL PROCEDURE IN CONTEMPORARY ART

We are fortunate to have abundant visual evidence to supplement and elucidate accounts of burial procedure preserved in contemporary literature. Painted plaques and vases are most informative, and a group of them by the Sappho Painter (about 500 BC), exceptionally rich in iconographic details, will serve as example.

On one of his plaques there is a *prothesis* of a youth with attendant mourners, most of whom are labelled: father, brother, mother, sister, grandmother and aunts (*Pl. 33*). The only representations of the *ekphora*—the two black-figure cups already mentioned— not by our painter—show us the *ekphora* with the body being borne along in a cart and on the other the cortège with pall-bearers (*Pls. 34, 35*). The lament, accompanied by music, which Solon had forbidden during the procession, is being performed on one of the vases. A bail-amphora by the Sappho Painter, in a private collection in Lausanne, shows the scene at the grave (*Pls. 37, 38*): it is not yet dawn, for lamps still burn, while the dead is being lowered into his coffin, apparently just completed by the carpenter, axe on his shoulder, who steps to the side. A woman takes up a box of *lekythoi* and a boy holds a *hydria*. The next scene, the entombment, occurs on another vase by the painter, a *loutrophoros* amphora: the body is being carefully consigned to the earth in the presence of mourners (*Pl. 36*). On the reverse (*Pl. 36*), the neck of the vase shows the burial mound marked by a *loutrophoros*, receiving homage from two mourners. On some unpublished funeral scenes on cups painted by the Theseus Painter there are detailed representations of *prothesis*, and oil bottles and a bowl of eggs (?) are carried.

WATER IN FUNERARY RITES

We have already mentioned the *miasma* of death which affected both gods and men, and the necessity of purification. For the Greeks water was a primary cathartic element, especially water from the sea since it was considered less susceptible to pollution. In funerary rites purifying waters were important to the dead and to the living.

One of the first duties of the women of the family was the bathing of the corpse. Those who knew they were about to die performed this ritual bath for themselves: Socrates, before he took the hemlock, bathed 'to save the womenfolk the trouble'; Alcestis, when she realized that death was near, bathed herself with running water and put on her funeral dress; likewise Oedipus, when the time had come, called upon his children to bring *loutra* of running water and *choai*. The former, administered to the dead before burial, prepared his body for consecration to death; the latter were offered by the living at the grave in honour of the departed. *Loutra* can, however, also be used broadly for the drink offerings made at the grave, although *choai* or *loibai* are more usual. *Spondai* were the libations to the gods above, and Thanatos, therefore, was a god *aspondos*.

The living become ritually unclean by their contact with the dead and sometimes they make themselves physically unclean to express outwardly their deep inner grief: Hecuba covers herself with dirt and Orestes refuses to bathe.

On the third day after death the house of the dead was purified, and so were the mourners who visited it, for the vessel of water standing outside the door was not only a warning of pollution, but also a means of purification from it. There is some evidence for a preliminary purification of the living at the grave itself: a fragment from the *Exegetikon* of the Atthidographer Kleidemos describes a rite in which a shallow pit was dug to the west of the grave, into which one poured water, then wine, with the offering of a prayer. The waters are called *aponimma*, and this has suggested to some scholars that the mourners purified themselves with water. Athenaeus, however, who has preserved for us the fragment of Kleidemos, seems to imply a more general use of the word: 'in Athens there is a special use of the word *aponimma* to describe a ritual in honour of the dead—*es timen tois nekrois*—and a purification of those who have made offerings to the dead—*enageis*.' *Enagizo* describes the act of making an offering to the dead or to the gods below; *thuo* being used for offerings to the gods above.

Now that we have examined some of the uses of water in funerary rites, let us look at vases found in funerary contexts which may have held water for some part of the ceremony of burial. Deep vessels with two handles, spout and low foot—a shape for which the ancient name is unknown—seem to have been designed for transporting and pouring water. Although this type of vessel appears to have gone out of fashion in the Classical period, earlier examples are reasonably numerous both in domestic

and in funerary deposits. The vases, sometimes miniatures, have
been found in graves, in offering places, and, in one instance, in situ
above a grave.

There is a group of rather diverse two-handled deep vessels
which have in common one feature—a high conical foot which
is occasionally fenestrated. Some of the vases have spouts, some
have lids. Some are very large and handsomely decorated; others
are smaller and more modest. The total number of examples
known is not large, nor do the vases continue beyond the Archaic
period. The best-known examples are from the cemetery at Vari
and the offering deposit in the *dromos* of a Mycenaean chamber
tomb at Menidi. We do not know the purposes for which they
were designed, but those with modelled snakes and painted
funerary scenes are almost certainly funerary. The names of these
vessels are unknown. There is some evidence for the use of the
word *louterion* to describe water basins equipped with stands, and
for this reason scholars have called the vases *louteria*. But this
name, which has also been applied by some to the spouted vessels
on low feet, is perhaps better restricted to the standed lavers.

A deep double-handled vase, regularly supported by a high
conical foot, but sometimes on a low base and covered by a lid,
was produced in the Late Archaic and Classical periods and it
has become known to us as a *lebes gamikos*, although evidence for
the name is inconclusive. There are black- and red-figure *lebetes
gamikoi* and their iconography leaves no doubt about their function: scenes of wedding preparation predominate. There are,
however, a few sherds of black-figure with mourners, and since
lebetes gamikoi, both black- and red-figure, have been found in
graves, offering places and offering ditches, sometimes two or
more to a deposit (*Pl. 21*), a funerary purpose seems likely.

One of the vases often associated with rites of marriage and
death is the so-called *loutrophoros*. The name of the vase is derived
from a passage in Demosthenes: when asked how he knew that a
man had died unmarried, Demosthenes replied that there was a
loutrophoros over his grave, but later writers and lexicographers
interpret *loutrophoros* as the person bearing the *loutra*, a boy or
girl depending on the sex of the deceased. *Loutrophoros* is used

adjectivally by Pausanias in his description of the priestess of Aphrodite in the sanctuary at Sicyon; other words, such as *hydriaphoros* and *kanephoros*, are known to have been used in a similar manner to describe the person bearing the object, not the object itself, and a line from the *Samia* of Menander seems to require this translation for *loutrophoros*: 'Chrysis, send for the women, the *loutrophoron*, the flute girl, and have someone bring us torches and garlands so that we may join the procession' (730–1).

In Athens it was customary, so we are told, to mark in a special way the graves of those who died unmarried, but the manner in which they were so designated is not made entirely clear. Although archaeologists recognize two types of *loutrophoros*—the *loutrophoros hydria* and the *loutrophoros* amphora, the former with three handles, the latter with two, it is by no means certain that the vase seen standing above grave mounds in paintings on vases, and adorned with ribbons on grave reliefs, was ever so named: literary evidence, as we have seen, weighs against this. Some of the vases we call *loutrophoroi* do have holes in their bases, and they were probably secured into position in much the same manner as the Geometric marker vases. The *loutrophoros* amphora is represented in low relief on gravestones very frequently, some having scenes of family groups, and on at least one two women and an infant are seen; we may therefore question whether all those whose graves were marked by the vase did in fact die unmarried. A more general use for the so-called *loutrophoros* is likely: a vase for the *loutra*, water for bathing. This broader interpretation corresponds better with the diverse iconography of the vases, on which battles, weddings, and funerals are most often represented, and with the many different purposes for which we see them being used in scenes on vases.

The concept of marriage in death, that is, the belief that persons who died unmarried received at death rites which 'may have been meant to help them to obtain in another world the happiness they had missed in this' finds less support among Classical authors than among the late nineteenth- and early twentieth-century scholars of Anthropology and Classical civilization. We have already pointed out the probable misinterpretation of *loutrophoros*

36 A black-figure *loutrophoros* by the Sappho Painter. The detail of the neck shows women by a grave mound topped by a '*loutrophoros*'; the body shows the coffin being lowered into the ground.

37 A black-figure vase by the Sappho Painter. The dead man is lifted into his coffin at night (lamps are burning) while his shield hangs above him. For other details see Plate 38.

38 Details of Plate 37. The funeral procession assembles, with baskets of food and *lekythoi*, *hydria*, *alabastron*, and the carpenter.

39–41 Hellenistic grave offerings from Athens: *above*, a gold wreath from an ash urn; *below, left*, gold 'ghost money' for Charon's Fee; and (*below, right*) an assemblage of fusiform *unguentaria*, the equivalent of the earlier *lekythoi*.

2 Spartan warriors return home with their dead, on a cup painted
about 550 BC.

43, 44 Clay figures of mourners: a sixth-century example from Thera (*left*) and a fifth-century one, with a woman seated by a *stele* with a *hydria*, from Boeotia (*below*).

45, 46 Magic in the grave: a curse tablet
of lead, folded and pierced by an iron nail
(*above*) and a small lead coffin with a
bound figure, found with curse tablets in
the Athens cemetery (*right*).

47 A Hellenistic Hadra vase (*below*), the
ash urn of a Chian envoy who died in
Egypt.

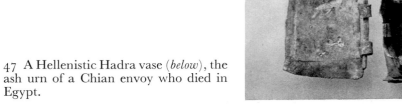

48, 49 East Greek *stelai*:
capitals showing volute and
palmette patterns from the Troad
(*left*) and from Samos (*right*).

and the importance of preliminary purification by bathing to ceremonies of marriage and death. It remains to consider the several well-known passages in Classical literature where unmarried youths and maidens lament that, owing to some tragedy, the only marriage they will enjoy will be in Hades. But these lines are laments—expressions of intense grief, not of established beliefs in marriage after death. Of such sorrow there could be no better expression than the words of Megara on behalf of her sons whom their father Herakles will kill in a fit of madness: 'But changeable Fortune now gives you *Keres* [spirits of death] for brides, and I have only tears to bring for your *loutra*' (Euripides *Herakles* 480–2).

Neither the name nor the function of the three-handled water vessel—the *hydria*—is open to question. Although the vase is often found in non-funerary deposits, it also occurs in some numbers, and occasionally in miniature form, in the graves of adults and children, and in offering places associated with them. The iconography is not often funerary, but the importance of the vase in funerary rites is clear from scenes on white-ground *lekythoi* on which women carry *hydriai* to the grave and *hydriai* stand around or on top of the tomb. But *hydriai*, metal as well as clay, were also burial urns for the inhumation of children and for secondary cremations, and there are some fine bronze *hydriai* still preserving bits of the cloth in which they were wrapped before being placed in protective stone boxes. Lastly, there is in later lexicographers mention of an Athenian festival of mourning called the *Hydriaphoria*, but at present we have no evidence for the festival in the Archaic or Classical periods.

CHAPTER VIII

THE HELLENISTIC PERIOD

Oblivion is not to be hired; The greater part must be content to be as though they had not been, to be found in the Register of God, not in the record of man.

HELLENISTIC BURIAL CUSTOMS in Athens, so far as we may judge from the archaeological material available at present, can be given no more than summary treatment.

In 317/6 BC, according to the *Marmor Parium*, Demetrios of Phaleron passed legislation which placed limitations not only on many aspects of Athenian life, but also on their rites of death. Although this traditional date has been questioned, it cannot be far wrong, since Demetrios' rule lasted little more than a decade. As a result of his sumptuary laws and of other factors affecting Athens at this time—her diminished importance as a political power in the Hellenistic world and her declining prosperity—Hellenistic burials show little variety, and almost all graves are very modestly furnished.

Few Hellenistic cemeteries in Attica have been properly published; attention has most often been concentrated on graves of earlier periods which are more diversely, and more richly, furnished. Consequently our knowledge of Hellenistic burial practices is somewhat limited. For the city of Athens, however, there is sufficient evidence to permit some generalizations. There are graves of this period on the outskirts of Classical cemeteries and these extensions to earlier burial grounds have been noted along roads leading from many of the city's gates (Map 4). In the Kerameikos burials continued, but towards the end of the fourth century many of the earlier graves were covered over and the land was artificially levelled. These measures permitted the land to be reused without undue disturbance to earlier graves. In the Kerameikos, and at other sites where the original plan can be determined, graves were set out in plots and sometimes enclosed within stone walls, which were regularly in alignment with the path or road along which the cemetery lay. As in the preceding periods plots were marked off by inscribed boundary stones, but the gravestones of the Hellenistic period were modest. The layout of the cemeteries was not, then, affected by Demetrios' legislation, only the sumptuous scale on which they had previously been adorned. There is, once again, no apparent rule of orientation.

Inhumation and cremation were practised, but the former is more common than the latter, both in the Kerameikos and, so far as we can tell, elsewhere. Primary cremations do not differ from those of the Classical period. Secondary cremations differ only in the variety of ash urns. There are some new clay shapes, for example cylindrical lidded pots with painted decoration. A clay urn in the British Museum, said to have come from Athens, has four modelled griffin foreparts (with horses' forelegs) on its shoulder. The vase and griffins were painted white with some gilt and coloured decoration. Inside were cremated remains, two obols adhering to the jawbone—presumably 'Charon's Fee'—a clay figure of a mourning siren, and bits of bronze and linen. There are some stone urns of the same shape, similarly decorated and with griffin attachments. There were several shapes of stone cinerary urn in use at this time and some of them were equipped with specially designed lead containers which held the ashes, and they were regularly closed by lids of stone or metal. There is less evidence for the use of metal ash urns at this time, but this may be due to the chance of excavation. Ash urns were placed in earth or rock-cut pits or they were given protective stone packings, and grave markers stood above them. In some of these secondary cremations, especially those which used stone receptacles, there were gold wreaths with the cremated remains (Pl. 39). Some of the leaves of gold foil show signs of burning, but most do not. Presumably the wreath adorned the dead during the *prothesis*, but was removed before the cremation.

Inhumation graves continue in the forms known from the

preceding period. There are simple earth or rock-cut shafts which were apparently left unprotected, and there are similar shafts which were covered by a few slabs, not infrequently broken slabs of earlier grave monuments. Limestone, marble, or a combination of materials were used for both the slab-lined and covered pits and for the sarcophagi, which were either monolithic or composite. By far the commonest form of burial in the Hellenistic period is the tile grave. These differ from those of the Classical period only in the more frequent use of round tiles. In many of the graves—pits, sarcophagi, and tile—there are nails of varying sizes. In some, bits of wood have been preserved, indicating the presence of a wooden bier or coffin, but in others there is no wood and the purpose of the nails is not clear (see pp. 216f.).

Children were buried in clay tubs, and occasionally this form of burial was used for adults. Painted decoration has been preserved on the inside and outside of a few. Infants and small children were buried in clay vases of different types, amphorae being especially common. There were also apparently cremation burials for children, but the evidence for this is slight (see p. 99).

Offering places, resembling those of the Classical period, are found over graves, under enclosure walls, and less closely associated with burials. Most are shallow and roughly oval in shape, although deeper, more rectangular deposits are also found. The contents are ashes, sherds, and occasionally animal bones. Most of the vases represent types which were regularly found in the Classical offering places—cups, bowls, and plates.

Generally speaking Hellenistic graves in Attica are not well furnished. The most characteristic of the rather uniform and modest offerings is the spindle-shaped oil bottle, variously known as 'tear flask' or fusiform *unguentarium*. Unlike the *lekythoi* of the Classical period, fusiform *unguentaria* show almost no variety in shape or style of decoration (*Pl. 41*). The earliest are bulbous, covered with a shiny black paint, and decorated with a few coloured stripes, red and white, on the neck, shoulder and body. In Athenian graves they appear to have supplanted the squat red-figure palmette *lekythoi* around the middle of the fourth century. By the end of the century the body of the vessel has become more slender and the black paint is given up, although the stripes, now generally white, are still painted on the fired grey surface. Later fusiform *unguentaria* are taller, more slender, and less carefully potted. In the late Hellenistic period the shape becomes very elongated, the neck swells and the foot is not set off. They are eventually supplanted by the footless, pear-shaped Roman oil bottle. Some graves had only one fusiform *unguentarium*, others several. In a simple pit grave on Lenormant Street, in Athens, there were more than thirty. They were cheap vases, produced in quantity for the grave, but they are not exclusively funerary, being found in domestic deposits, cisterns and wells.

Other clay vases are not well represented in Hellenistic graves. There are cups, bowls, jugs, *pyxides* and occasionally lamps, but many graves had none of these. The *alabastron* which had been quite common in Classical graves seems to have gone out of fashion. Apart from clay vases, few objects occur with any regularity. Men have strigils, women have mirrors, children toys. There are figurines—'Tanagras', grotesques, animals and dollies, but they are not numerous. There is some gold jewellery which perhaps reflects the greater availability of the material at this time. We have already mentioned the leaves made of gold foil and the gold wreaths which were made from them. These continue into the Roman period, and may be found in both cremation and inhumation burials. Whether they were made especially for the grave or were worn in life on festive occasions remains unknown. There are also gold bands, at least one of which has been found in situ on the head of the dead. In a few graves there are bits of gold thread which perhaps once ornamented the funeral dress. Most of the jewellery, rings for fingers and ears and bracelets, were simple ornaments of baser metals, although there are some finer gold pieces, such as the earrings with tapering hoops and animal head finials found in a sarcophagus burial near the Academy Road in the Kerameikos. In the same area another grave produced many pieces of ivory which look like inlay for a wooden chest, and a miniature ivory column with Doric capital and Ionic base, probably the handle of some luxury item.

'Charon's Fee' (see p. 211; *Pl. 40*) is first noted in Athenian graves in the Hellenistic period. Although the sex of the dead can rarely be determined accurately, men seem to have been supplied more frequently than women. In some graves several coins were scattered about in no apparent order.

Demetrios of Phaleron included in his programme for the city a revision of its legal code. An account of his funerary legislation occurs in Cicero—the only documentation we have for the reforms which Demetrios himself recorded in five books *peri tes Athenesin Nomothesias*. Demetrios reinforced the restriction on the *ekphora* to the early morning hours, but his legislation seems to have been directed primarily against the construction of new tombs. The types of monument which could be erected were specified: a *columella* providing it did not exceed the height of three cubits, a *mensa*, or a *labellum*. Demetrios also provided for a magistrate whose special duty it was to see that these regulations were enforced. The influence of Demetrios' teacher, the philosopher Theophrastos, has been seen in his reforms, especially in the funerary laws, for in his will Theophrastos requested a modest burial without undue expense for ceremony or monument (Diogenes Laertius v 53).

Although Cicero's account of funerary legislation is an invaluable source of information on Athenian burial rites, we have already encountered the problems which his terminology creates. Unfortunately, his terminology for Hellenistic Athens is equally equivocal. The *columella* is, however, without question the small column or *kioniskos* found in large numbers in Attic cemeteries of this period (Fig. 27a). The monument admits little variation in size, shape or decoration. The bottom of the *kioniskos* was left rough for insertion into the ground or into a thin square or rectangular base. This base, which was most often of limestone, occasionally accommodated a double column whose inscription explains that here a husband and wife lay buried. Columns may taper slightly towards the top. On the upper shaft there is a torus moulding, on which there are occasionally preserved traces of painted decoration. Above this moulding some columns have ivy-berry sprays or olive leaves rendered in low relief; it therefore

ΙΕΡΩΝΥΜΟΣ

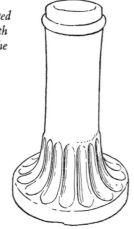

Fig. 27 Hellenistic markers: (a) an elaborated kioniskos with a wreath in low relief; and (b) the foot of a standed laver converted to use as a kioniskos

a   b

seems likely that these mouldings were designed to hold in place a garland or some other form of decoration, perhaps ribbons. Below the moulding there is a short inscription, and below that often decoration painted or rendered in low relief. By far the commonest relief decoration is the *loutrophoros* bound with ribbons. On some *kioniskoi* objects are rendered in relief which are thought to denote the profession of the deceased. On others, late Hellenistic and Roman, there are two upraised hands, palm open, held either parallel or at a slight angle. The hands are, in fact, 'crossed', since the thumbs are next to each other, or are impressions rendered in relief. A few *kioniskoi* decorated in this way are said to bear inscriptions invoking curses on the murderer of the dead whose grave is so marked and on one there is an entreaty to the gods by the dead begging redress for an injustice suffered in life, but the significance of the gesture on other *kioniskoi* is not clear. A hand performing what looks like a similar gesture occurs among the Archaic shield devices found at Olympia, being interpreted by the excavators as an apotropaic sign.

Mensae are not so easily identified. In the Athenian cemeteries there are horizontal slabs and block-like monuments of different shapes, sizes and almost certainly of different purposes. Because *trapeza* is occasionally mentioned in Greek literature in descriptions of funerary monuments, notably the tombs of Lykourgos and Isokrates, and because *trapeza* is considered the most plausible translation of *mensa*, all of these diverse monuments have been grouped together under that name. But if Cicero had in mind tombs like the *trapezai* of Isokrates and Lykourgos, *mensa* could not be a new form, since both men died before Demetrios came to power; rather a modest version of an established type, in much the same manner as the *kioniskos* is a diminutive column. But unlike these grand tombs of the orators with their sculpture and relief decoration, most of the monuments we consider here—and we are forced to consider only those with recorded provenances—are unimpressive. Some are thin stone slabs, not infrequently of Hymettan marble, resting on one or more foundation slabs or supporting masonry courses. Others are higher, slightly grander monuments with mouldings for base and finial, and on the vertical faces inscriptions, or occasionally decoration in relief, *loutrophoroi* and wreaths being most common; panels with relief decoration are not regular. On the horizontal faces of some the name of the dead was inscribed (see below) or cuttings, circular or rectangular, were made to receive stone vases or *stelai*. Indeed some of these monuments are little more than large bases—grave monuments, not gravestones, the actual site of the grave being marked by a *kioniskos* or small *stele*—and they could be set along the façade of the plot just like other grave monuments (Fig. 20). This type of *mensa*, therefore, presumably antedates Demetrios' funerary legislation. Different are the *mensae* which actually covered graves. Although their number is small, there can be little doubt that burials lay beneath them and in this respect they resemble the earlier rectangular earth mounds and built tombs. In one plot on West Road three lay side by side. One was only a limestone slab, the covering marble having been removed, but the other two were marble slabs (approximately 0·20 × 1·30× 0·80 m.) still in place above limestone foundation courses. On the horizontal faces of the marbles the name of the dead had been inscribed.

Labellum defies identification. Apart from Cicero's use of the word, we find it in Cato and Columella to describe a vessel into which, for example, grapes were placed during the preparation of wine. On the analogy of a standed laver tomb monument on a number of South Italian vases, *labella* have been restored as standed lavers, despite the absence of lavers in Athenian cemeteries. This apparently incredible restoration is partially explained by a few laver stands in the Kerameikos and nearby areas which may have been cemeteries. But as Conze realized when he compiled the great corpus of Attic gravestones, these laver stands with their fluted shafts and flaring bases (Fig. 27b) were reworked in antiquity, the flutes being tooled down and inscriptions added. The laver stands and *kioniskoi* were so similar in size and shape that the translation of the former into the latter must have been common.

Demetrios' restrictions on sepulchral art and architecture seem to have been observed rigorously, for it is not until the second century that relief monuments of some size and magnificence reappear in number. For non-Athenians, however, the legislation may have been waived (see p. 264). Simple slab markers, generally without base and finial, and bearing only the name of the dead, did continue to be used throughout the late Classical and early Hellenistic periods. Just as in the early Classical period, when other funerary monuments were restricted by the *post aliquando* legislation, the small slab markers remained unaffected. Some of these have been found in situ above graves, others have been found along the façades of enclosed plots.

THE GREEK WORLD

CHAPTER IX

THE EARLY PERIOD

BURIALS OF THE EARLY Iron Age in Greece, described in Chapter I, present little variety and are generally poorly furnished. With the full Geometric period of the eighth century there is far greater diversification in burial practice and this persists through the seventh and most of the sixth centuries. The sequence is clearest in Athens, but this is by no means typical of all Greece. Indeed, the funeral monuments of Attica in this and later periods are in many respects remarkably unlike those of the rest of Greece, except in the matter of some sculptured monuments for which much of Greece seems to have followed Athens' lead. This, however, is a feature best explained in terms of art history and not of burial rites.

The eighth to sixth centuries saw rapid change, growing wealth and an increasing population which led to trade and colonization around the shores of the Mediterranean and the Black Sea, and renewed contact with the civilizations of the east and Egypt. We can observe this change in Greek life and literature, and the individuality of the various Greek cities is in no way better expressed than in their art. There were changes in religion too, in man's view of his gods, and, although burial customs tend to be the most conservative, there may have been other factors to dictate the variety of practices. Even so, the differences are mainly superficial, and, although the burials of the early period are most conveniently surveyed by geographical areas, there is nothing to suggest that different cities had radically different ideas about how they should dispose of or serve their dead. In fact, the differences hold more to interest the excavator and archaeologist than the historian of religion.

CRETE

The island of Crete affords clearer evidence for some continuity of culture at the period of transition to the Iron Age than most of Greece, and it is not therefore surprising to find there strong continuity of burial practice. This takes the form principally of tomb architecture, and there are several instances of graves designed for inhumation in the old manner receiving cremation burials in the new. But there is also a remarkable variety of practices, sometimes within a single cemetery and period.

The built 'tholos' tombs of the Bronze Age, with their stone-lined approach dromoi, blocked doors and corbel-vaulted chambers, were recalled in various towns. At Karphi, the mountain-top refugee town which seems to typify the unsettled conditions of the eleventh and tenth centuries BC, the tholos tombs, barely worthy of the title, have round or rectangular chambers on rectangular foundations, and are built free-standing, not dug into the ground. Sometimes a retaining wall is built against the hill slope above them. The chambers are quite small, about 2 m. across, and they received inhumations. They were used as family tombs with successive burials, possibly inserted through the roof rather than through the tiny doors.

The rectangular and circular tholoi in some other Cretan cemeteries are more rarely free-standing. Some continued in use into the eighth and even the seventh century, but with a variety of types of burial. At Afrati a cemetery which is basically an 'urn-field' also contained rectangular built tombs for inhumations and three larger circular tholoi containing cremation urns. There are other important cemeteries with tholoi at Kavousi, Kourtes, Rotassi, A. Paraskioi (near Heraklion; an above-ground construction), and we may probably take with them the rectangular built tombs at Vrokastro where inhumation and cremation are found side by side. This apparently arbitrary behaviour, in a single tomb, let alone cemetery, and in one period, can be remarked elsewhere in Protogeometric and Geometric Crete.

At Knossos the survival of Bronze Age practice takes a different form. There are several rich Protogeometric and Geometric cemeteries in the area of the old Minoan city. They are of rock-cut chamber tombs which resemble the Late Bronze Age graves but generally have rather short *dromoi* with a step in them, which are rare features earlier. There is, however, evidence that some of the tombs were Bronze Age ones, cleared and reused (as a Bronze Age *tholos* at Knossos was: see below) and it is possible that the majority are. Thus, in one Protogeometric cemetery a Late Bronze Age grave was overlooked. The chambers were used for repeated burials, all of which were cremations, but for some isolated Protogeometric inhumations. In the eighth and seventh centuries large ovoid jars were used as the ash urns with other offerings placed within or beside them, sometimes on slabs. Occasionally the urn is a bronze cauldron, once set on a slab hollowed for it. The vases were placed in the chambers side by side and after the floor was covered a second layer was begun, over the first (Fig. 28). Sometimes the *dromos* was used for burials, or a niche cut in the wall of the *dromos*. One tomb appears to have contained over eighty burials ranging from the mid-ninth to mid-seventh centuries, and deposited with increasing frequency as the family grew. Some patches of burning near the *dromoi*, once described as 'pits', might be the cremation or offering areas. Only one cremation is reported not in a regular tomb, and this may be within the town limits.

At least one of the larger Bronze Age *tholoi* near Knossos was cleared and reused. Judging from its finds it could have been the family tomb of immigrant eastern goldsmiths who used it for well over a century. For its first use, in the later ninth century, it seems to have been 'reconsecrated' in a non-Greek manner by two vases full of jewellery buried, like foundation deposits, just within the doorway. *Tholoi* like this would have been rediscovered from above and we may have a contemporary record of such a find in the clay model of what could be a *tholos*, discovered by two men, with their dog, who peer in through the vault to the mysterious underground 'shrine' which the artist has sanctified with the figure of a goddess. Such old tombs could easily be reused but they were also sources of treasure. Recall the Treasuries (*thesauroi*) of Mycenae, and perhaps the old Cretan story recorded in 'Dictys' of how Odysseus and Diomedes killed Palamedes by

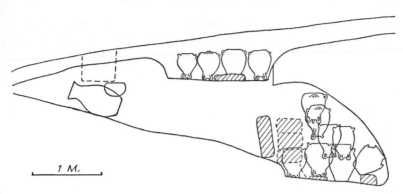

Fig. 28 A Geometric chamber tomb at Knossos with storage jars containing cremations

dropping stones on his head after he had climbed into a 'well' after treasure. This story might have been inspired by the discovery of a well-furnished Bronze Age grave.

Perhaps the strangest of the early Cretan cemeteries is that at Afrati, where we have already noted *tholoi* and rectangular chambers. Here there is clearer evidence for cremation areas—rectangular stone-lined platforms covered with the debris of clothing and offerings. The ashes were put in lidded pots of clay or bronze, which stood on flat dishes or stones, the whole being covered by an inverted clay storage tub, sometimes supported on a ring of stones. Earth and stones were piled around but the urns seem to have been mainly above ground (Fig. 29a, b). This was the common form of seventh-century burial, and the urns were placed in the same area as the built tombs, which were in use in the same period. The extraordinarily close resemblance between these burials and a contemporary and earlier cemetery (Fig. 29c) at Carchemish on the upper Euphrates (see p. 322) seems not to have been remarked before. Could this be another symptom of immigration from the east?

RHODES

The Dorian settlement of the Dodecanese must have taken place very early in the Iron Age. In Kos the earliest graves (*c.* 950 BC) were cut into the area of an old Mycenaean town. They are cists, a type of grave still current there in the eighth century, the only unusual feature being the piling of offerings of pottery and terracottas around the outside of the cist. Most of the burials were of children, who were also buried in pots, but two adults in simple pits were found laid out in a contracted position, as in the local Mycenaean graves. Otherwise, however, the Geometric and Archaic cemeteries of Rhodes and adjacent islands show some remarkable originality of burial practice and tomb architecture. Early ninth-century cremations at Ialysos, with amphorae as

Fig. 29   Seventh-century cremation burials at Afrati in Crete (a, b) and, of Iron Age date, at Carchemish on the Euphrates (c)

urns, are the first indication of any change in practice, but later cremations are differently arranged. Rectangular pits were dug and, to judge from their hard-baked sides, the bodies were burnt within them. Cavities in the lower corners of the pits (*pozzetti*) are distinctive and puzzling features—not, it seems, for the legs of a bier, since they sometimes undercut the sides of the pit, and occasionally offerings were found in them (Fig. 30). Might they have been made by the ends of crossed beams which supported the fuel for the cremation? These pits are found at Exochi (Late Geometric), Kameiros and Ialysos (seventh-century) and Vroulia (around 600 BC), but cremation and the ubiquitous burial of children in pots do not exhaust Rhodian local practices.

At Vroulia, a seaside barracks occupied by fewer than a hundred people for about fifty years, the primary cremation pits were found in four main groups, as for families. Some pits were used more than once, and flat slabs at the surface seem to have marked their position. But there was one communal inhumation grave too, for four men. It was set closer to the walls and included at least one weapon: perhaps they fell in defence of the com-

Fig. 30 A cremation pit at Vroulia in Rhodes

munity. On the island of Nisyros the primary cremation areas were oval mounds of ashes and offerings.

In the sixth century inhumation again becomes the more popular method of burial, although not exclusive. At Ialysos there were elaborately fitted cists, and all-stone sarcophagi with gable lids—a type persisting into the fifth century. They seem to have been buried with extreme care, the interiors sometimes being almost hermetically sealed with stuccoed joints, while rows of slabs outside, over the lid of the sarcophagus and along its sides, offered further protection. At Kameiros the sarcophagi were of stone or clay, but the finer sixth-century burials were in small chamber tombs which have a broad court-like *dromos* (Fig. 31). The dead are laid on two or three rock-cut ledges against the walls of the roughly square chambers; once in a *pithos*, once in a clay sarcophagus. If the shape of these graves recalls the Bronze Age, the arrangement of benches anticipates the Hellenistic tombs, but it might well be that these graves in late seventh- and sixth-century Kameiros are directly inspired by Cypriot practice. This could even mean immigration from the island and there is much else of Cypriot inspiration in Rhodes at this time. There were some plain *stelai* in this cemetery and a stepped base was associated with a late sixth-century cist.

Fig. 31 A chamber tomb and tile-covered grave at Kameiros in Rhodes

IONIA AND AEOLIS

The community of culture and art in the East Greek world is not much reflected in the burial customs, and the Rhodian cremation pits and chamber tombs are by no means characteristic also of the more northerly cities and islands on the Asia Minor coast. These are distinguished rather by their above-ground monuments and elaborate sarcophagus burials, usually beneath tumuli, a practice which certainly owes much to Anatolian neighbours. In Chios, Ephesus and Clazomenae we find Archaic cists and clay sarcophagi beneath small earth or stone tumuli. A cemetery in Chios town contains large sarcophagi beside a group of pot in-humations around a pyre. Some of the Old Smyrna tumuli over sarcophagi or cists have fine ring walls to support the mound, in the Anatolian manner. The cemeteries on Samos are more elaborate and have yielded important monuments in the form of *stelai* and *kouroi*. The North Cemetery was used principally in the second and third quarters of the sixth century and most burials are in monolithic stone sarcophagi (also found in Ephesus). The interiors of some are shaped to the body, rather like mummy cases (Fig. 58). The comparison may have point since this is a period of Samian interest in Egypt (Amasis and Polycrates). The bodies were laid on sand or pebbles. Offerings were sometimes found in clusters above the graves and one or two amphorae, protected by slabs, could be set at the end of the sarcophagus at lid level. There were a few clay sarcophagi or simpler slab-covered pits, pot burials, and even cremations, one in the North Cemetery being covered by a tumulus in a stone ring and perhaps marked by a *kouros*. Another statue base stood by an apsidal built terrace, covering a sarcophagus, while higher walls of shorter radius stood over other sarcophagi and presumably supported mounds. Small chamber tombs, rather like those at Kameiros, may have been dug first in the Archaic period. At Miletus a chamber tomb with a long *dromos* approach may owe more to Anatolian practice. The cemetery there seems to have been well supplied with sculpture—lions, seated figures, a *kouros*.

Farther north, in Aeolis, we find the low tumulus burials with the mound edged by stones or low walls. At Pitane the tumuli cover pyres, the ashes being gathered in pots, but there are also Archaic inhumations in *pithoi*, cists and plain pits. At 'Larisa' in the Hermos valley, and so in close communication with Sardis and the massive Lydian tumuli, rather better revetted tumuli cover cist graves, and there are also some rectangular enclosures with cists (Fig. 32).

Fig. 32   The tumulus cemetery at 'Larisa' in the Hermos valley

THE ISLANDS

The extreme diversity of early burial customs among the Cyclades islands cannot easily be explained in terms of their relative isolation since in other respects they show signs of the closest contact with Greeks of the mainland, Crete and the eastern Aegean. Several, moreover, may have been settled, or resettled, only in the advanced Protogeometric or even Geometric period.

That the Therans should have preferred cremation burials might be due more to the influence of their southern Dorian neighbour, Crete, than to the fuel offered by their bare, treeless island, or the example of their reputed original home in Laconia. Perhaps the shortage of cultivable land encouraged this practice, and the choice of the bare windswept slopes of Sellada for the main cemetery. The finest seventh-century tombs are chambers,

Fig. 33 A chamber tomb with cremations on Thera

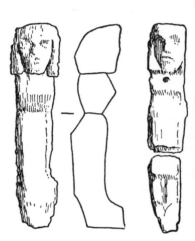

Fig. 34 Stone statuettes from a possible cenotaph on Thera

usually rectangular with a few oval or round, partly built out from the hillside and many with doorways large enough for a man to enter. The ash urns were placed on the floor in these family tombs. There are also smaller niche-like chambers with smaller entrances (Fig. 33). The ashes are usually deposited in clay vases, occasionally in bronze, and rarely in stone boxes. Apart from the chamber tombs there are burials in urns set in the hill slope and sometimes protected by a shallow terrace wall. There are also grander terraces supporting whole series of tombs, and for later burials the family terraces are elaborate and monumental (Fig. 48). Offering pits, lined with stones, were closely associated with many burials. In them were burnt offerings of food as well as pottery and other articles like those deposited with the burials. The bodies were burnt in large prepared areas cut into the hillside, but there is evidence too for the burning of the body in its grave, lightly terraced on the slope beside the road. Only children were not burned: the remains of three were deposited in vases packed in a rectangular tower of stones, like a small, solid chamber tomb. One burial, 'Schiff's grave', was remarkable for the number and variety of vases and metal objects found within it. It was taken for a rare example of inhumation, but the few small bones (no skull) were not specifically identified as human. It also contained two crude stone statuettes which at this date, before the mid-seventh century, are unique (Fig. 34). They may be substitute figures, and the tomb a cenotaph for a mass disaster, perhaps at sea. These were hard years for the island, with drought and famine, leading to the dispatch of a colony to Libya in about 640 BC. The Thera cemetery is in later years rich in its variety of grave monuments—incised and plain *stelai* and '*trapezai*' (Figs. 45a, 47a), an Archaic palmette *stele*, *kouroi*, Classical reliefs and cube markers, a '*phallos*' (Fig. 51c). On another southerly island, Kimolos, there are Geometric pits each containing several cremations. This seems an odd practice but we await the full publication.

In the heart of the Ionian Cyclades inhumation may have been preferred, and there are eighth-century cist graves on Tenos and Naxos, and later ones on Paros and Delos. But cremations are also reported on Paros, and Archilochus approved it (fr. 10), while a cemetery at Tsikalario on Naxos contains some unique burial complexes which are mainly eighth-century with some later Archaic intrusion of cist graves. Rough lines of stones marked out enclosures, usually circular and up to 10 m. across, within which were traces of one or more pyres, apparently for the bodies. Pots were placed over the pyres but also in smaller compartments within the enclosure and outside it, where separate pots were often protected by slabs as though they were ash urns. They were found full of clean sand only, but it is hard to understand them merely as offerings, and the condition of the site is clearly hostile to the preservation of traces of bone. Two *pithoi* set mouth to mouth in one tomb certainly suggest inhumation, although possibly later. A small rectangular walled area outside one of the enclosures is declared a pyre for offerings only. The entry to the cemetery area was marked by a large upright slab. It seems likely that the enclosures mark low mounds over main and secondary burials, which may be cremations.

THE PELOPONNESE

This is the only major area of early Iron Age Greece whose known cemeteries display any marked uniformity of burial practice, and the evidence for the Geometric period is particularly rich. Inhumation in cists or pots (for adults and children) is the normal practice, with minor variations of grave construction dictated by local conditions or wealth. In Corinthia and the Argolid the body is normally buried in a contracted position, with the knees drawn up towards the chest. There are several instances of the reuse of graves within a generation or two of the first interment (Argos, Mycenae), the earlier offerings being removed and reburied in the fill above the grave. A child cremation is reported at Nauplion, perhaps Asine, and partly burnt bodies in cists at Nauplion and Tiryns, but these are the only, and equivocal, exceptions to the rule of inhumation. There are several examples of multiple burial in a grave: a group of four at Nauplion, two head to toe at Mycenae where also we find a woman with two children (Protogeometric) and a man and woman (Early Geometric). More unusual are two pairs of linked burials at Corinth (Late Geometric). In each case one grave was cut across the head of the other. Spits were apparently laid on the intervening shelf of one pair, occupied by a man and woman; the wider shelf between the graves of the other pair, where the burials had been robbed, was pierced by a channel.

The Corinthian cemeteries have been most informative about grave construction. A shaft was usually dug, sometimes to a depth of two or three metres. The body was protected by a single slab above, probably supported on ledges cut in the shaft side, or by a regular built cist, but already early in the Geometric period we find all-stone sarcophagi being cut for the inhumations, while some of the slab cists have carefully mortised corners. The graves were deliberately filled with earth after interment in most instances—not by any means a regular Greek practice. Some burnt material in graves is taken to be food, and in the fill over some graves a jug and cup were buried. Burials are grouped, as for families, a Geometric group being set in an enclosure of upright slabs. The sarcophagi, which are of course simply an elaboration

of the cists, continue into the Classical period. But here, and elsewhere in the Peloponnese, a simple pit could suffice. Near
Perachora, opposite Corinth, and in the Megaris sarcophagi were
also used in the Archaic period.

Sparta is inevitably a special case. Plutarch describes sumptuary
laws (*Lyk.* 27) which are attributed to the lawgiver Lykourgos and
therefore undatable, but probably represent practice in the
Classical period. Burials are to be made within the city, even
near temples, so that folk should not fear death. There were to
be no funeral offerings, the body wrapped simply in a red robe
and olive leaves, and no name on the *stele* except in the case of a
man killed in war (cf. *Pl. 42*) or a priestess who died in office.
In later practice women who died in childbirth were also thus
honoured. Eleven days were allowed for mourning, with a
sacrifice to Demeter on the twelfth. A group of early sixth-
century graves was found recently in the Mesoa district of ancient
Sparta. They were cist graves near a small pyre for offerings and
food, and a fine clay relief vase which was carefully buried but
empty. The graves seem to have been dug in a yard immediately
beside a potter's kiln—clear evidence for intra-mural burial.
There were no offerings with the dead. Of the famous Laconian
'hero reliefs', which begin in the sixth century, none demonstrably celebrates the recently heroized dead and so might be
regarded as a tombstone.

Aegina may conveniently be considered here for its geographical position although its burials in the Archaic period have
nothing in common with the Peloponnese and little enough with
other parts of Greece, except perhaps the Rhodian chamber
tombs. The earlier graves are cists, like the Peloponnesian, but a
Late Geometric burial with the body laid in a stone slab hollowed
to receive it is reported. An important series of chamber tombs
begins in the early sixth century with the simplest form—a
sloping shaft leading to a niche containing a stone sarcophagus.
This is followed by a variety of forms which continue in use into
the fifth century. Two chambers may open out on either side of a
vertical shaft, or the approach to a whole series of chambers may
be made down a stepped tunnel. The burials are in sarcophagi or

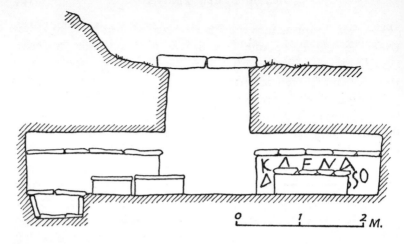

Fig. 35 A sixth-century chamber tomb on Aegina, with sarcophagi, one with the name of the dead painted on it

laid on sand on the floor. There are also simpler pit graves with cover slabs. The name of the dead may be inscribed on the entrance slabs at the lip of the vertical shaft or on the chamber walls. One family grave of the late sixth and early fifth century was approached by a vertical shaft and held six sarcophagi, one of them sunk in the floor, and some with several burials. The long side of one sarcophagus has the occupant's name inscribed in large cut and painted letters (Fig. 35). Strabo says (viii 375) that the Aeginetans were called ants for the way they dug up earth to spread for cultivation. Their interest in tunnelling is shown by their early graves.

CENTRAL GREECE

In Boeotia the evidence for early burials is rich, but from a few sites only since robbers have been more actively successful than excavators. At Vranesi tumuli cover tenth- and ninth-century cist graves with, it is said, both inhumations and cremations. The cemetery at Rhitsona, ancient Mykalessos, is our best evidence for Archaic Boeotian practice. The usual type of grave was a shaft, up to 2 m. deep, with ledges cut in the sides to support covering slabs over the burial. It is attested from the late eighth century to about 400 BC, and there are Classical examples at Thebes also. A very few shallower pits had burnt contents and may have been for primary cremations. Of the deep graves a few lacked stone covers but there may have been wooden coffins. Otherwise there was a large number of Archaic *pithos* burials and a few seventh-century cists. The Rhitsona graves are probably most remarkable for the number rather than the quality of the offerings, some containing over four hundred objects. The shaft graves superficially resemble their grander Bronze Age predecessors, but there is no real connection, and the only remarkable feature is the depth at which the Boeotians were prepared to set their dead. Of course, not many Greek towns enjoyed burial grounds with such a generous depth of soil.

In Phocis an interesting cemetery at Medeon has Proto-geometric primary cremations in pits, into which a jug had first been broken. Some Geometric burials in cists have the body contracted, but cremation persists to the sixth century.

In Euboea we might have expected early burials to resemble those of Boeotia or Attica. Recent excavations at Lefkandi, the site between Chalcis and Eretria, have revealed pyres and primary cremation burials in pits (as in Geometric Eretria) but in many instances some ashes had been gathered and deposited with offerings in ordinary, although generally small, cists, and occasionally in ordinary ash urns. Inhumations in full-size cists are also found. Only in the Late Archaic and Classical periods do we find in Eretria shaft graves at all resembling those of Rhitsona, with clay sarcophagi and slab lids. Earlier burials are generally cremations. A group of six, in bronze cauldrons carefully set on stones hollowed for them or beneath stone covers, was found near the West Gate. Near by were nine burials of children in shallow pits, but all were furnished with offerings. The whole complex had been contained in an enclosure and above them a structure like a *heroon* had been later constructed (Fig. 36; see p. 298). The graves are Late Geometric and may have something to do with the founding family of the city. Other Geometric cremations are simple pits for the pyre with its heap of ashes and offerings. The child burials in amphorae are only remarkable in Eretria for the

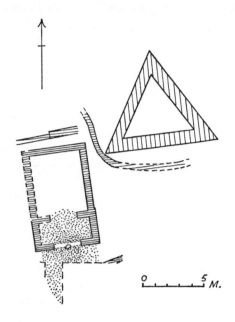

Fig. 36 A heroon *at Eretria. The triangular structure covers the graves, and there is a later shrine over an offering pit near by*

elaborate decoration of the vases and the possibility that they had been deliberately made for this purpose. The series begins by about 700 BC and can be traced beyond the mid-sixth century with little variation in shape—cylindrical neck, double handles, conical foot. One of about 600 BC is inscribed *thea*, 'goddess'. The latest are influenced by Athens both in style and shape since they borrow features of the shape and decoration of Athenian *lebetes gamikoi*.

NORTH GREECE

In the early period two main areas have to be distinguished—Thessaly, and Macedonia with Thrace, and in the last the case of the seventh-century colonial foundations is somewhat different from that of the indigenous population which was Greek neither in culture nor race. Thessaly is one of the few places where inhumations in *tholos* tombs in the Early Iron Age continue the Bronze Age practice. At Chyretiai there is even one tumulus covering four or five small *tholos* tombs, allegedly Geometric.

Otherwise the early burials are in cists, some of the adult dead being buried in a crouching position. By the eighth century, however, Halos presents an interesting cremation cemetery, with sixteen separate pyres, each covered with slabs and rocks, and the whole complex covered with a tumulus.

In Macedonia the tumulus cemetery at Vergina has been well explored and appears to have been in use from the tenth century on, the main period ending in the eighth. The burials are in simple cists, pits or *pithoi*. They are sited in groups of between five and twenty-five, often radially around a central burial, and enclosed in a ring of stones up to 20 m. in diameter, which edged a low tumulus of earth into which the later graves were dug at varying depths (Fig. 37). The *pithos* burials are carefully arranged,

Fig. 37   A tumulus at Vergina in Macedonia with pithos, pit *and cist tombs*

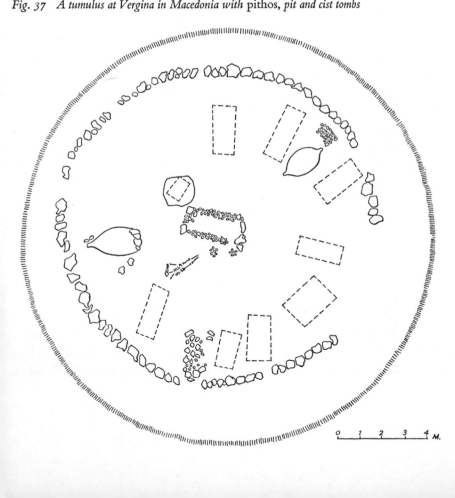

often in two vases set mouth to mouth, embedded in stones, with the body laid on a bed of pebbles within the vases. At Chauchitsa, in burials of much the same date, the bodies were simply covered with piles of stones; and, far to the west at Vitsa Zagoriou in Epirus, there is a similar arrangement for graves, persisting into the Classical period, with the stones sometimes more carefully arranged around the body, like cists. The low tumuli with cists in the cemeteries of North Greece have much in common with burials to the north and north-west.

The Greeks who lived on the island of Samothrace preferred cremation in the Archaic and Classical periods, as did the 'Tyrrhenians' of Lemnos before the occupation by Greeks in about 500 BC.

HOMER

Studies of early Greece no longer begin with Homer, but the epic poems can still be used to illustrate practices which archaeology proves to have been current in the Geometric period. Homer's view of death and burial is almost wholly in keeping with Geometric and later Greek practice, and not at all with that of the Bronze Age. Cremation is the normal method, but inhumation is not unknown (*Iliad* iv 174–7). The washing and oiling of the body are presented as practical rather than ritual matters. Homer may have known of embalming (*Iliad* vii 84–6; xvi 456f.) or at least of measures for the temporary preservation of a body (*Iliad* xviii 350f.; xix 38f.). Mourning, wailing, the cutting and offering of hair, and a ceremonial procession around the body indicate rites on a scale which we might credit from scenes on Athenian Geometric vases but not later. The offerings at the pyre are of honey, oil and wine. Animals are slaughtered, including pet dogs and horses—a practice of the Greek Bronze Age and Archaic Cyprus—but the sacrifice of twelve Trojans for Patroklos may have been more a matter of sheer revenge and anger than ritual. The embers of the pyre were doused with wine, the burnt bones wrapped in a cloth and consigned to a gold dish, amphora or box. The wrapping of the bones has been noted in several Greek graves. The tumulus and *stele* were the last due of the dead, and the rites were paid even for a cenotaph (*Odyssey* i 289ff.). The ashes of the dead at Troy could be returned to their homes (*Iliad* vii 333–5), but this may be an interpolated 'archaeological Atticism'. The great funeral games too find their echo in later Greek practice but the Greeks of Homer and no doubt of Geometric Greece at large were more intemperate in their funerary display than Classical mores would allow, and in this respect at least later Greeks did not look to Homer for guidance.

CHAPTER X

EVERYMAN'S GRAVE

*Many have taken voluminous pains to
determine the state of the soul upon
disunion; but men have been most
phantasticall in the singular contrivances
of their corporall dissolution: whilest the
sobrest Nations have rested in two wayes,
of simple inhumation and burning.*

THE VARIETY OF BURIAL practices current in different parts of
Greece in the Geometric and Archaic periods gives place in the
fifth century to an overall uniformity with a few local variations
or distinctions of wealth. The Attic cemeteries have been described in detail and it would be tedious to survey individually all
other Classical cemeteries in Greece, so we may begin to generalize
about burial practices, noting only the significant deviations.

Cemeteries are regularly situated outside areas of habitation or
beyond a city's walls. In Athens intra-mural burial seems to have
persisted through the sixth century with a few later examples but
only in Sparta were adults regularly buried within the town.
Another possible exception is in the Greek trading town at Al
Mina, at the mouth of the River Orontes in North Syria. Here
fourth-century sarcophagi and cists are found beneath the floors
of buildings which are taken to be warehouses, and so presumably
not regarded as truly domestic. But since house burials are commoner in the Near East this may reflect rather on the nationality
of those buried at Al Mina.

Children's graves, however, are often found near houses. The
rites and regulations affecting their burial must have been less
exacting and presumably no danger of pollution was feared from
lives lost so young. The fear of pollution was only one reason for
keeping the main cemeteries outside a town: land within an

occupied area, especially if it was walled, was too valuable to waste on the dead. For the same reason, if good land for ploughing or pasture was scarce, the graves would be dug in shallow earth or bare hillside. The cemeteries often flank roads away from the town. At first it would have been a matter of sheer convenience. Later, access for the *ekphora* was easier along a road, and monuments could effectively be displayed along it. Cemetery areas must have been determined early in a town's history, but they were rarely defined by walls and the ground was generally not filled in a systematic manner. Some early cemeteries do show signs of this 'horizontal stratigraphy', but by the Classical period it was more common for graves to be grouped, presumably for families. This grouping appears in some early cemeteries where low tumuli cover a group of graves and are dug into for later burials. Otherwise plots may be defined by low walls, or be more monumentally conceived, as in Athens.

Cemeteries are good places for trees and the alleged graves of heroes are sometimes associated with trees, but there is no clear evidence that the planting of a tree as a marker or symbol was at all a common practice. Plato recommends a grove for the burial place of his Examiners, in the spirit of the later *kepotaphia*.

In a sanctuary area or *temenos* birth, death and burial were normally forbidden. On the sacred island of Delos the rule against burials was applied strictly only in the main sanctuary, but the whole island had twice to be 'purified' at Athenian instance, in 543/2 BC and 425 BC, and the burials removed to Rheneia opposite (see p. 198). All that was left behind was the prehistoric 'Grave of the Hyperborean Maidens' and a group of Archaic burials which was enclosed and attached to the sacred area of the Archegesion. After 425 BC there were no more burials except for one or two hasty interments at the time of the troubles with Mithradates and pirates in the first century BC. In Hellenistic Greece there is a little more evidence for priests being buried within sacred precincts. At Pergamon some simple burials in and around the Hellenistic incubation rooms in the sanctuary of Asklepios may indicate what became of unlucky patients.

Children were normally buried, and not burned, even in

communities which otherwise preferred cremation, and, as we have seen, the children's burials could be intra-mural. Pliny observed that children were not usually cremated if they died before their teeth had grown (*Nat. Hist.* vii 72). If this was a valid criterion in Greece it must have applied to the growth of their adult, not infant, teeth. The commonest receptacle for the body was a plain jar, the body inserted through its mouth, or through a hole cut deliberately in its side. The jar was buried on its side, sometimes supported by smaller stones, and the mouth closed with a slab or tile. Small cists or made-to-measure sarcophagi were also used in some places, and simpler burials involved single tiles, large sherds, incomplete pots or bath tubs. Sometimes a child is found buried with an adult, presumably its mother. Areas in some cemeteries were set aside for children, and there is the exceptional cemetery for the victims of the Smyrna epidemic in the mid-seventh century, where children were buried in pots sealed by sherds or querns, buried in the brick ruins of the city wall. In the Classical period children were presumably buried with their families, if not at home, and at Corinth it was noted that children's graves were grouped near the larger family complexes, although there was one contemporary cluster of fourteen.

For adults inhumation was the usual method of burial in the Classical period and, of the earlier cremation cemeteries, cremation was still practised to any marked extent only in those of Thera, Euboea and Athens. Nevertheless, it is not uncommon to find isolated cremations in Classical cemeteries, and in some the proportion is just high enough to make it clear that both types of burial were practised at the same time. Cremation was convenient too for some mass burials, after battle or in the extremities of the pestilence in Athens (Thuc. ii 52). If a death occurred away from home the body might be cremated and the ashes returned home for burial. This was a practice known to Homer, and remarked by later poets: 'instead of live men their arms and ashes come home' (Aeschylus *Agamemnon* 434–6). It probably accounts for the isolated cremation burials already noted: one example of a warrior's grave we may cite is the early fifth-century sarcophagus burial at Corinth containing armour and a bronze ash urn. Only the Spartans on occasion made some effort to return the whole bodies, and we hear that King Agesipolis was brought home from Chalcidice preserved in honey, and King Agesilaus from North Africa, in wax. We may recall the mid-sixth-century Spartan Hunt Painter's cup showing warriors returning home bearing the bodies of the dead (*Pl. 42*), a scene not repeated in Greek art of this period. Apart from the record of the Spartan kings there are no other known attempts by the Greeks at even temporary embalming of a body, but they were well aware of the Egyptian practice and later writers alleged that 'the ancients' buried their dead covered with honey for its cleansing and preservative properties. In Cretan myth the child Glaukos was drowned in a pot of honey, which may indicate knowledge of the practice, and there are pots of honey in the Paestum cenotaph (see p. 299).

Classical burials differ only in the manner in which the pit to receive the body is prepared. At the very simplest a rectangular pit is dug in the bare earth. It would need to be deep enough to discourage attention from animals, and at Chauchitsa in Macedonia stones were piled directly on the body possibly with this danger in view. There is no evidence to suggest that anything put over the grave was intended to 'keep down' the dead and restrict any malignant activity. The varieties of cist grave have been described already, with slabs at the sides, sometimes for the floor and lid. Where slabs were not available the sides of the grave were built up as walls. Alternatively the body, or coffin, could be laid at the bottom of a shaft into whose sides ledges had been cut to support a cover slab. The slabs for the cists may be carefully cut or even jointed at the corners. Some at Ialysos are quite elaborately fitted, and have end stones with rounded tops, like bed ends, projecting above the gable roofs of two lines of slabs (Fig. 38). In Hellenistic Myrina the cists are constructed in rows

Fig. 38 An elaborate cist grave at Ialysos in Rhodes, with pottery offerings

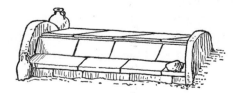

and sometimes three deep, economizing in both covers and space. The all-stone sarcophagi are normally provided with a lid and in this respect perform some part of the functions of the coffin without being so portable. Traces of wooden coffins and occasionally of *klinai* have been observed within stone sarcophagi. The sarcophagus must have been the most expensive form of inhumation burial, and a few are found in most cemeteries. In some they are more generally used, as at Corinth. Decorated sarcophagi are an eastern feature, discussed in Chapter XV. Plain clay sarcophagi are used occasionally in Greece, but especially in East Greece where we also find the only decorated examples.

Ancient clay roof tiles are larger than those with which we are familiar today, measuring up to 90 by 70 cm. Sometimes they were used as lids for cists or sarcophagi, but from the Late Archaic period on they were increasingly used for the whole construction of the grave. Two or three tiles could serve as floor. The tiles for the walls were rarely set upright, and usually leant together over the body, giving the grave a triangular section. Upright tiles or slabs covered the ends and ridge tiles could be used to finish the gable. Far simpler structures with tiles were possible and children might be laid out on tiles with or without a broad convex cover tile over the body.

Where a regular cavity was created for the body, by a cist, sarcophagus or tiles, it was not usually filled with earth before being closed (there are exceptions at Corinth). A bed of pebbles, sand, branches or seaweed was sometimes laid for the body, which was stretched out on its back, hands to the sides. The only exception to this position is met in the Geometric period and seventh century in the graves of Corinth and the Argolid, occasionally in Geometric Phocis, Thessaly and Kos, and at Halai in Boeotia in the sixth and fifth centuries. Here the bodies are 'contracted'—laid on their sides with the legs drawn up or occasionally on their backs with the knees raised. After the first half of the sixth century all burials at Corinth are extended in the normal way, and when the old shorter sarcophagi were later reused their ends were sometimes knocked out to accommodate the extended burials. In the earliest Iron Age tombs in Athens, and occasionally later, the extended body has its hands, or one hand, on its belly—not necessarily the warrior's death-spasm, seizing his genitals, described by Tyrtaeus (10b, 25). Contracted burials are not uncommon in many of the non-Greek communities around the Aegean—the position is the natural one of sleep. In some Hellenistic burials traces of the pillow beneath the head have been found—or at least of the stuffing: straw (as at Gremnos), sand (as at Pergamon) or seaweed (in South Russia). Deliberate partial cremation has been observed in European Hallstatt graves and suspected in Greek ones (see p. 180), but the instances are probably merely of incomplete burning. There are, however, some burials from which the skull is missing (Myrina and western colonies) and it is possible that these are burials of visitors part of whose body was returned home. Ashes travel more easily but cremation was expensive.

A large plain vase laid on its side could serve as a convenient burial chamber, with one-piece floor, walls and roof. The bodies could be bedded in it, extended, as in other graves, and two jars set mouth to mouth could accommodate a tall body. Otherwise the projecting limbs were covered with slabs, or the body contracted for insertion into the jar. The mouth of the jar was usually covered with a slab and the jar might be securely packed round with small stones in the pit where it was buried.

Chamber tombs went out of fashion in the Classical period. The small chambers on Thera and the Cretan chamber tombs and *tholoi* were not used after the seventh century and the chamber tombs and cremations in the cemetery of Kameiros gave place to cist graves in the fifth century. At Pontamo in Rhodes, however, there are groups of Classical chamber tombs, with separate small chambers opening out of rectangular vestibules, and in Hellenistic Myrina round pits gave access to small trapezoidal chambers. In Aegina the tombs of Archaic type with their shafts or stepped entrances were still dug in the fifth century (Fig. 39), and with the fourth more elaborate tombs are constructed with vaulted ceilings and painted walls. A small chamber was built for a mass burial at Delphi in the fifth century. It is in the north of Greece that we find the forerunners of the Hellenistic

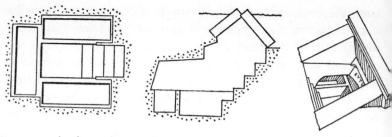

Fig. 39   A chamber tomb on Aegina, about 460 BC

'Macedonian' tombs. At Olynthus, before 348 BC, there was a chamber tomb little over 2 m. square, with a stepped approach and covered by a tumulus (Fig. 40). The chamber's plastered walls were painted with stripes and marbling. Non-Greek chamber tombs in tumuli, in North Greece and Asia Minor, will be discussed in Chapter XVI.

Sometimes more than one body is buried in a single grave or sarcophagus. The obvious combination would have been of mother and child or man and wife. The bodies are laid out neatly, side by side, sometimes head to toe, and these burials are readily distinguished from the reuse of graves in which earlier interments are often unceremoniously pushed aside. But this reuse is not particularly common. A Classical grave at Kozani was cut in the form of a cross, with one body laid across the other: it contained weapons.

Solon demonstrated that the Megarians buried their dead facing east, the Athenians facing west (Plutarch *Solon* 10). We have no evidence for Megara but in Athens, in Solon's day and earlier, we cannot say more than that there was a tendency to place the body facing west (that is, feet to the west), certainly not a rule. There was no uniformity of Greek practice even within a single cemetery. In many the graves lay roughly parallel but the orientation was usually dictated by the slope of a hill, the position of a road or the convenient and economical use of the area available for burials. Homer and later Greeks placed the home of the dead to the west, if anywhere. A number of Greek cemeteries lie to the west of their towns and perhaps, if there was a choice, the west was preferred and the dead were laid facing it, but we cannot believe that divergence from east–west orientation meant significantly different beliefs.

In some Classical cemeteries cremations still account for a proportion of the burials. On Thera cremation and inhumation may be found within the same family plot. The body was burned in the grave (primary) or on a separate pyre and the ashes gathered in a pot (secondary). At Eretria too the bodies were burned in the pit of the grave, one of which shows a central trough which may have been for ventilating the fire. But in some the ashes were gathered and deposited in the cremation pit within a stone urn, or in a clay vase covered by an upturned stone 'flower pot'. The offerings were left with the burned debris. In North Greece, at Olynthus, nearly ten per cent of the burials were cremations, treated rather as at Eretria, with the ashes gathered in a clay vase. It is not always possible to be quite sure that the body was burned in situ, but careful excavators note whether the sides of the pit have been hardened by fire. At Oisyme, a colony of Thasos, near Kavalla, most of the burials were cremations, the urns being protected by slab boxes, and amphorae or cylindrical clay bins used for the ashes. The fullest evidence for Archaic cremation practice comes from Athens. It must be remembered that the cremation of a human body was a difficult and expensive operation.

Fig. 40   A fourth-century tumulus and chamber tomb at Olynthus in North Greece

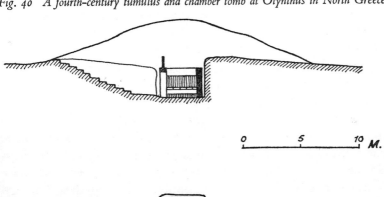

0   5   10 M.

There is no great variety in the vessels used as ash urns in Classical Greece. Plain clay vases are favoured, including wine amphorae, but figure-decorated vases are also used. Bronze cauldrons and *hydriai* are more expensive alternatives. The vessels are lidded or closed with a slab, a small clay vase or a lead lid. They are sometimes further enclosed in a hollowed stone container, also usually lidded or inverted over them. Otherwise a small slab cist sufficed or a packing of small stones in the cavity where the urn was buried, usually at no great depth. Lead boxes begin to be used for ashes in the Hellenistic period, and at Arta a lead disc inscribed with the name of the dead served, with a clay disc, as lid to an urn, and a similar lead disc cover also dates the burial by the archonship. Where there are grave markers there is no distinction between cremations and inhumations. At Ialysos in Rhodes a sixth-century burial consisted of an ash urn (a bronze cauldron) placed within a sarcophagus designed for inhumation, and in a later sarcophagus there was a red-figure vase with ashes. These may be burials of folk who died away from home.

Inevitably the digging of new graves often disturbed or destroyed older burials. Generally the sextons seemed unworried by this and there are rare examples of special attention being paid to the disturbed dead. One instance is the Mycenaean tomb in the Athenian Agora which was disturbed in the fifth century and amends made by the deposit of seven *lekythoi*. When an old grave is reused we cannot be sure (except with chamber tombs) whether this is a marked family grave which has been reopened or an unexpected opportunity seen and taken. The bones and offerings of earlier burials are usually pushed to one side and it often looks as though the offerings were removed. The vases taken from a Middle Geometric cist at Mycenae which was reused for a Late Geometric burial, were reburied over the covering slabs of the pit. When the Geometric chamber tombs of Knossos became too full burials were sometimes removed to the *dromos* or to a niche cut in the *dromos* wall, and a similar practice is observed in Hellenistic chamber tombs. Sometimes there is a more general clearance of burials and we find deposits of bones, stored together, although not generally with any offerings, which might have been con-

Fig. 41   A Hellenistic cist tomb with grid divider, in Arcadia

sidered by then to have served their purpose. A sixth-century pit at Delphi, however, contained up to forty skulls with other bones and vases indicating that graves of up to a century earlier had been cleared, possibly from a sacred area. An economical way of disposing of earlier burials is seen at Theisoa (Arcadia) where there are Hellenistic graves in the form of double-decker cists, with a stone grill as the divider (Fig. 41). The bones of the old interments fell or were pushed down into the lower cavity and the latest body laid out over the grill. But this neat arrangement is not repeated elsewhere.

The wilful or even accidental disturbance of a grave seems to have been a matter of greater seriousness in the Classical period and later, to judge from some threatening epitaphs. Nevertheless, it was possible to reuse old tombstones to construct cists. A fine example is a Late Hellenistic cist at Thebes whose cover slabs are almost all old *stelai*. And there were, of course, occasions when graves had to be removed or when there seemed to be good reason to destroy them or overthrow the monuments. This happened to the Alkmaionid graves in the purification organized by Epimenides after the Kylon affair in Athens, and again at the insistence of Kleomenes the Spartan king in his liberation of Athens in 510 BC. The breaking and immediately subsequent reuse of monuments in the Samos cemetery in about 540 BC might have been due to Persians or to local politics, but the breaking and reuse of monuments was a lesser matter than the removal of burials—the Themistoclean Wall of Athens was well packed with pre-Persian War grave *stelai* and bases, and state burial monuments were sacrificed to Athens' defence needs in 338 BC.

The purifications of Delos were another matter and the burials were respected. The Peisistratid purification in 543/2 BC removed bones, ashes and pottery to a shallow pit on Rheneia, just opposite the sanctuary area of Delos. This was incorporated in the arrangements for the purification of 425 BC when an enclosure measuring 22 by 23 m. was prepared. Twenty-nine stone sarcophagi, carefully bound up in lead strips, and presumably the latest of the Delos tombs, were moved over bodily and laid out neatly at one side of the enclosure. The rest was divided by upright slabs into rows, with separate compartments, making it look as though the intention had been to keep the remains and offerings from each burial separate after removal—a laudable one, totally nullified by the methods of the late nineteenth-century excavator.

There are only two other classes of common burial to discuss—of criminals and slaves. Executed criminals were certainly not accorded burial in town cemeteries. From ancient authors we learn that their bodies were thrown into the sea or into open pits and quarries. On sacred Delos, where none were allowed to die or give birth, two hasty burials may be of pirates dealt with summarily by Delians in the first century BC: one was beheaded, the other crucified. At Phaleron a pit grave containing eighteen bodies, shackled at necks, hands and feet, cannot be closely dated.

Slaves, like any other men, were entitled to burial but, to judge from the poets, the Classical Greek did not consider that a slave had expectation of any form of after life, so ritual and offerings were unnecessary. No 'slave cemeteries' have been identified, and it is likely that in the early period, before Classical class-consciousness had set in, they would have been buried in the family plot with other members of the household. If so they would be difficult to identify and we have no reason to believe that all burials without offerings must be of slaves. In Sicily it has been thought that secondary burials laid over the cover slabs of cists were of slaves. Certainly it was the owner's duty to see that his slaves were properly buried. Only by dying in battle did they lay claim to share some of the funeral honours of free men. In Athens' cemetery the slaves who fought faithfully against Aegina, probably in the seventh century, were buried and commemorated with their masters in the state burial, but in the fifth century the mood was different. After Marathon the slaves were buried in a separate tomb, together with the Plataeans; and after Plataea the Spartans buried their helots separately from their young men and citizens, while in the later rites at the Plataea graves no slave was allowed to take part since these men had died for freedom. Clearly, slaves could not share the honours of heroized citizens who died for their country.

In the Hellenistic period there is better evidence for the burial of slaves, even some tombstones and epigrams. The tombstones bear their names only, indicating that they were slaves by naming their masters or professions. Their own beliefs were respected, and in a third-century epitaph by Dioskorides (XXVIII) a Persian slave asks that he should not be cremated and that water should not be poured at his burial since he held both fire and water sacred. He writes another epitaph (XXXVIII) for a slave, Lydos, buried as a free man. A holocaust, with slaves and free killed together, might seem an embarrassment, but not to the epigrammatist Theaitetos (V):

> On a winter's night the great house of Antagoras, steeped in wine, was surprised by fire. Eighty free men and slaves perished together in the terrible pyre. Their kin could not separate their bones so they shared a common urn, funeral and tomb. But Hades distinguishes them easily, even in the ashes.

CHAPTER XI

RITES AND OFFERINGS

*Now that they accustomed to burn or bury
with them, things wherein they ex-
celled, delighted, or which were dear
unto them, either as farewells unto all
pleasure, or vain apprehension that they
might use them in the other world, is
testified by all Antiquity.*

THERE MUST HAVE BEEN, it seems, some danger that an ordinary
Greek funeral might degenerate into a display of money and
noise: wailing at the bier, the carrying out and burial; a richly
dressed bier and body; splendid offerings; guests to be entertained after the burial; a tomb monument which would do as
much honour to the survivors as to the deceased. While most
other religious activities in public were conducted by professional
priests, this was one conducted by private persons—the next of
kin. It is not surprising, therefore, that nearly all the evidence we
have about legislation for burials is concerned with limiting
expense, noise and the period of mourning.

A late fifth-century inscription from Iulis in Keos (off the coast
of Attica) gives us most information and is worth quoting in full:

These are the laws concerning the dead. Regulations for burial:
    in three—or less—white coverlets, *stroma*, *endyma* and
    epiblema, of total value not more than 100 dr.;
to be carried out on a plain bier and only the head not to be
    covered;
up to three measures of wine and one of oil may be brought
    to the tomb, and the vessels must be removed;
the dead to be carried in silence and covered to the tomb;
the preliminary sacrifice (*prosphagion*) to be carried out accord-
    ing to ancestral custom;

the bier and coverlets to be brought home from the tomb;

on the next day a freeman should cleanse the house first with sea water, then with plain water, having scattered earth;

once it has been purified the house is clean and household offerings should be made;

the women attending the funeral should not leave the tomb before the men;

no rites to be observed on the thirtieth day;

no cup to be set beneath the bier or water poured or offerings (*kallysmata*) brought to the tomb;

once the dead has been taken from the place of his death only the polluted women are to re-enter the house—these are the mother, wife, sisters and daughters, and apart from these not more than five others, the children of the daughters, of cousins and no one else; . . .

(there follow the regulations for decontamination)

There were, of course, earlier laws. Evidence for those of Athens has been discussed (pp. 70, 90, 121f., 166). In litigious Crete fragments of laws from Gortyn date from the seventh to fifth century. They define the responsibility for arranging *prothesis* and lustration, and regulate the carrying of a body over private land. At about the period of the Iulis code the Labyad phratry at Delphi restricted the total expense on a burial to 300 dr., including the value of material taken from home. The body could have a spread (*stroma*), cloak (*chlaina*) and pillow, and had to be carried in silence. Demetrios' sumptuary legislation for Athens at the end of the fourth century seems not to have been matched by comparable restrictions elsewhere, to judge from the magnificence of some Hellenistic tombs. A third-century law of Gambreion (near Pergamon) restricts the period of post-burial rites to three months and of mourning to four months for men, five for women; it also prescribes the dress for mourners—dark for women, dark or white for men.

Plato, in his *Laws*, envisaged funeral regulations defined in much the spirit of these codes. For ordinary folk the grave was to be dug on otherwise unusable land; the tumulus no bigger than five men could raise in five days; the *stele* big enough to accommodate an epitaph of no more than four lines; the *prothesis* no longer than to demonstrate that the man was really dead; total expense limited according to class; no wailing or uncovering of the body out of doors; and the journey to the tomb to be over by daybreak. But when it was a matter of burying the Examiners he allows a magnificence near-Homeric or Hellenistic: a cortège with hymns, vaulted stone tomb chambers with *klinai* for the dead, a tumulus, grove of trees and annual games, but no general mourning, only eulogy.

The austerity of Spartan rites has been remarked (p. 181 and see p. 265) but from Herodotus (vi 58) we learn that for kings there was compulsory mass mourning. It was said that in Thessaly even in Aristotle's day it was still the practice for a murderer to be dragged around the tomb of his victim by the next of kin, a heroic ritual recalling Achilles with Hector's body at Troy.

How far the restrictions on wailing affected the composition and performance of dirges is not wholly clear. For Hector the bards sing, the women wail the refrain and Andromache herself leads them. These are the highly personal expressions of grief which appear often in the works of the tragedians in a fairly direct and simple form, often making much of word-repetition to conjure the attention of the dead. The Athenian Geometric vases suggest the sort of mass mourning which was not acceptable later. Legislation was intended to confine the noisier expressions of grief to the *prothesis* at home and the grave side. Professional mourners (Carian women had some reputation here) were discouraged, but Lucian could still complain of the excessive wailing and self-laceration which left the living in a sorrier state than the dead (*de Luctu* 12). The more sophisticated dirges, as those composed by Simonides and Pindar, may have been intended for commemorative occasions. Simonides' song for the dead of Thermopylae was not sung where they fell and were buried but at a cenotaph shrine at home—'an altar is their tomb' (fr. 5D).

Funeral games were appropriate to the hero cults and all the Greek national games were thought to have their origin in honour of the dead. Athenian Geometric vases may suggest that there were funeral games in the Homeric manner, but generally games are reserved for the heroized dead like Miltiades in Thrace, Leonidas in Sparta or Timoleon in Syracuse. The need for some sort of contest, if only a boxing or wrestling match, which served to avenge or appease the dead, was felt in many ancient societies, and could well have been a regular feature of Greek funerals.

These stray references to burial rites in the Greek world add little to the evidence provided by Athenian sources already discussed. Except in the matter of the grave offerings themselves, the archaeological evidence is hardly more informative, while the non-Athenian artist seems generally uninterested in funeral representations. In the Geometric period the only scenes of *prothesis* outside Attica are on a Boeotian and a Samian vase—both probably inspired by the Athenian vases and adding nothing to them except that in the Boeotian a rectangular fan is held over the body.

The grave offerings should prove a valuable source for speculation about views on death but before we consider them there are some general points to be made. In this as in all archaeological studies we are restricted to consideration of what has survived. If it had been a regular practice to bury dolls or models of wood, wax or rags we would know nothing of it since these materials do not survive. It must also be remarked that the majority of grave groups show no uniformity of practice; that many graves have no offerings at all and that this is not an indication of poverty since these often lie beneath elaborate tomb monuments. We are bound to concentrate on the few local customs which can be distinguished, and the exceptionally well-furnished graves. Here are three examples of grave groups which are not typical, but which do indicate what opportunity such finds give us for deductions about the purpose of the offerings. In a late eighth-century cist grave at Argos, which had been disturbed and partly robbed, the buried warrior was left with nine clay vases, a corselet and helmet, two iron axes, twelve spits with fire dogs in the form of ships and three gold rings. In a late Archaic shaft grave at Rhitsona (grave 80) the offerings were mainly pottery, piled in masses at each end. The number of vases was exceptional, even for Rhitsona: 6 Boeotian 'kylikes', 13 Corinthian aryballoi,

60 'kothons' (probably scented-water containers), about 150 plain cups, most of them Boeotian *kantharoi*, and of decorated black-figure vases 29 *lekythoi* and 8 cups. There was also a silver necklace at the centre of the grave, iron nails in a corner, a glass bottle, three clay figures of 'goddesses' and scraps of unexplained worked bone and bronze. In fourth-century Olynthus a child was buried in a tile grave (no. 191), a bronze coin in its mouth, adorned with bronze earrings and a bracelet, and accompanied by six clay figurines, mainly of women and set by the shoulders but with one by the legs, and a mask and a donkey-rider by the left hand. This, then, is the kind of evidence we have to use, but it is exceptional, and the average grave may be empty of offerings or have no more than one or two vases or a strigil.

First, the placing of the offerings. Most are set beside the body itself. Clusters by the head, or the feet, or along the sides may be observed in single cemeteries but there was no common practice. Small offerings like jewellery or oil bottles may be placed in the ash urns, but generally the offerings are piled around it. We have to distinguish the broken and burnt pots which accompanied the body on the pyre or were disposed of in an offering pyre, and the unburnt offerings made once the ashes had been gathered for their final resting place. Even in the early period, when cremation was relatively common, the practice differed widely. In Thera a large proportion of the pottery in and outside the grave was broken and burnt, while in Crete, where the burials are otherwise very similar, the vase offerings are generally unburnt. On Ischia the vases are burnt but an unburnt jug was often added to the pile of ashes. In Athens the burnt pottery was left in the offering ditches while unburnt was placed with the ash urns. Pots burnt with the body were no doubt mainly containers of food for the dead.

With inhumations larger vases, usually an amphora or water jar (*hydria*), may be placed outside the burial, whether in readiness for the dead or as a token of a last rite paid after the grave was closed. In Samos and at Ialysos (Fig. 38) a pot and cup were often placed outside the grave at lid level or over the head. At Olynthus the pot was outside at the foot and on Ikaria the pots stood over the corners of the cists. At Corinth most of the offerings were sometimes to be found outside the sarcophagus. At Locri finely decorated vases stand on the tile covers of a grave (Fig. 81b). The four Panathenaic vases at the corners of a sarcophagus at Tarentum (Fig. 84) refer rather to the career of the dead. At Halai in Boeotia clay figurines were often put outside graves, the vases within. These extra-burial offerings are by no means the rule in Greek cemeteries but the jugs and cups outside the graves seem to indicate immediately post-burial rites or offerings of honey, water or wine.

Often the offerings were disposed of by burning on the ground or in pits, which can sometimes be associated with individual burials, as at Athens and on Thera. These offerings are not a substitute for offerings in the grave itself, but it is not always possible to tell whether they were made at the time of burial or in some subsequent rites. Rarely, as at Athens, such offering pyres are detected over burials (pp. 65, 75). The burnt material, usually food, is sometimes put in the grave before it is closed. Occasionally the offering pyre is actually on the tomb lid, as at Derveni, over the tomb which yielded the famous bronze crater, where the pyre included scraps of a papyrus scroll with a commentary on Orphic theogony.

On occasion there may be a mass deposit of offerings, apparently not for a particular burial, like the Archaic 'Massenfund' on Thera with its clay figurines of types not well represented in the graves, or what appears to be a communal offering pyre. An early example is the pit by the *heroon* at Eretria (Fig. 36), and in a recently explored Hellenistic cemetery near Navarino there are big pyres with burnt pots, bones of birds and animals, and nuts. It is likely that some areas or pits for burning offerings have been mistaken by excavators for cremation areas.

In chamber tombs offerings may be put with the body, in wall niches or hung on the walls, where there are often signs of peg holes. In Eretria (Fig. 64) the paintings show what might be hung there—wreaths, fillets, a sword, a shield, a mirror, vases.

Access to the tomb for liquid offerings made after burial was provided for in the Roman period by pipes leading into the grave. The broken bases of Athenian Geometric vases have been thought to have served this purpose (p. 58) and the same feature is observed in later and smaller vase markers on Thera (p. 241). In the Great Bliznitza tumulus in South Russia (p. 319) there was a pipe closed by a limestone slab with a central orifice. But we are not told where it led nor can we be sure that it was not installed later.

Any attempt to classify the grave offerings prejudges conclusions about their purpose. No ancient author gives any clear account of the principles involved and it is likely that the Greeks would have given widely differing reasons for the offering of many objects—'because it belonged to him', 'because he may need it', 'because I value it', 'because it served the ritual of death and cannot be reused', 'because we must honour the gods below'. It is difficult for man wholly and abruptly to dissociate the dead from life. If objects useful in life are offered this need not imply a belief in continuance of life as such. 'Man, I take it, feeds his dead for the same sort of reason as a little girl feeds her doll; and like the little girl, he abstains from killing his phantasy by applying reality standards' (Dodds, *The Greeks and the Irrational* 136). It is likely that for the Greeks in the period with which we are dealing the impulse to make offerings came from an inner need to satisfy a sense of loss or reluctance to credit total separation from the dead, rather than any positive belief in the value of the offerings to the departed. That the offerings are so disposed and chosen as to appear of use to him, or that explanations are given for their use, is in keeping with that lack of logic which informs man's views and emotions in the face of death. But some belief in an after life, or at least a journey to the other world, seems implicit in many offerings, and is made explicit in the Orphic instructions to the dead.

It is to be expected that the idea of the offerings being of physical value to the dead is the one best recorded. Lucian, in his diatribe against burial practices, comments that the dead are thought to be sustained by our offerings, and that without them they starve (*de Luctu* 9)—a proposition which the simplest Greek could have thought out to its absurd conclusion. In one of Aesop's fables (Budé no. 88) the dead drunkard complains that his wife brings him food when what he wants is booze. And in Herodotus' story (v 92) Periander's wife complains from the other world that she is cold because her clothes had not been burnt with her. The tyrant (incidentally, our first Greek necrophil) obliged her by stripping the women of Corinth and burning their clothes in a pit. A late Hellenistic epitaph from Astypalaia (*GV* 1363) is more realistic, rejecting food and drink—not needed now—but, for the sake of remembrance, requesting saffron and frankincense, appropriate gifts for the gods below. The dead in the other world were generally thought to be in much the condition they had been in during life, still bearing their wounds, but Aristotle expected them to become better and stronger.

We return to the archaeology of burial. The artefacts buried with the dead can be discussed in three categories: probable personal possessions; objects of everyday use but in this context having a possible funerary significance; and objects made for the grave.

There is not a great deal of evidence from excavation for the body being elaborately dressed and crowned for burial although this—the 'adornment of Hades' (Euripides *Medea* 980, *Alcestis* 613, 631-2)—is often referred to by ancient authors. Some warriors may be buried with their armour, but not in it. Several Geometric graves show from the position of dress pins that the body was dressed, and gold diadems may be worn. The normal Classical practice may have been to leave the body naked in its shroud but with the fourth century some of the richer burials have jewellery in situ on the body. The wreathing of the dead is often referred to and there are several gold wreaths in burials from the fourth century on. Some take these to have been deliberately made for the burial because the gold is so thin, but they may underestimate its pliability and toughness.

Other objects are appropriate to profession, age or sex. Weapons are commoner in graves before the Archaic period, but not so rare later as has been made out. Iron fire dogs (for the spits, see below) with supports in the shape of warships have been found in warrior graves of the years before and after 700 BC at Argos,

in Cyprus at Kouklia and Salamis, and in Crete at Kavousi. They
are not indicative of local interest in marine warfare, as has been
suggested for Argos, nor are they symbolic of the voyage to the
other world, which was not a concept popular with the Greeks
(Charon had a punt, not a warship). In Homer the warriors see
to their own cooking and a rich one might be expected to have
his own equipment for the purpose.

In burials of men and even children strigils (body scrapers for
use after a rub-down with oil) are often found, in the Classical
period and later. Already in the Archaic period it was fashionable
to characterize the dead as an athlete, and basic *palaistra* equipment included strigil and oil bottle. It was the sort of intimate
personal possession we could expect to be buried with its owner.
A fifth-century burial in Argos has a strigil laid across the forehead
like a wreath, a use of the *stlengis* attested by ancient authors. In
the Late Archaic and Classical graves of Delos and Rheneia
curved blades (*drepana*) seem to have taken the place of strigils,
and may in fact have been used as strigils since similar implements
were given as prizes to young Spartans later, and dedicated by
them. At Syracuse a man was buried with an iron discus as his
pillow.

There are no comparable surviving objects which regularly
appear in women's graves. Mirrors, the finer *alabastra* and toilet
vessels are sometimes found and once an *epinetron* (Rhodes,
Pontamo) used in spinning. We might expect loom-weights or
kitchen utensils but these are rare.

Astragals—knuckle-bones—are far more commonly found.
They could be thrown like dice, played with like our 'jacks',
strung as necklaces or made up into whips. We suspect that they
may have served the ancient Greek in much the way the *kombologi-*
beads do the modern. They are not uncommon in Greek graves
but the remarkable feature is the number found with single
burials—far more than required for any of the purposes named.
There is an extreme example at Locri where hundreds are strewn
over the lid of the sarcophagus of an old woman, with more
inside as well as a mirror and *alabastron*. They seem appropriate
for men, women and especially children. Sometimes they are

deposited in little boxes. Polygnotos showed the game being played in Hades (Pausanias x 30. 2). Children's graves are otherwise easily furnished—with miniature vases (which may also have a more adult connotation), models, rattles, toy clay dolls or clay feeders.

There are many other pretty objects which may be possessions and so appropriate offerings. These include most of the clay figurines found in graves. We must resist the temptation to identify death goddesses or concubines here since the types are usually exactly the same whether found in funerary or votive contexts. They are at any rate comparatively rare as grave offerings except in Boeotia, in Hellenistic Asia Minor and in some Western Greek cities. We cannot always decide whether the 'possessions' are of the dead or gifts of the living, and so not always appropriate to sex. The number of apparently inappropriate offerings is considerably reduced when we reflect that mirrors and even earrings need not be unmasculine, that adults keep their toys, even that some women might wash or exercise and use strigils.

We come now to the objects of everyday use which may acquire funerary significance in a grave. This is usually explicable in terms either of ritual in burial, or of specific expected needs of the dead in the other world. The most numerous class is of oil flasks—the early *aryballoi*, Classical *lekythoi*, and the fourth-century and later fusiform *unguentaria*, popularly miscalled 'tear-flasks'. The oiling of the body was an important part of the ritual but the offering of oil after the burial seems also to have been a regular practice, at least in Athens, and at the time of burial the offering of one or more oil flasks may have become a normal practice for kin or guests. There is not usually more than one or two in each grave, and many have none at all, but occasionally they may be counted in dozens.

Cups are equally common as offerings. The dead are always thirsty and there is much written about drinking of waters of the rivers of the other world, of Lethe and Mnemosyne, as we shall see. At Halai the plain jug at the head and cup in hand observed in some graves seem a fair indication of purpose. Water jars—

hydriai—are a special case. For the ash urn itself a *hydria* was commonly but by no means exclusively chosen. Archaic examples are mainly from Western Greek cemeteries, but they are more frequent in the homeland in the Classical and Hellenistic periods, many of them being superb works of bronze. If the shape had any special significance as an offering, this would not necessarily explain its choice for ashes. It is just possible that the choice bore some reference to the belief that, in the other world, the dead had to drink of the waters of Lethe, but this may not have originally suggested the use of a water jar. For the Orphics the analogous act was drinking the waters of the lake of Memory. A fourth-century bronze ash *hydria* from Pharsalos contained an inscribed gold sheet with instructions for the dead:

> In the halls of Hades you will find on the right a spring with a white cypress standing beside it. Go nowhere near this spring, but farther on you will find cold water running from the lake of Memory. Above it are guards who will ask you what you want. You tell them the whole truth, and say 'I am a child of Earth and starry Heaven; my name is Asterios. I am dry with thirst; allow me to drink from the spring'.

There are similar Orphic instructions from somewhat later burials at Petelia (South Italy), Eleutherna (Crete) and Thurii.

Decorated clay *hydriai* from Hellenistic Alexandria (the 'Hadra vases') seem to have been made deliberately to serve as ash urns. Some third-century examples are inscribed with the name of the dead and the date (*Pl. 47*). A few were exported to Greece and South Russia.

Pouring vases—*oinochoai*, but not exclusively for wine—may have served much the same purpose as *hydriai* and were especially appropriate for libations. In Ischia they were regularly placed with the early cremations and burials, but elsewhere they appear simply as part of the customary furniture of drinking vessels. In fifth-century Corinth the jugs are sometimes placed by the skulls, mouth to mouth. We may recall the Homeric dousing of the flames of the pyre with wine, but this will not explain all the jugs, and at Medeon they were broken before the primary cremation or burial.

Lamps are found occasionally in late graves, but are a regular feature only at Corinth from the fourth century on. Burials took place before dawn but it may be that the dead were thought to need lighting on their way. Another problem of the journey to the other world was the payment of ferryman Charon over the river Styx. Aristophanes (*Frogs* 140, 270) mentions a fee of two obols—a sum possibly determined by the dramatic context since later writers mention one obol or coin placed in the mouth of the dead. In an age of no pockets small change was conveniently carried in the mouth. No charge was made in places reckoned to be close to Hades, like Hermione (Strabo 373). Excavation shows that the practice was not universal. The coin was usually bronze, rarely silver or gold, and it is found in the mouth, in the hand or loose in the grave. One has been found in an oil flask. They were offered with cremations as well as burials. Pseudo-coins—'ghost money'—made of gold plaques and sometimes bearing the impression of a real coin, may take their place. These are found especially in Sicily and South Italy, and later in Sicyon, Athens (*Pl. 40*) and Megalopolis. Larger sums of money may have been offered for their intrinsic value in the other world. A grave at Nikesiani held 124 bronze coins and one gold. At Oisyme there is one with six obols and we may recall the Geometric graves at Argos and in Cyprus with six and twelve *obeloi*, spits—pre-coinage currency. The spits in other and later graves may be domestic (pp. 180, 203 and note the Paestum cenotaph 'bed', p. 299).

Shoes may also have been considered a necessary aid to the last journey. Three pairs hang in the athletes' grave at Tarentum and real shoes have been detected in graves in Argos, South Russia and Alexandria. A pair hang painted with *palaistra* equipment on a fourth-century *stele* from Athens. Clay substitutes are provided in pairs in Geometric Athens (*Pl. 8*) and Eleusis, and there is a clay shoe-vase in a grave at Palinurus. In Rhegion a Hellenistic clay sarcophagus was found shaped like a shoe (Fig. 42).

We have already discussed some of the things made deliberately

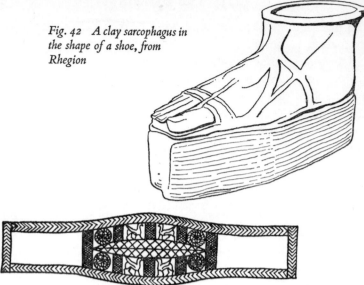

Fig. 42   A clay sarcophagus in the shape of a shoe, from Rhegion

Fig. 43   A gold lip band from Rhodes

for the grave—substitute money and shoes and certain funerary *hydriai*. It is debatable whether any of the gold wreaths found on bodies or in urns were capable of everyday use or not. There are, however, several examples of substitute jewellery from graves, usually in the form of necklace pendants, rosettes or earrings made in gilt or painted clay. These are fourth-century or later and found especially in Tarentum, North Greece, Athens and at Pergamon.

In the *prothesis* as shown on Athenian vases the dead has his mouth held shut by two bands around the head. There is a gold version of such a device, composed of head band and mouth piece, said to be from Athens but undated. Few of the Geometric gold bands may have been so used and there is difficulty in understanding the purpose of other gold sheet ornaments in burials unless their position on the body is known or their decoration betrays their purpose. Gold mouth bands are found in Late Bronze Age Cyprus and ninth-century Tell Halaf, decorated with lips. In early seventh-century Rhodes, at Kameiros, there are gold bands showing lips (Fig. 43) and plain versions of the same shape and size, presumably for the same purpose; but two of these were found in a pit in a chamber tomb (LXXXII). The mouth bands reappear in Cyprus in the fourth century.

Lozenge-shaped plaques from tombs in Chalcidice and Macedonia may have been fastened over the mouth and are sometimes, in fourth-century and later graves, associated with long narrow bands which could have gone over the eyes. The 'mouth pieces', however, go back to the ninth century and are found also in Thrace. For complete gold masks, like the Mycenaean, we have also to turn away from Greece, to the Illyrian tombs of Trebenishte (p. 316) where there are also gold hands, sandals and pectorals, or to a much later period in South Russia where there are also separate eye and mouth pieces in gold.

Athens yields the fullest series of vases and other clay artefacts made especially for the grave (pp. 76ff., 100ff.). There is little to match them elsewhere. It is not certain how many of the large Archaic amphorae from Boeotia, Euboea (see p. 184) and the islands were made especially for the grave as containers or markers, but an island vase from Delos has what appears to be a male mourner painted on its back. Mourners are painted on Late Geometric vases from Eretria and Ischia. A seventh-century *hydria* from Kavousi in Crete has painted on it three mourning women tearing their hair and there is one woman with hand to hair painted on an ash urn from Afrati. In fifth-century Corinth there was a limited production of some rather poor white-ground *lekythoi* imitating the Attic. It has been asserted that the Tarentine clay *rhyta* (animal-head pouring vases) of the fourth century were designed for funeral purposes, and the same might have been true of the many Apulian vases with grave scenes. It has been suggested that the scenes on many Athenian black- and red-figure vases were deliberately chosen with a view to their use as grave offerings, and even that the *kalos* inscriptions praising handsome youths had a purely funerary significance. We are not impressed by these arguments. Miniature vases were made in most Greek potteries. In children's graves they might be regarded as toys, in adults' graves, where they are rare, as substitutes for finer offerings. They are very common in votive deposits.

For most of the clay figurines found in graves no specific funerary connotation can be proved, but there are several Athenian representations of mourners on funeral apparatus from graves (pp. 64, 78f.) and a few elsewhere. Raised arms alone are not sufficient identification for mourners, but there is a fine sixth-century figure from a Thera grave of a woman tearing her hair and cheeks (*Pl. 43*), another with both hands to her hair, and similar figures from Boeotia with hands to hair, and to hair and breasts. In seventh-century Afrati in Crete a lid handle is formed by a seated woman with hands to her hair, so the whole vase, like many other Cretan *pithoi*, may have been intended for the grave. There are two primitive clay women from the same site making the same gesture and a fragmentary 'Dedalic' one from Lato. Kameiros offers clay figures of the seventh century with their hands to their hair and once to the cheeks, while one figure has streaks of red for blood on cheeks and breast, and in Ischia modelled mourners are attached to a vase, but it was not found in the cemetery. As in Attica the Archaic period provides the greatest variety in funerary terracottas. Fifth-century Boeotian figurines stand like the Attic with their hands to their hair or are shown as mourning women seated in the 'Penelope' pose, also adopted for tomb sculptures (p. 133). These may have been intended for the grave, and there are later groups with the figure beside a *stele* with a *hydria* at its foot (*Pl. 44*). There is a clay mourner from a Hellenistic grave near Navarino but the production of such figures for graves was clearly not a common practice by this time, and the graceful 'Tanagras' were for use in the home as much as the grave.

An unusual clay group from a Late Archaic tomb at Ialysos anticipates some features of the 'death-feast': it has a woman seated on a bier by the feet of the body which is covered with a shroud and pillowed on a prominent head-rest. There are no clay models from non-Attic graves to match the Vari death cart (*Pl. 16*), except in Cyprus, but a model clay *kline* from Tanagra of fourth-century date is probably from a grave where its purpose must be judged in terms of other *klinai* in graves and in funerary ritual. There is another from Athens. The rattles and pomegranates in some graves might have been made for them but could have served other votive or practical purposes.

The offerings in graves were not usually inscribed for the occasion, but in a sixth-century grave on Thera several vases are inscribed by scratching with the name Timosthenes, on one associated with the word *sema* while a plain vase was labelled *nekys*, 'corpse'. In the same cemetery a group of vases found intact over a pyre included a Late Archaic cup with the graffito '*sema* of Hegemon', and the name incised on the base of a later ash urn may be that of the dead. We have also the Alexandrian Hadra vases with painted inscriptions (*Pl.* 47) and for the rare examples from Attica see pp. 72, 98.

Foodstuffs in burials are represented by the bones of small animals, birds and fish, sea shells, eggs and nuts. They are found in the pits or pyres in which offerings were burnt and occasionally in the grave itself. They were all presumably for the benefit of the dead. Stone eggs (as on Rhodes and Thera) or clay models of animals may be food substitutes.

Other burials of animals with human interments have no cult significance, and may simply be of pets—the bird at Berezan (p. 318), piglets and dogs with burials in Athens, Rhodes and Thessaly. There was a separate grave for a horse at Olynthus (grave 437) and by the Roman period pets claim their own gravestones and epitaphs. The separate burial of a ram at Pilaf-Tepe is a special case (p. 282). Animal sacrifice, as to a hero, only becomes appropriate once the dead are heroized and the evidence is literary or from epitaphs. The late grave altars may have served in this.

There is no clear evidence for human sacrifice although Lucian's account (*de Luctu* 14) of the way folk killed horses, concubines and cup-boys to serve them in the after life is not specifically referred to heroic antiquity. Secondary burials on the lids of cists or sarcophagi have sometimes been taken for the burial of slaves killed for their masters. There are several examples in Sicily but the explanation seems improbable.

The food and some other offerings were regularly burnt (rather than cooked) and thus 'killed' so that they could accompany the dead. But only on rare occasions have excavators been

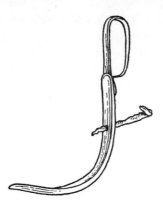

Fig. 44   *A strigil cancelled by an iron nail to render it useless. From a grave at Gela*

convinced that unburnt vases were deliberately broken in or outside the tomb, and many have survived intact, to the satisfaction of museum curators and art historians. Some Athenian white-ground *lekythoi* show broken vases by the *stele*. In the Geometric period swords were 'killed' by folding them in half or bending them in a circle around the ash urn (Fig. 5). This cannot have been to guard against reuse by the living since it would not have been difficult to straighten them in a forge. In Longus' *Daphnis* (i 31) at the funeral of Dorkon many syrinxes are broken. At Gela a strigil is cancelled by an iron nail driven through its blade (Fig. 44). This is very odd, and nails, of course, have a magical significance. In a fifth-century grave at Camarina the dead man had both his coin for Charon and six nails in his hand. Nails found in other graves have generally been thought to be from a coffin or bier. Their size is seldom stated and Greek carpenters usually glued or pegged their work. At Olynthus the nails were observed at the corners of the rectangular pit or in rows at either side of the upper part of the body. They were often found standing point up and their length was 10 to 15 cm. It is difficult to see how nails of this size and in this position could be from a coffin or bier, or indeed any ordinary furniture. Admittedly, most are from graves which could have held coffins, but single nails are also found in a tile grave and with two cremations, and there are nails in tile graves in Athens.

Another magical use of nails was to pierce folded lead plaques (*Pl. 45*) inscribed with curses (*katadesmoi*). These are intended for the attention of the underworld deities and were placed in pits, rivers, drains, the sea, or any place likely to afford ready access to their destination. An obvious place was a cemetery or grave, and several have been found in graves in Greece, Sicily, Asia Minor and Cyprus. The inscriptions on some indicate that the graves of those who died by violence or before their time were the favoured post boxes. Otherwise they have no special relevance to the burial they accompany. The earliest are late fifth-century but most are Hellenistic. More sinister still are the tiny lead figures with their hands bound, placed in lead coffins and set in or over Athenian graves in the late fifth century (*Pl. 46*). As with the curse tablets advantage is being taken of a burial to work malignant magic against the living. Quite different are the Orphic and Pythagorean lead or gold inscribed plaques (p. 210) with instructions for the dead.

One last 'magic' practice for which there is material evidence may be noticed. In many early cultures it was the custom to smear the body or bones of the dead with red pigment, a practice apparently intended to restore blood to the lifeless corpse. There is no evidence in Greece for this treatment of the body, and only the Spartans insisted on a red shroud, but in many parts of the Greek world from the eighth century on it has been observed that some stone cists, stone or clay sarcophagi and wooden coffins have been painted red on their inner surfaces. This is usually taken to be an analogous custom to that of smearing the body, but it is not self-evident and we may wonder whether the colour used in this way signified fire rather than blood.

CHAPTER XII

GRAVE MARKERS AND MONUMENTS

Great Persons affected great Monuments,
And the fair and larger Urnes contained
no vulgar ashes, which makes that dis-
parity in those which time discovereth
among us.

ABOVE-GROUND MARKERS of the site of a burial may perform one
or both of two functions. They may mark the position of a grave
so that it shall not be disturbed by later burials; or they may
commemorate the dead by a decorative monument which may
even name him. The commonest marker, for which perhaps no
particular function was envisaged, was provided by the surplus
earth, piled over the ground as a low mound, but there is often
some more deliberate, even if anonymous, marker—a *sema* in the
true sense of the word. This may be something built, of earth,
brick or stone, or, in its most basic and popular form, it is the *stele*
or gravestone. This, together with the tomb mound, was for
Homer the due of the dead.

Much has been written about the significance of the *stele* and
its possible function as a form of surrogate or symbol of the dead.
This is easiest argued when the *stele* approximates to human form,
carries the representation of a human figure, or is replaced by a
statue. Classical gravestones in Athens were the focus for post-
funeral rites and offerings, and the *archon* of Plataea washed and
anointed the *stelai* which recorded those killed in the battle as if
they were the dead themselves (Plutarch *Aristeides* 21). But
although this view of the *stele* may have obtained at some times
in some places it is not likely, to judge from the early evidence,
to have been its prime function, which was more practical; and

in later periods old *stelai* were casually reused. We should bear in mind also other types of marker which might not have survived, for instance, those made of wood, or which designated the dead in other ways—like the rudder which Odysseus' companions set up on Elpenor's tomb (*Odyssey* xii 13f.) or the oar and basket for a fisherman's tomb (*Anth. Pal.* vii 505). The *stelai* could be set on top of the tomb mound or structure, or in front of it; an epitaph from Eretria (*GV* 1210) describes one as on the very top of the mound, while several from Athens are 'near the road', presumably in front of the tomb.

EARLY STELAI

The practice in Attica was typical of much, but not all of the Greek world, and we have seen full evidence there for the use of an upright slab as marker, which is not embellished with an inscription or figure decoration until at least the mid-seventh century. Plain *stelai* of this sort are attested elsewhere throughout the Early Iron Age, but there is clearer and possibly earlier evidence outside Attica both for the inscribing of *stelai* and for their assimilation to figures or use as a field for figure decoration. Rough-hewn long slabs with the name of the dead written vertically up them are known from the middle and second half of the seventh century on Thera (Fig. 45a) and Corcyra and in Aetolia and Achaia. These are from 0·50 to nearly 2 m. tall. From Corinth, perhaps as early as the mid-seventh century, comes a *stele* with more monumental pretensions, having a projecting ledge above, and a lengthy epitaph in horizontal lines beneath.

Early decorated or decorative *stelai* are more difficult to place. There are two from Greece which have been assigned to the late eighth century but the evidence for their date is purely circumstantial, from their discovery in the area of Geometric cemeteries. One from Kymisala in Rhodes is in the form of a fat disc on a broken pillar, topped by a rectangular 'abacus'. The disc has shallow cut figures of birds (?) on one side and a rosette on the other. It does not look more Geometric than Byzantine. It is from an area otherwise known only for a Bronze Age to Geometric cemetery, yet it was strangely overlooked when the cemetery

Fig. 45 Gravestones from the islands: (a) a seventh-century stele from Thera; (b) a figure stele from Kimolos; and (c) a Classical stele from Melos

was excavated. The second *stele*, from Kimolos, is in the form of a slab with its upper part fashioned as a bust with arms crossed (Fig. 45b: height 62 cm.; the head is missing). It was found close to a Late Geometric cemetery and is certainly 'primitive' but not securely datable. At Neandria in the Troad the slabs have a centre-top projection like a head, and they taper downwards, as does the Kimolos *stele* and few from seventh-century Attica, like a human figure. The Neandria *stelai* are 2 to 4 m. high, but the cemetery in which they were found seems hardly earlier than the sixth century. Some other figure-decorated *stelai* of seventh-century date have been described as gravestones but this has never been clearly demonstrated. They are a slab from Paros showing a seated woman, and a series of slabs from Prinias in Crete, showing women or warriors, one of the latter being accompanied by the small figure of an attendant or adorant.

RELIEF AND DECORATED GRAVESTONES

The only important series of grave *stelai* outside Attica in the sixth century is that from East Greece. The most informative group is from Samos, but there are related examples also from the north (Perinthos, Stryme, the Troad, Thasos and Kerch) and from other Ionian cities (Chios, Smyrna, Erythrai). The shafts are plain except for the inscription but they are topped by exquisitely carved scroll-and-palmette *anthemia* (*Pls. 48, 49*). The Samos *stelai* begin before the mid-century and continue through the third quarter: examples from other areas may be later. It was during its floruit that the type was introduced to Athens by Ionian artists and replaced the older Attic *stelai*, with their sphinx crowns, having already influenced the volute members beneath the latest of the *stele* sphinxes (Fig. 13). The Ionian type was also copied in Lydia, and stood beside tumuli at Sardis. One with relief decoration on front and back was found at Dorylaion in Phrygia (*Pl. 50*). The reliefs are purely Late Archaic Greek but the tomb may have been that of a Phrygian or Persian. Other *stelai* from Daskylion, the Persian satrapy capital in Phrygia, have more Persian content and style in their panel reliefs, and it has been suggested that they were Greek *stelai*, reused. Volute finials in clay may have been used in Archaic Corinth, and there is a stone *stele* with floral crown in Aegina.

The East Greek *stelai*, unlike the Attic, carried no figure decoration, but in the later sixth century, little before the time the Attic series ended, examples with relief figures are found both in the East Greek area and elsewhere in the Greek world, notably the islands but including mainland Greece and some colonies. It is tempting to associate this activity with the dispersal of artists from Attica, or to explain it in the light of the restricted sculptural activity in Athens in the first half of the fifth century, since these non-Attic *stelai* continue through the Early Classical period with much the same proportions, changing only in style and the form of *anthemion*, which may occasionally be replaced by a low pediment. There is no clear evidence for this from their style or from sculptors' names—the Naxian Alxenor worked in Boeotia—but not all Athens' sculptors were Athens-born, and the overall unity of the *stelai* from such diverse sites is striking. Many of the figures on the *stelai* broadly resemble those on the earlier Attic series but there are several important new types for the male figures as well as more radical innovations. The old man leaning on a stick and feeding his dog appears on stones from Boeotia (Alxenor's), Apollonia (the Milesian colony on the Black Sea) and on the Borgia *stele* in Naples (*Pl. 51*) which is probably from Asia Minor, perhaps from Sardis; but this is a type which originates in Attica. There are more athlete figures, fewer warriors, and occasionally a boy slave joins his master. On the tall figure-*stelai* of Athens the fair sex was only admitted as a young girl beside an elder brother, but now we see some women alone on gravestones: the Esquiline *stele*, from a colony in South Italy, perhaps Locri, or the exquisite Early Classical Giustiniani *stele* in Berlin (*Pl. 52*), which may be Parian.

There are some interesting variations too in the form of the *stelai*. Stones with reliefs on both sides (*amphiglypha*) have a limited vogue in Thrace and the Black Sea cities, and they include Deines' *stele* from Apollonia. The type was copied once in Athens for a *stele* showing a lion and lioness. There is a general tendency for the *stele* to broaden. Really broad *stelai* were rare in Archaic Attica. They seem to commemorate women and the breadth may have been intended to accommodate a seated figure. There are other broad reliefs of the Archaic and Early Classical periods showing a seated figure or figures, sometimes with one or more attendants. These are often discussed with the gravestones but are probably votive, albeit showing 'heroized dead'. The best known examples are the Laconian 'hero reliefs' with a couple seated, approached by attendants, and there are single seated figures from other parts of Greece. More clearly funerary, perhaps, is a *stele* from Chalcedon showing a seated woman with attendants and a mourner. She may be dying or in childbirth, to judge from the attention paid to her. The date is mid-sixth century. A *stele* from Kos shows an erotic scene and may not be a gravestone, but a Hellenistic epitaph (*GV* 1181) alludes to a similar subject. In the first half of the fifth century we find the grouping of seated woman and attendant, and even if these are not gravestones they may reasonably be understood to influence the iconography of the main series of Athenian relief gravestones which begins around 430 BC. Before this date we find such grave reliefs from Sinope (*Pl. 53*), on the south coast of the Black Sea, in Thessaly and Thrace, and we have already seen that the North Greek area seems responsible for some innovations and originality in gravestone design.

Most *stelai* of the Classical period are, of course, quite simple slabs with, at the most, a moulded pediment or *anthemion* above the inscription. Our attention is attracted naturally to the minority with figure decoration. Of the plainer *stelai* those of fifth-century Melos may be mentioned: they are flat, with gable tops, the whole shaft filled with the inscription giving name and patronymic, cut within bold guide lines (Fig. 45c).

The simplest of the ornate Athenian *stelai* of the Classical period carried palmette *anthemia* elaborated with acanthus leaves. They owe nothing to Ionian models, and the series begins by the mid-fifth century, to judge from representations, lasting until the decree of Demetrios, and with a brief late Hellenistic return to fashion. The type was widely copied in Greece, best in the nearby cities of Euboea. After Demetrios the Athenian type is transplanted to the islands, Boeotia and the new city of Demetrias in Thessaly, and persists in much of the Greek world, though often in a 'fossilized' style, through the Hellenistic period. Only Alexandria and South Italy seem to have ignored it.

In about 430 BC begins the great series of Attic relief gravestones. Those of the rest of Greece are readily comparable with the Attic in general form and iconography, but it would be wrong to minimize the importance of some local variants and we have to remember that the tradition of gravestone reliefs in the first half of the fifth century was maintained in Greece in the islands and East Greece and not in Athens at all. Moreover, the decree of Demetrios, which brought the Attic series to an end before the fourth century was through, had no effect on practice outside Attica. The richer cemeteries of most parts of the Greek world offer examples of Classical gravestones with reliefs. We shall dwell only upon some of the more distinctive local schools.

The earliest figure *stelai* from Thessaly antedate the Attic series and betray their debt to the islands in their palmette finials—a form which persists into the fourth century although the pediment finial had already been introduced around 450 BC. The best are Early Classical in style and some carry the unusual group of two women standing, facing each other (Fig. 46). Otherwise subjects are as the Attic, with a fondness for children shown with

Fig. 46   A Classical Thessalian stele *with two girls*

adults, and for girls holding balls. By the end of the century there is more conformity with Attic and in the fourth century multi-figure groups become popular. The material is local marble, the style increasingly provincial once the apparently direct influence of Early Classical island schools was replaced.

The *stelai* from Boeotian cities are predictably much influenced by Athens, yet there are some distinguished Classical series and, especially later, considerable originality of form. In the Late Archaic period some *stelai* seem to have been imported from Athens and are of the usual Athenian type, while Alxenor came from Naxos to make the famous *stele* found near Orchomenos. Through the Classical period plain upright slabs, later with pediment tops and carrying only the name of the dead, serve most burials. A very fine group of relief gravestones from Thespiae (as *Pl. 54*), and mainly of the third quarter of the fifth century, is evidence for a good local workshop, using local marble and, if trained in Athens, showing some measure of independence from current Athenian iconography. Later in the century come the first of a series of painted gravestones from Thebes and Tanagra, the earliest being flat slabs, some with pediment tops, while later there is a fuller architectural form (at Tanagra) with free-standing

50 East Greek *stelai*: a rare example with relief figures from the inland city Dorylaion. It shows an eastern Artemis with her lion.

51–3 Relief gravestones of the Early Classical period: from Asia Minor (*left*, the Borgia *stele*); from the Greek islands (*centre*, the Giustiniani *stele*); and from Sinope (*right*) on the south coast of the Black Sea. The first two retain the Archaic form, the third looks forward to the Classical in shape and composition.

ΣΑΥΓΕΝΕΣ

54, 55 Two
Boeotian *stelai*:
one with a
horseman, of the
Thespiae group,
Athenian in style
but not shape
(*above*); and the
painted *stele* of
Saugenes (*left*).

56 A Boeotian gravestone with architectural decoration and devices including the Boeotian cavalry helmet and Celtic shields. These stones were supported on slender pillars.

57 A western Greek type of gravestone with mourning sirens holding a plaque bearing the name of the dead.

58 A high-relief gravestone from Boeotia, the figures carved almost wholly in the round, like *kouroi*.

59 Gravestone of Krito and Timarista from Rhodes. Contrast this
with the Athenian for its shape and the composition of the figures.

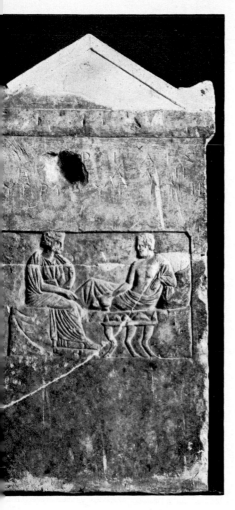

60, 61 Two typical late Classical gravestones: one from Athens (*left*), with an early example of the death-feast motif on a gravestone; the other a Hellenistic *stele* from the East Greek world.

62 Painted *stele* from Demetrias in North Greece.

side columns. The painting, direct on to the marble, has seldom survived well, but a few late fifth-century *stelai* were differently prepared, the backgrounds being roughened, presumably to carry a white stucco, with the figures polished on the flat stone, to take encaustic painting, with all details incised. The colour has gone, but the linear detail and figures are clear. The three best—of Mnason, Grynchon and Saugenes (*Pl. 55*)—show charging warriors, and have been associated with the battle of Delion (424 BC). There may have been yet earlier warrior *stelai*, to judge from the allusion in an epigram on a base recently found, and apparently for a victim of the battle at Oenophyta in 457 BC.

Apart from the figure reliefs a common Boeotian gravestone in the fourth century and Hellenistic period takes the form of a low rectangular block, socketed beneath to be supported on a slim pillar, and probably copying a simpler wooden type with a plaque on a post. Some *stelai* show the whole T-shaped monument over a round burial mound. The simplest stones have just the name of the dead in a horizontal panel. Most have relief pediments with various architectural features below—a triglyph frieze, a colonnade or scrolls—and a panel for the name. The relief emblems sometimes figure armour (*Pl. 56*), notably the 'Boeotian helmet' with crinkly rim which is also executed in the round in stone to top a funeral monument. There are plain pediment *stelai* too, like the Attic. The simpler Boeotian *stelai* set a pattern followed largely in central Greece and the western islands, where too the name of the dead is also regularly given without patronymic. On some grander West Greek pediment *stelai* of the Hellenistic period two mourning sirens are shown standing on a high base and holding a plaque between them, bearing the name of the dead (*Pl. 57*).

There are a few good Classical relief gravestones from the islands and East Greece. The Rhodian gravestone of Krito and Timarista is Attic in style but not shape (a rounded top), nor in the poses of the two standing women (*Pl. 59*). Hellenistic Rhodian reliefs also show some originality with emotional scenes of the type we expect only for subsidiary tomb figures of mourners.

Some of the types of gravestone already described persist in use throughout the Hellenistic period but there are also some special local groups of the late period which deserve mention. The most numerous of these are from East Greece, belonging mainly to the Hellenistic period but continuing with minor variations well into the Roman. The shapes recall the Attic, with pediment top and architectural frame, or are wide and rectangular resembling votive reliefs in form and subject. Standing and seated figures are shown, often with attendants or slaves who mourn and may be shown at a reduced scale (*Pl. 61*). This is a feature of votive reliefs showing a deity and adorants, and since the major figures on the *stelai* are often specifically identified as the dead, this is in keeping with the new mood of 'heroization'. The dead are shown in a funerary setting of pillars topped by various objects (animals, boxes, baskets, vases), herms and altars. These may give some idea of the appearance of a Hellenistic cemetery, and if the plain pillars have not survived this may mean simply that the slabs were more readily turned to other uses than the relief sculpture could offer. The pillars most resemble those seen as gravestones on fourth-century Apulian vases.

The normal theme for the broad rectangular reliefs is the death-feast (*Totenmahl*) with the dead reclining on a *kline*, a side table with food, often a woman seated at its foot and smaller figures of attendants or worshippers. The form and figures are exactly those of the votive reliefs for heroes and this is a specific indication of the dead as a hero. The origin of the motif is not easily established but we have no good reason to believe that the dead was thought to be present at any meal actually consumed in the course of or after the burial rites. The banquet motif for votive reliefs appears in Greece by the end of the sixth century. In a funerary context it is seen on a Cypriot sarcophagus and on Lycian sarcophagi, including the Satraps sarcophagus at Sidon, before the end of the fifth century. In Greece it is seen in the pediment of the Boeotian *stele* for Saugenes of the late fifth century (*Pl. 55*) and occasionally on Attic gravestones from about 375 BC on (*Pl. 60*). In the Hellenistic period it appears also outside the East Greek area.

Reliefs which broadly followed the Classical pattern but without the variety and circumstantial detail of the East Greek, are found throughout the Greek world in the Hellenistic period. They are sometimes accompanied by painted *stelai* on which the subjects are the same. Those from Alexandria will be discussed below, and there is only one other group which deserves mention—those from Demetrias (Pagasai), a new foundation of 294 BC. The *stelai* were found built into the city wall a century after foundation. Some have pediment crowns but most are rectangular and the finest, though fragmentary, are excellent examples of Hellenistic painting (*Pl. 62*). Most, however, are more simply executed. The scenes are of the usual funerary repertory, and we may note the one of a woman dying in childbirth. The *stelai* were apparently mounted in shallow built *naiskoi* or niche-shrines.

BLOCK MONUMENTS

One class of grave markers is worth considering on its own. The form is generally a long low block with a flat upper surface, and although it may advertise the name of the dead or carry relief decoration, like any gravestone, its shape suggests other possible functions. Though few actually resemble tables—*trapezai*—this is the name generally given them and some are thought to have served as platforms for offerings—a use for which there is, and perhaps can be, no direct evidence. The use of the name is misleading and may have been encouraged by its application to Hellenistic Athenian monuments and perhaps by association with presumed 'funeral feasts'. Outside Attica, where the use of such monuments is obscure (see p. 168) and at any rate not pre-Classical, they may stand instead of *stelai*. The blocks were perhaps regarded as more substantial markers than upright slabs, but flat slabs inscribed on the upper face (as from Methana, about 600 BC and a hollow block from Krommyon of somewhat later date) seem simply to record without attracting attention and may have had no '*trapeza*' function.

The fullest evidence for the tables and blocks is seen in the cemeteries of Thera where we have also found some of the earliest inscribed *stelai*. The 'tables' are low blocks with three rough-hewn legs, the inscription being on the sides (Fig. 47a), but there are also plain low blocks, similarly inscribed. Some could

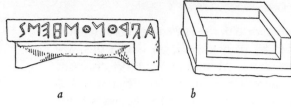

Fig. 47 Some block markers: (a) from Thera in the form of a low, three-legged table; (b) an altar-shaped block from Tanagra; and (c) a block from Boeotia with a kantharos cup in low relief

serve to mark several burials, and one of about 600 BC carries nine or ten names, some inscribed on the flat top. This Archaic usage is succeeded in the fifth and fourth centuries by the use of stone cubes inscribed with the name of the dead. These are sometimes arranged neatly on family plots standing on small built terraces over the burials. A good late fourth-century example has five cubes in line, one of them exceptionally bearing a relief scene of a seated and standing woman, of the usual funerary type (Fig. 48).

Similar cubical stone monuments from East Greek sites, as Samos, are not inscribed and we may wonder whether they served simply as grave markers. In Chios the usual East Greek palmette *stelai* were followed by block markers which in the later fifth and fourth centuries are tall in proportions, but later become flatter and more like tables. Most are simply inscribed but some of the earlier group were painted, the stone being prepared as for the finer Boeotian painted *stelai*, with incised polished figures and rough background. The most elaborate is the early third-century gravestone of Metrodoros, in Berlin. The front bore the inscription; on one side was shown a youth out hunting; on the other a still life of *palaistra* equipment (Pl. 63). There are subsidiary friezes of sirens, a centauromachy and Nikai in chariots. Simple low 'tables' are found in some areas of North Greece, as at Dion, and there is one from Samos.

Boeotia has some comparable monuments to offer—near-cubes decorated like the ordinary gravestones by painting or in low relief. Most are fourth-century or later and odd subjects are the *kantharos* cup (Fig. 47c) and three painted pomegranates. Stranger are the Tanagra 'grave altars' (Fig. 47b). They run from Late Archaic to the fourth century and take the form of stone blocks hollowed like a seat, or with a cavity on top. These are very much more like real offering tables, logically taking the form of altars, but some of them are inscribed and so they could presumably serve as a form of grave marker.

This aspect of the tomb marker serving as a receptacle or resting place for offerings to the dead may have been implicit in some earlier monuments, like the grave vases. Only with the Hellenistic period, and its freer heroizing of the recent dead, do we find wholly explicit grave altars and these are especially common in East and North Greece (see p. 301). In Thrace the practice may go back to the fifth century but we may reasonably suspect that some of the other block monuments we have discussed were regarded as altars as well as markers.

STATUARY

Stelai in human form—if there are any in early Archaic Greece—prefigure the use of *kouroi* or *korai* as grave markers, a practice best observed in Attica from about 600 BC on. Rather earlier *kouroi* from Thera seem to have served this function which may then be traced back to the beginning of true monumental sculpture in Greece and may possibly have been inspired or encouraged by the same source—Egypt. From Tanagra in the early sixth century comes a pair of *kouroi*, arms round each others' necks, not wholly worked in the round but left attached to a

Fig. 48 A grave terrace on Thera with cube markers, one carrying a funeral relief scene

flat *stele*-like background with projecting cornice (*Pl. 58*). These are interesting because the inscription on the base names the man who erected the *stele* and separate inscriptions beside their legs identify each figure, Dermys and Kittylos: specific identification even if not portraiture.

The evidence for the placing of *kouroi* over graves is not often clear. The famous Tenea *kouros* was apparently found fallen over a grave, and that from Keos near a pyre of ash and bones. The feet and base of a *kouros* on Thera were found in situ on a hill slope just in front of a cleft in the rock face which concealed an ash urn. In the North Cemetery on Samos fragments of two *kouroi* and two columns were found beside a tumulus which covered an ash urn, and a *kouros* was found in the cemetery at Pitane. There is an unfinished *kouros* from the Miletus cemetery.

Fragments of *korai* were found in cemeteries in Attica, Samos, Chios and perhaps Thera but it is by no means certain that they all served as grave markers. Seated figures were also used as grave monuments in Athens but again the evidence is vague elsewhere. There are three seated female figures from the Miletus cemetery. There may also have been riders as grave markers in Archaic Athens. The early Attic *stelai* supported sphinxes, and columns may have supported statuary. Early fifth-century Attic vases show low boxes which may be tombs topped by a cock, a sphinx or a siren, with visitors.

In the Classical period the range of statuary types on tombs is somewhat different and we have to distinguish accessory figures which served as sculptural decoration to a family plot or the more elaborate single monuments. The best evidence for these is in Attica where we find pairs of lions, dogs and sirens, of Scythian archers and of seated mourning women. Outside Attica the mourning woman type is met on Mykonos (see also p. 214) and a pair of lions in the cemetery at Ialysos.

In Athens single animals were found appropriate, like the butting bull or reclining dog from the Kerameikos, where Plato's tomb was said to have been marked by an eagle—the symbol of his soul, flown to Olympus, according to the epitaph in the *Anthology* (vii 62). By far the commonest animal marker was a lion. In an epitaph by Simonides (*GV* 1173) a lion explains why, but here he also serves as a canting device for the dead man, Leon:

> I am the strongest of beasts, as was he, whose grave I stand to guard in stone, of mortals. But if Leon had not possessed my spirit as well as my name I would not have set my feet on his tomb.

The same sentiment is expressed in Hellenistic epitaphs. It is possible, however, that originally the creature was adopted as guardian of the tomb rather than for its symbolism. The earliest tomb lion known is the fine reclining creature from Corfu which used to be associated with the tomb of Menekrates (*Pl. 65*). This is of the years around 600 BC and there is the fragment of another smaller lion from the same cemetery. Other Archaic examples are found in cemeteries in Athens, Kythera and Miletus (*Pl. 64*) and later ones in Athens, East Greece, the islands, Epirus and Boeotia. They were the usual marker for communal tombs for those killed in battle and are often referred to in epitaphs. The Archaic lions are recumbent or sitting while the Classical commonly crouch, bottom in air.

We might have expected snakes to appear as tomb monuments but although they are not uncommon in representations of tombs and on tomb vases, they were clearly not considered appropriate for individual monuments. They were thought to embody the souls of the dead or, Plutarch says (*Kleomenes* 39), to be born from rotting bodies. Thus they may appear in relief on late grave altars and a large one is carved on the rock in the late cemetery on Thera. A Hellenistic epitaph (*GV* 1260) reveals that the snake monument—'fierce guardian of the tomb'—is there because a snake was the dead warrior's shield blazon.

Sphinxes topped the early Attic *stelai* and grave monuments. Later they are usually only accessory figures but they sit on *tymboi* attacked by satyrs on two early fifth-century Athenian vases. In a fifth-century epitaph from Pagasai one is addressed: 'dog of Hades, whom do you guard?', but the title probably derives from this occasional function on tombs since in Greek art sphinxes are not usually in any funerary context and the representations of them carrying a body can be referred to the Theban story.

Sirens, however, are far more commonly associated with the dead. They may be shown carrying a body, as on the Xanthos Harpy tomb, and from the fourth century on they often appear on grave monuments mourning and playing musical instruments. We cannot be sure that all sirens carved in the round are funerary, unless they are mourning, but there are examples from Athens, Andros, Amphipolis and Marmara.

We have noted one example of a canting device, a lion for Leon—and there were others. From her epitaph (GV 1802) we learn that Boidion had a stone bull. She was the concubine of the Athenian general Chares, and died on the Bosporos at some time after his campaign there in 340 BC.

In Hellenistic Greece, outside Athens, statues of the dead, even if not portraits, become more common as grave markers. They are often alluded to in epitaphs (see pp. 262f.). Some monuments are described as of bronze but none in this material has been preserved.

COLUMNS AND VASES

A column may seem a perfectly reasonable substitute for a *stele* slab as a grave marker, but its function is in some respects different since it serves to support a statue or other object which is presumably the focus of attention. Columns commonly served as bases for dedications like *korai* or even cult statues.

Doric columns seem especially favoured for tombs but, unless an epitaph tells us, we do not know what they carried. Most are of the sixth century—from Assos, Corfu (described as a *stele*), Troizen (put up in one day), Samos (perhaps for *kouroi*) and near Argos. Two in Attica carried works by Aristion. Fifth-century examples are from Corfu and Pagasai (for a sphinx). A Late Archaic Ionic column from Asia Minor (now in Ankara) carried the figure of a reclining lion, cut in one piece with the capital (*Pl. 66*). Not all, however, took a canonical architectural form and there are faceted pillars from Troizen, to support a tripod won by the dead in games and from Eretria (early fifth century). Descriptions and representations show that such tomb columns might support a vase, especially a *hydria*, shield or helmet, while sirens, sphinxes and lions are other likely subjects. The cynic Diogenes' tomb was appropriately marked by a dog on a column.

Columns supporting marble cauldrons with griffin protomes, such as appeared in Athens' cemeteries in the fourth century, are found also in Chalcis and one is represented on a relief in Mykonos. Urns are shown on columns on Hellenistic gravestones and epitaphs have been cited—not wholly convincingly—to suggest that ash urns were thus prominently displayed. The analogy with Lycian pillar tombs seems weak and the top of a column is a precarious place for something usually carefully bestowed below ground and protected by a stone box or cist.

Stone *loutrophoroi* are not found only in Attica: there are examples from Camarina and Verroia, but we do not know how they were mounted. The Attic use of clay vases to mark graves is paralleled only, and rarely, in Thera in the fifth and fourth centuries. The vases were propped up with stones or set on slabs, and they include two red-figure Athenian *lebetes gamikoi*—marriage vases—with pierced bases.

HERMS AND PHALLOI

Cicero's use of the word 'herm' in describing sumptuary legislation in Athens has encouraged the belief that herms were used as gravestones. The appropriateness of Hermes and herms to cairns, roadways and the escort of souls, would explain representations of the god in any form in or near cemeteries. There is no clear evidence for the use of herms as grave markers in the Classical period. They are carved on some Hellenistic gravestones, below the inscriptions on Thessalian *stelai*, on the borders of painted *stelai* and in the field of some East Greek reliefs, where there are also some Herakles-herms. On a Hellenistic gravestone from Verroia, of the type otherwise most familiar in East Greece, a herm shares a base, inscribed for Hermes Chthonios, with the god himself, with the human figures standing to one side (Fig. 49). A herm is also carved prominently in a niche on a phalloid

Fig. 49 A gravestone from North Greece showing Hermes and a herm on a base, beside the figure of the dead woman and attendant

second-century gravestone for a woman at Daskylion (Fig. 50). Only once the herm type was adopted as a base for portraits can we credit their use as gravestones, and there is evidence for their use thus in Greece in the Roman period.

The mushroom-like stone finials on tumuli in Asia Minor (Fig. 51a, b) are generally described as *phalloi* and the few analogous markers for which there is evidence in Greece are similarly explained. It would be easier to accept these as *phalloi* if any one of them bore the slightest resemblance to the organ with which Greek artists were well familiar. The asymmetry of the glans, the duct and the testicles are never shown, and the knob is often flat, hemispherical or spherical. The only group of objects which

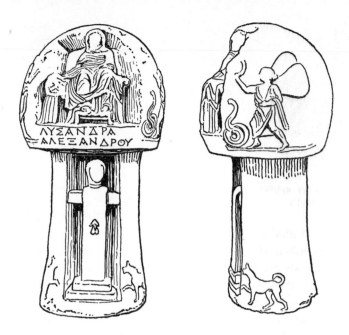

Fig. 50 A 'phallos' monument with relief decoration, including a herm. Hellenistic, from Asia Minor

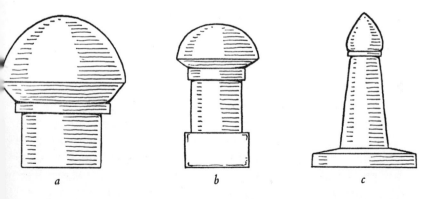

a   b   c

Fig. 51 'Phalloi': stone markers from graves in Asia Minor (a, b) and on Thera (c)

Fig. 52 *Grave markers from Corinth: a faceless head, a 'phallos' and a simple block and cylinder*

all these '*phalloi*' can be said to resemble is fungi—mushrooms and toadstools of different varieties, no more nor less appropriate to tombs than *phalloi*. Most Greek examples are Hellenistic and from East Greece, as Pergamon, or Macedonia, near the homeland of this type of marker. But Archaic examples are reported in the Greek cemetery at Old Smyrna. We may discount the small conoid markers in this context. Some earlier examples from Greece are more plausibly phalloid since the shafts and knobs are roughly conical although all other distinguishing features are lacking. Examples are from Thera (Fig. 51c) and from what may be the debris of a fourth-century cemetery at Corinth (Fig. 52). With the last was another marker of similar form but with part of the knob carved as human hair—a simple aniconic bust. Whatever the explanation of this piece may be, the possibility that others of these stone knobs on stalks are basically anthropomorphic should be considered.

OTHER STRUCTURES

The magnificent family burial plots of the Athenian cemeteries have no rivals in Greece, but single graves and groups of graves are occasionally given some architectural elaboration, other than a stone-edged tumulus of earth. Thus, on Thera, there are both low stone terraces before individual burials and bigger terraces for groups of graves supporting the cubical stone markers (Fig. 48), rather like the larger Athenian terraces with their graves and statuary. The top of a large third-century terrace at Anaktorion

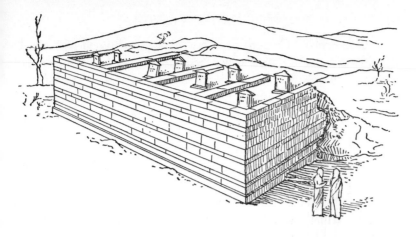

Fig. 53   A Hellenistic grave enclosure at Anaktorion in West Greece

was divided by low walls into four compartments, each with a
row of inscribed *stelai* (Fig. 53).

Sometimes a stone structure over the grave may take the place
of a *tymbos* mound or the mound may be contained by quite
substantial walls. In late seventh-century Corfu the grave of
Menekrates was topped by a built cylinder of stone, nearly 5 m.
across and 1·20 m. high, crowned by a conical roof (Fig. 54).
This is the earth tumulus turned into stone, which we see later in
East Greece and Cyrenaica. In fifth-century Ikaria the structure
above ground was rectangular, of upright slabs enclosing a mass
of stones and earth, or else a massive stone 'base' enclosing the cist
grave.

Fig. 54   The grave monument of Menekrates at Corcyra

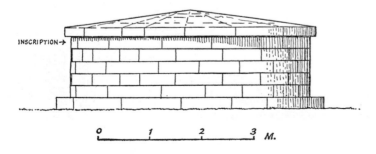

In Late Archaic Corinth four graves were crowned by a single massive stone base which supported four *stelai*. A grave or small group of graves may be enclosed by a low walled *peribolos*—a complex which safeguards and renders prominent individual burials, or which defines a family plot. There is an apsidal enclosure in sixth-century Samos, but the shape is usually rectangular— as in fifth- and fourth-century Pharsalos, and the arrangement is met in various North Greek cemeteries, especially in the Hellenistic period. At Preveza one such enclosure seems to have been adorned with statues, gravestone and *exedra*, while in Hellenistic Euboea statues and *stelai* stood before the wall enclosing graves facing a road.

There are stranger monuments too, like the fourth-century structure at Olynthus, 4 m. wide, with a straight back wall and projecting wings. Possibly this originally supported a *stele* and was a cenotaph. The general form would resemble some of the Athenian monuments, and, more closely, a Hellenistic tomb at Alipheira in Arcadia (Fig. 55), where the gravestone is partly preserved and the burial lay behind the monument. At Sicyon a comparable monument with projecting wings enclosed three compartments with burials let into them, but we know nothing of the *stelai*.

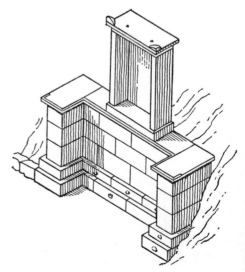

Fig. 55 A Hellenistic monument with stele *in Arcadia*

CHAPTER XIII

COMMUNAL GRAVES AND CENOTAPHS

The certainty of death is attended with
uncertainties, in time, manner, places.
The variety of Monuments hath often
obscured true graves: and Cenotaphs
confounded Sepulchres. For beside their
reall Tombs, many have found honorary
and empty Sepulchres.

AFTER A BATTLE the victors normally paid the defeated the
courtesy of permission to pick up their dead; this practice among
the Greeks being variously attributed to Theseus and Herakles
(Plutarch *Theseus* 29). Even when the foe was barbarian the due
of burial was observed, and Pausanias says that at Marathon the
Athenians tossed the Persian bodies together in a trench. The usual
practice, except by Athenians in the Classical period (see p. 108),
was for the dead to be buried on or near the field of battle. Six
polyandria from recorded battles have been properly investigated.
At Marathon the bodies were cremated and a tumulus raised
over a brick platform which some have seen as the cremation
area, together with some vase offerings, mainly *lekythoi*. The
stelai with the names of the dead were set on top and at the side
was another brick offering trench. The dead were treated as
heroes and later visited by youths (ephebes) who presented
offerings and wreaths—so much we learn from excavation,
Pausanias and an inscription. Pausanias adds that there was a
separate mound at Marathon for the Plataeans and slaves together.
This was identified in 1970, about one mile west of the Athenians'
tomb. The dead were not cremated but buried—the cheaper
method—in a single trench, beside which was a pyre of offerings.

A mass of bones noted in 1884–5 might have been the Persians'.

At Thespiae a terraced enclosure (32 × 23 m.) probably supported a mound over the cremated remains of men killed in the battle of Delion (424 BC). They seem to have been burnt on the site, so their bodies had been brought home over 50 km. from the battlefield. Some inhumations beside the ash layer may have been of men who died later from wounds. Eight *stelai* named the ninety-four dead, and from Tanagra there is a casualty list from a *polyandrion* of the same battle. At the centre of the north side of the tomb at Thespiae stood a marble lion. At Chaeronea, after the battle with Philip of Macedon in 338 BC, a similar rectangular enclosure (24 × 15 m.), with the lion monument which has been restored (*Pl. 67*), covered 254 bodies laid out neatly in seven rows, with a few small offering vases and strigils. Pausanias was told that the tomb was that of the Theban Sacred Band (of three hundred men), but it has been doubted whether Philip would have permitted the defeated such a grand memorial, and it is possible, although perhaps not likely, that it is the Macedonians who are buried here. Out on the battlefield, near where the Sacred Band was annihilated, a tumulus covers a pyre of bones and weapons.

The tomb of the Spartans who died fighting in Athens in 403 BC has been described already (p. 110) and there are other mass graves in Athens whose identity is not known. We have the gravestone of the Corinthians who fell at Salamis and were buried there, and in Athens, but in Argive script, of the Argive and Kleonaian allies who fell at Tanagra in 458/7 BC. In the latter instance the allies were treated as though they were Athenians and brought away from the battlefield for burial, although not to their own homes. There are several other epitaphs extant or recorded from *polyandria* at Athens and elsewhere. The Spartans were buried where they fell at Thermopylae and *stelai* erected. Herodotus says that after Plataea each state buried its dead separately, the Spartans in three *thekai* for the young men, the citizens and the helots. He adds that other states who had not fought there erected empty tombs to share their glory. The Plataeans were responsible later for rites at the *stelai* of the fallen.

63 Painted *stele* from Chios, prepared like the Boeotian (Plate 55). It shows friezes of sirens, a centauromachy and chariots, with a large still life of *palaistra* equipment (strigil, sponge, sandals, etc.) and a vase on a pillar.

64–6 Three Archaic lions
marking graves: one from
Miletus (*top*); one from
Corcyra of about 600 BC
(*centre*); and one seated on
the Ionic capital from a
column marker, from Ana-
tolia (*left*).

67 The lion marking the communal tomb at Chaeronea for the
battle of 338 BC.

68 The tumulus cenotaph of King Nikokreon at Salamis on Cyprus, showing (a – *above*) the brick platform (b – *below*) the tidied pyre, and holes for the pillars which carried the clay portraits of the dead (c – *opposite*).

69 A sixth-century sarcophagus from Samos, in an architectural form.

70 A Clazomenian clay sarcophagus painted in and out; the lid removed.

71 A wooden
coffin from South
Russia, its lid
missing (*above*).
The appliqué
decoration is in
wood painted,
and gilt.

72 The 'Lycian'
sarcophagus
from the royal
cemetery at
Sidon, about
400 BC.

73, 74 Two of the royal sarcophagi from the cemetery at Sidon: *above*, the Mourners sarcophagus in architectural form, mid-fourth century; and (*below*) the Alexander sarcophagus, late fourth century.

An inscription of about 400 BC from Thasos regulates common burial of war dead, allowing no more than five days' mourning for the brave, requiring their names to be displayed and allotting privileges for their sons and fathers.

A few other mass burials have been found, mute records of military or domestic disasters. In late seventh-century Acragas, some time before its official foundation from Gela, a pit held dozens of bodies and over 150 Greek vases, perhaps an indication of difficulties experienced by the Greeks in becoming established in this area. Multiple burials in sarcophagi are not uncommon but in Syracuse we may suspect a family disaster in the burial of two adults and a baby within a sarcophagus, with two older children buried on its lid. At Vroulia in Rhodes, about 600 BC, four men were buried together, away from the main cemetery of cremations and close to the wall which they may have fallen defending. At Delphi little before the mid-fifth century a small chamber tomb was built against the rock face to hold eight dead, laid in two rows. At Olynthus a number of men, with a few women and children—forty-four in all—were buried in three broad trenches. They were perhaps the victims of local skirmishes in the years around 430 BC.

Cenotaphs were constructed for a variety of circumstances. On the field of battle, if all the bodies could not be recovered, a cenotaph was built and due offerings paid to it as to a tomb. The Athenian tomb robber found no defence in pleading that it was a cenotaph that he broke into (Demosthenes xxi 512). If a communal tomb had been built on the battlefield a cenotaph might be erected in the home city to record the names and event. There is evidence for this in Athens, although it is a matter of opinion whether the memorial for Marathon was sufficiently like a tomb monument to be regarded as a cenotaph.

When individuals died away from home their bodies might be cremated and the ashes returned home for burial. This probably accounts for the occasional ash urns which are found in what are otherwise purely inhumation cemeteries. Otherwise a cenotaph memorial could be erected at home, and it is probable that these resembled ordinary tombs. It has been suggested that the famous lion monument at Amphipolis was a cenotaph for a distinguished companion of Alexander's, but it may be rather earlier. A similar lion at the Persian capital Ecbatana may have been erected by Alexander for his companion Hephaistion who died there in 324 BC but was taken for burial to Babylon (p. 305). For heroes whose remains could not be identified cenotaphs were also required (Tiresias at Thebes, Achilles at Elis, Odysseus at Sparta; and see p. 299). Occasionally burials have been noted which are normal in all respects except for the absence of a body. This seems to suggest that the whole rite of burial might be carried out, but perhaps only when the body was missing and no rites had been performed elsewhere. Other evidence for these personal cenotaphs comes from funeral epigrams (see p. 265) where disasters at sea seem the commonest occasion. Euripides gives an account of Greek practice in his *Helen* 1239ff.: an empty shroud is buried and offerings cast into the sea—but the other details may be 'heroic'.

The most remarkable excavated cenotaph was discovered at Salamis in Cyprus in 1965–6. A low tumulus covered a stepped mud-brick platform (11·5 × 17 m.) and ramp. At the centre a neat cairn covered the remains of a pyre, containing *alabastra*, strigils, jewellery and similar offerings or articles of dress (*Pl. 68*). With them were pieces of several life-size clay statues which had been modelled over wood and preserved by the baking heat of the pyre. The statues must originally have been fastened in the sixteen holes found around the pyre. The heads are portraits or near-portraits, of women and men, old and young. There were no bones, and the style of the heads suggests a date towards the end of the fourth century. Karageorghis is surely right in seeing here the cenotaph of the family of the last King of Salamis, Nikokreon, who died in the suicidal holocaust of his palace in 311/10 BC.

A similar disaster is recorded in a Hellenistic epitaph (p. 199). For the use of sculptured substitutes we may recall the two statuettes in 'Schiff's grave' on Thera (Fig. 34) and Herodotus' account (vi 58) of the burial of Spartan kings who were killed in war and whose ashes only, presumably, were available (when they had not been 'preserved'; see p. 191). Images of the Spartan kings were made and carried on the bier like the funeral effigies of French and English kings. In Athens an empty bier in the *ekphora* represented the 'unknown soldier' (Thuc. ii 34.3). Other substitutes for missing bodies may be the stone block in a late sixth-century Athenian grave, and possibly the Classical pot 'burial' at Locri in South Italy, containing only the clay bust of a woman and a cup (Fig. 56). We would like to know more about the fifth-century grave at Karystos containing a small column with lead strips bearing names wrapped around it.

Fig. 56   *A burial without bones or ashes at Locri: possibly a cenotaph, the dead represented by the clay bust*

CHAPTER XIV

EPITAPHS

*Gravestones tell truth scarce fourty years
(Old ones being taken up, and other
bodies laid under them): Generations
passe while some trees stand, and old
Families last not three Oakes. To be
read by bare Inscriptions . . . to hope for
Eternity by Aenigmaticall Epithetes, or
first letters of our names, to be studied
by Antiquaries . . . are cold consolations
unto the Students of perpetuity, even
by everlasting Languages.*

IN A HIGHLY LITERATE society like that of ancient Greece a degree
of personal immortality was ensured by the epitaph which, at
the least, gave the name of the dead, at the best, gave an account
in verse of his virtues, the manner of his death, and the example
he set, and which bid for a measure of sympathy from the
passer-by who was often directly addressed. The name was usually
accompanied by that of the father, and occasionally, where
appropriate, by an ethnic or indication of the deme to which the
dead man belonged. But there are variations even on this simple
convention, from the Boeotian and West Greek tombstones
which usually omit the father's name, to the fifth-century Chian
Heropytho whose family must have had something special in
mind when they set up his tombstone and traced his genealogy
on it back through fourteen generations. The name is generally,
and understandably, written in either the nominative or genitive.
In the rare cases where a dative is used an element of 'offering to'
the dead may be inferred—either of the monument itself or of
articles placed on or by it.

There are also, of course, many more informative epitaphs,

almost all of them in verse. The art of the Greek epigram is perhaps nowhere better displayed than in these poignant memorials. It is not their art which must concern us here, but their form, as records of interment, and whatever information they may incidentally convey about burial customs. A very large number of them are known from surviving tombstones. The earliest are often the only inscription on the *stele*, and in Archaic Attica they are inscribed on the *stele* base. On the larger relief gravestones of the Classical period room is found between the relief and the crowning member, but most of this and later periods appear on gravestones which are either not decorated with figures or on which the reliefs are confined to a small area leaving more room for the verses, generally written below. Another important source, especially for Hellenistic and later epitaphs, is the *Greek Anthology*, a compilation of the Roman period from earlier sources. While we are regularly told the poet's name for these, the date is sometimes uncertain, and there is usually no indication of the setting or location. Many, indeed, must be simply literary exercises—like the epitaph for an ant, or some of the more contrived circumstances of death and burial which are described.

Verse epitaphs appear as early as any inscribed grave monuments. On a rock on Amorgos we read 'For Deidamas his father Pygmas . . . this house', in lettering of the first half of the seventh century. And the epitaph of Deinias, from Corinth, may be as early as the mid-seventh century, and it tells us how he died—'This is the *sema* of Deinias, destroyed by the ruthless sea' (*GV* 53). As we might expect, the father's name often finds a place in the verse, but features of later Archaic epitaphs are the record of the name of the man who set up the *stele*, not necessarily a parent, and of the sculptor of the monument. Thus, from Sounion and with a Homeric touch such as is not uncommon in early epitaphs—'Peisianax set up here the *sema* of Damasistratos, son of Epikles; for this is the due of the dead' (*GV* 156). And an earlier Attic epitaph, naming a famous sculptor—'This is the *sema* of Archias and his sister Phile. Eukosmides made it fair, and clever Phaidimos set the *stele* upon it' (*GV* 74).

The last is in iambic hexameters, the others are Homeric hexameters, the commonest metre for early epitaphs. With the sixth century a variety of new metres is used, both exploiting the new riches of Greek prosody and accommodating a number of personal names of awkward scansion. The commonest metre and form for epitaphs was to be the elegiac couplet.

The *sema* may itself address the passer-by—a common and popular device which appeals immediately to the reader. In sixth-century Attica we have the simplest, direct form, from the base of a *kouros* monument (*Pl. 20*)—'Stand and mourn at the *sema* of dead Kroisos, whom one day, fighting in the front rank, wild Ares slew' (*GV* 1224). Sometimes it is not the stone but the sculpture which speaks. The mourning figure on the tomb of the Phrygian king Midas says 'I am a bronze maiden' (*GV* 1171) but the epitaph must be late if there was really such a tomb figure. From fifth-century Amorgos—'I stand here in Parian marble in place of the woman, a memorial to Bitte, a tearful grief to her mother' (*GGG* 54). And on the late fifth-century tombstone of Ampharete in Athens, showing a seated woman holding a child (*Pl. 31*)—'I hold here this dear child of my daughter. When, in life, we both beheld with our eyes the rays of the sun, I held her thus on my lap; and now, both dead, I hold her still' (*GV* 1600).

The Classical epitaph was more informative about the virtues of the dead, as well as giving the bare details of his death and family or surviving kin, but the finest epitaphs of the fifth century are for the *polyandria* or cenotaphs of the war dead. In the fourth century the imagery is enriched by the example of tragedians' works, while in the Hellenistic period the rich symbolism of death, loss, courage and Hades is fully exploited and we are occasionally told something relevant to the present enquiry. For instance, we find more often now a 'conversation piece' between the *sema* or the occupant of the grave (even on occasion from a cenotaph) and the passer-by, and these also sometimes tell something about the form of the monument or the poet's interpretation of the sculpture set upon it. Our sources for this period are richer too. We give some examples.

Erinna's epitaph for her friend Baccis (I) lets the dead girl address the *stele*, sirens and funeral urn on her tomb. Anyte writes an epitaph (VIII) for a mother who sets over the tomb the statue of a girl of like size and beauty to her dead daughter. An epitaph by Perses (VII) suggests a grave relief showing a man and wife mourning over a portrait (*graptos typos*) of their daughter; others imply a bronze statue of a charging horseman or a warrior with raised shield. An epitaph by Antipater (XXXI) addresses the lion on a tomb, who explains his presence as symbolic of the excellence and strength of the dead man. There are more pedantic, sophisticated and rarely witty explanations of the symbolism of figures on a tomb monument, usually of animals, but also of dice and astragal throws, or the stone cup on the tomb of a bibulous old woman. A late Hellenistic tombstone set up by the people of Sardis (*GV* 1181) carries lines which draw attention to the elegant lady shown in the relief and, in a conversation, explain the symbolism of other objects on the stone—the lily for her youth, the A because she was an only child, the book for her wisdom, the basket for her domestic virtue and the wreath because she had served as *stephanephoros*. An epitaph by Leonidas (XXII) explains the astragal on the tomb—it lies in the position of a 'Chian' throw, the poorest one, and the dead man died of Chian wine. A large stone astragal was found in a Hellenistic tomb mound in Messenia.

These may not all be real epitaphs but they are clearly inspired by the sort of decoration which we see especially on the Hellenistic tombstones from East Greece. Other epitaphs reflecting on the appearance of the tomb refer to the appropriateness of flowers growing over it, and Heraclitus, who himself inspired one of the best known of ancient epigrams, writes (I) of 'the freshly turned earth; on the sides of the *stele* flutter the wilting garlands of leaves'. Some epitaphs threaten would-be desecrators of the tomb and epigrams regret tombs disturbed by road-making or the plough. Family tombs may be built and appropriately dedicated with verse even before they are occupied.

It is not often that we have both the figure monument and the epitaph which refers to it. Ampharete's tombstone was an example, and we cite two others, of different type. A fine but

Fig. 57 *The gravestone of a Phoenician who died in Athens, inscribed in Aramaic and Greek*

fragmentary Hellenistic painted tombstone from Demetrias shows a dying woman in bed, and the epitaph describes her death in childbirth (*GV* 1606). By far the strangest is the early third-century gravestone from Athens for a Phoenician visitor who died there. It is inscribed in both Phoenician and Greek (*GV* 1601). The relief shows the dead man laid out, attacked by a lion which is being fought off by a man whose upper part is in the form of a ship (Fig. 57). The epitaph helps us explain the strange circumstances. The body was in danger from evil spirits, represented by the lion, if it was not properly buried. The man, Antipatros of Askalon, was saved from this by the timely arrival of a ship carrying Phoenician priests from Sidon, who saw to his obsequies in the proper manner and commemorated them with this stone. Their request for a graphic representation and record of their services taxed the ingenuity of both the Greek sculptor and the epigrammatist.

Spartan pride in her war dead and her austere attitude to ritual (see p. 181) are well expressed in Hellenistic epitaphs. The simplest are properly laconic—a name and 'in battle' or 'in bed' (i.e., childbirth). Dioskorides writes one (XXX) for a Spartan father whose son was brought back honourably upon his shield, with his wounds to the front, and is placed on the funeral pyre; and another (XXXII) for a Spartan mother who buried her eight dead sons without a tear—'O Sparta, for you I bore these sons'. Six brothers who fell outside Messene were cremated by their surviving brother who brings their ashes home for burial (an epitaph by Nikander, I).

For other Greeks who died away from home and not in battle, epitaphs beg the passer-by to take news of their death and burial back to their homes, but some were luckier and their epitaphs record the hospitality of strangers who sent their ashes home in a bronze urn. A third-century epitaph from Smyrna marks a cenotaph and describes the real tomb farther off inland:

> Mount Tmolos hides the bones of Hermias beneath its lowest slopes, and the mound of earth over them is far seen; on it a polished stone with mute voice tells the name of the dead. This empty tomb has been raised on the shores of Smyrna by his yearning friends (GV 1745).

The virtue of burying the dead is often commemorated, and in an epitaph by Karphyllides (II) is rewarded, for the fisherman who 'catches' a skull and buries it finds hidden treasure where he digs the grave. Callimachus (L) records the sailor who finds and buries the body of a fellow mariner on the shore, but his wit is more bitter in the conversation epitaph (XXXI):

'O Charidas, how are things below?'

'All dark.'

'And what about the way up?'

'A lie.'

'And Pluto?'

'A myth.'

'Then we're done for.'

CHAPTER XV

DECORATED SARCOPHAGI

*Playstered and whited Sepulchres were
anciently affected in cadaverous, and
corruptive Burials.*

IN THE EARLY PERIOD all-stone sarcophagi appear to serve as
expensive alternatives to the slab-lined cists, constructed for the
reception of the dead, or to wooden coffins, in which the dead
might be carried out to burial and interred. Certainly no one was
carried to burial in a stone coffin; so in a way these all-stone sarcophagi, which we find already in Early Geometric Corinth, may
seem to confuse the functions of a portable coffin and a built
receptacle for the body. Our only representational evidence for
the *ekphora* is from Athens where, in the eighth century, the body
is carried on its bier, set on a cart (*Pl. 5*), while in the sixth century
it may be carried in the same way or by pall bearers (*Pls. 34, 35*).
So perhaps the early sarcophagi should be equated only with the
stone cists and not with the wooden coffin. Certainly, some of the
cist graves are constructed with extraordinary care, the corners
jointed and the inner walls plastered over and sometimes decorated, so there seems to have been some concern that the body
should have a snug resting place. In the western world today the
coffin is used for both *prothesis* and burial.

Plain stone sarcophagi are best known from the early cemeteries of Corinth, and, in the sixth century, at Pharsalos, on
Samos and Rhodes (Ialysos). They were buried out of sight in
the ground, like the cists. When *decorated* sarcophagi first appear,
however, we have to consider whether, as in later periods, they
stood uncovered in tomb chambers where they could be viewed
by mourners and visitors or on the occasion of later interments.
The earliest are by no means the slab-cist cut in a single block,
but imitate woodwork with lightly picked decoration recalling

the nails and corner struts of a wooden chest. Massive seventh-century examples in Chios (one is nearly 1·5 m. high) were certainly buried, as was probably a fragmentary sixth-century example on Samos. On both islands there are also plain sarcophagi, but mid-sixth-century Samos has also yielded an elaborate marble sarcophagus which sets other problems. The box resembles the woodwork of chests, but is provided with Ionic columns cut in low relief between corner pillars (*Pl. 69*). The lid is purely architectural, gabled and with acroteria. It is generally regarded as a translation of wood into stone, 'architecturalized' under the influence of the 'normal' gable lid, but there are difficulties—it was not easily portable, like a wooden coffin; and in vase representations sixth-century wooden chests or coffins always have flat lids; and if this resembles a building should we not recall the house-tombs of nearby Asia Minor and the east? The circumstances of the finding of the sarcophagus are not clear. It was probably buried, but there is evidence for sixth-century chamber tombs on Samos. On the other hand, in Rhodes, the Archaic chamber tombs of Kameiros contain no sarcophagi, while the sarcophagi of Ialysos are not only buried but often further protected by outer rows and roofs of slabs. A sixth-century sarcophagus like the Samian, simpler, but again with an 'architectural' lid, was found in Cumae where there are chamber tombs. The plain sarcophagi on Samos sometimes have the inner cavity roughly shaped to the body, resembling Egyptian mummy cases (Fig. 58). From the later sixth century on, plain stone sarcophagi, some with gable lids, are found in chamber tombs on Aegina and in Tarentum. A fragment from Athens has a moulding at the rim. It may be Late Archaic but is not certainly from a burial and, unlike other stone sarcophagi, it has cuttings for separate feet.

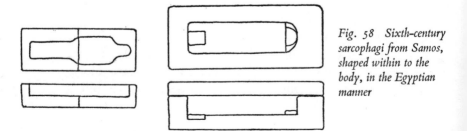

Fig. 58 Sixth-century sarcophagi from Samos, shaped within to the body, in the Egyptian manner

The decorated clay sarcophagi of East Greece are mainly of the sixth and early fifth century. They do not imitate wooden chests so much as baths, with broad flat rims and sometimes steeply gabled lids. A few have relief decoration: a fragmentary example in Chios with a relief scene of mourners; one from Kameiros with bulls' heads at the lid corners; an architectural 'bead and reel' on a lid from Samos. At Assarlik in Caria an elaborate series of sarcophagi are decorated with impressed linear and circular motifs recalling the decoration of relief *pithoi* in the islands. The commonest class of painted clay sarcophagi is the so-called Clazomenian, which have been found in some numbers at Clazomenae, Smyrna and Rhodes, with a few examples also from Erythrai, Ephesus, Lesbos, Pitane and Chios (?). They were made from about 530 to 460 BC. The decoration resembles that of contemporary vase painting, imitating the incising black-figure technique by using white linear detail, occasionally imitating Athenian red-figure, and adding some quaint animals in the old-fashioned Wild Goat style. The subject matter is never specifically funereal. The main scene is set in the broad rim at the head of the sarcophagus, generally with patterns along the sides and animals at the foot. Some more elaborate examples have figure decorated friezes on the lid and even on the inner walls of the sarcophagus itself (*Pl. 70*). Most had lids of stone slabs or tiles. At Smyrna they were buried beneath small tumuli of stones. To judge from the finds and some features of the painting Clazomenae in North Ionia was a principal centre of production.

Plain clay sarcophagi, like the Clazomenian in shape or more like rectangular chests, were also used in Samos, Chios, Rhodes, Abdera, Kavalla and Oisyme, and are reported sporadically in mainland Greek cemeteries. A greater range of clay containers was in use in the Western colonies, and there is an important series of relief sarcophagi from Gela (Fig. 79).

Wooden coffins, which might have been decorated in relief or with paintings, have normally not survived in Greek soil. Remains of a wooden coffin were found within stone sarcophagi in a Hellenistic tumulus in Thessaly, and a wooden coffin from the Piraeus is said to have been found in a marble sarcophagus.

Sometimes nails found in tombs are taken for evidence of wooden coffins, but most would not have been nailed together, but pegged, bound or glued (see p. 216). Cut out clay plaques with mythological and domestic scenes rendered in low relief were made on Melos in the Early Classical period, and probably decorated wooden furniture. The many found on Melos were probably from tombs and so may have been fastened on to coffins. A few were exported. There is better evidence for the appearance of Greek wooden coffins from the chamber tombs of Egypt and South Russia, where conditions for survival were more favourable. Of the fourth-century examples those in Egypt (Abusir) have high gabled lids with painted panels and sometimes relief stucco decoration, while those from South Russia have lower, roof-like lids with gilt wooden relief appliqués (*Pl. 71*). An occasional example from both areas has a semi-cylindrical lid. From the later fourth century on in South Russia there are more explicitly architectural coffins with columns or pilasters rendered around the box. These give valuable evidence for the persistence of a type sparsely represented in stone. In fourth-century Tarentum gilt clay appliqués appear to have decorated coffins.

For Classical stone sarcophagi decorated by Greek hands we have to go outside the Greek world to Phoenicia where, within the Persian empire, the kings of Sidon employed Greek artists. In the interconnecting series of royal tombs several different sarcophagus types are represented. All are now in the Istanbul Museum. For the chest-like the form is strictly architectural, with acroteria on the roof lids. On the first and last of the graecized series—the Satraps sarcophagus of the mid-fifth century and the Alexander sarcophagus of the late fourth (*Pl. 74*)—the box is decorated with panel reliefs showing hunting, fighting and court scenes. Both were made for kings of Sidon, the latter for Abdalonymus, Alexander's man, and its reliefs may show Alexander himself in battle and hunt. Its lid had pedimental reliefs at either end but the architectural illusion is carried further on the Mourners sarcophagus (about 360 BC) where the box has colonnaded sides, with figures of mourning women set between the columns (*Pl. 73*). A different sarcophagus type is the Lycian,

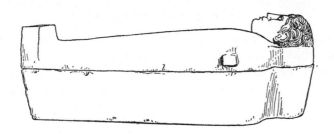

Fig. 59 An anthropoid sacrophagus—a hellenized version of an Egyptian type for a Phoenician burial at Sidon

which takes the form of the open-air house tombs of Lycia (p. 283), with steeply pitched, rounded roofs, here converted for use as an ordinary coffin. The example from Sidon, of about 400 BC, has pairs of griffins and sphinxes at each end of the lid, a lion hunt and a boar hunt on the sides, and mythological scenes (centaurs, Kaineus) on the short sides (*Pl. 72*). Another type of sarcophagus in the Sidon tombs which owes something to Greek art is the 'anthropoid'. The earliest examples were purely Egyptian in appearance but from about the mid-fifth century in Sidon (and, after Sidon was burnt in 350 BC, for a while at Tortosa) the three-quarter human heads on the coffins are rendered in a Classical Greek manner, with some characterization of male heads recalling East Greek art (Fig. 59). The rest of the block-like body was also better shaped, with the arms and outline of the back sometimes rendered. The material was usually Greek marble, and examples were carried by Phoenicians to Spain and Sicily, Corsica, Malta and Cyprus.

The relief stone sarcophagi most familiar to us in museums are nearly all of the Roman period but we have to look for evidence of continuity for some of the types already current in the Classical period, through the Hellenistic. The earlier decorated sarcophagi all belong to the East Greek world or beyond it, as we have seen, and it is in Asia Minor that the tradition is likely to have been maintained. This is readily demonstrated for the Lycian house-sarcophagi with their high rounded lids, of which apparently Hellenistic examples are seen at Trysa and elsewhere. The type with panel reliefs on the box is represented by an example from

Ephesus, now in Vienna, which may not be later than the fourth century but at least shows that the type was known outside Phoenicia. Its reliefs show Amazonomachies. For the type with columns around the box, like the Mourners sarcophagus and the later Roman Sidamara sarcophagi, the evidence is slighter, but the wooden sarcophagi in South Russia help to bridge the gap.

Some sarcophagi, for burial in the earth, may be decorated to resemble houses from the point of view of the dead rather than the living: some Hellenistic sarcophagi in Thessaly are made of closely fitting slabs with Ionic colonnades painted or in relief on the inner walls. There are isolated examples of decorated Classical sarcophagi elsewhere—the Athlete's tomb in Tarentum (Fig. 84) and we may compare the painted slab sarcophagi of Paestum (Fig. 78). From Acragas there is a fine fifth-century example with a triglyph frieze on the body, and from South Russia a late Classical sarcophagus of marble from Taman and another, probably later, with an architecturally painted interior.

The word *sarkophagos*, 'flesh-eater', was not used in Classical Greece and was later applied to a type of limestone coffin whose carnivorous qualities were especially esteemed.

CHAPTER XVI

MONUMENTAL TOMBS, HEROA AND HELLENISTIC GREECE

Man is a noble animal, splendid in ashes,
and pompous in the grave.

IN THE HELLENISTIC PERIOD Everyman remained content with his simple sarcophagus, cist, tile grave or ash urn. The important innovations are the monumental tombs for the rich and their families, taking the form generally of elaborate chamber tombs or of above-ground mausolea. The origins of both types will be traced back into the fourth century and earlier, and, for some features, outside the Greek world. This was the age of the individual, and for the first time we have abundant evidence for the individual's belief in his own immortality, while the example of Alexander and his successors indicated a clear claim to divinity for those dead who could afford it. This new attitude is reflected in some aspects of the tomb architecture. There is some evidence, too, for earlier cult of the privileged dead which can be reviewed. The Hellenistic burials of Athens, blighted by Demetrios' legislation, have been discussed already and have little in common with the finer burials in the rest of the Greek world.

TUMULI WITH CHAMBER TOMBS: MACEDONIAN TOMBS

The classic type of Hellenistic chamber tomb is the Macedonian, of Alexander's homeland, which influenced the construction of monumental tombs elsewhere. We may conveniently describe these Macedonian tombs before considering their origins and influence. They are not uncommon in Macedonia itself but barely thirty have been described and of these less than half are adequately published. They are situated along roads, but not always near a city and some may lie on family estates. All were covered with an earth tumulus but most of the tomb construction was under ground level. They have a *dromos* approach, which may be vaulted or, if very short, stepped or like a broad sloping forecourt. The tomb façade is generally of finely dressed masonry which may be stuccoed and painted. The finest have elaborate marble doors set in an engaged columnar façade, Ionic (as Vergina, Langaza) or Doric (as Dion, Salonika, Angisti, Lefkadia) and with a pediment above. Exceptionally, on another tomb at Lefkadia (Naoussa) there is a two-story façade: Doric below with paintings of the dead warrior, Hermes, Rhadamanthys and Aiakos between the columns; an entablature with painted metopes imitating relief sculptured centauromachies; an upper story of Ionic columns with false doors between, and a pediment with figure painting (*Pl. 75*). Simpler façades have the door set in a rectangle of fine masonry (Fig. 60) and the most basic have more roughly cut ashlars and a doorway blocked by a slab or wall. All façades were covered by the tumulus earth, which accounts for the good preservation of the painting on the stuccoed masonry.

About half of the tombs have a shallow antechamber behind the façade (Fig. 61), usually vaulted but with a flat roof at Niausta and Dion, where there are also interior engaged Ionic columns. In one tomb at Amphipolis relief *stelai* were found in the antechamber, and in another there was a couch (*kline*) for a burial. In a tomb at Lefkadia the tiny flat-roofed antechamber had painted on its walls a holy-water basin and an altar.

The main chamber is rectangular and vaulted, and usually provided with one or two *klinai* along the back or side walls. One tomb at Verroia has a large square side chamber. The *klinai* may be simple block benches or cut in stone, stuccoed and painted like real couches. The dead were laid out upon them but a few examples are hollowed and lidded, to serve as sarcophagi for a body or ashes. Some *klinai* have figures painted on their sides and from Pydna there is a lion (*Pl. 80*) and snake in relief on two *klinai*. Occasionally the burial is in sarcophagi, usually set

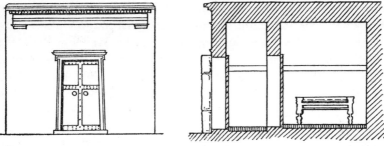

Fig. 60 *The Macedonian tomb at Palatitsa showing the façade with monumental door, and a section showing the antechamber and* kline

below the floor of the tomb (Langaza, Philippi, Nigrita). At Amphipolis, Philippi and Lefkadia tombs have wall niches to receive the ashes of the dead. At the last site one had twenty-two niches in two rows for ashes and offerings, the names of the dead being painted over the niches. In a simpler rock-cut tomb there the niches seem to have been used for the bones displaced by later burials, but still named. At Lefkadia and Salonika the pyres were identified, behind the tombs. In the latter case there was a bricked rectangular area full of ash and animal and human bones. At Vergina the chamber held a throne as well as a *kline*, and some chambers boasted pebble mosaic floors with simple patterns: diamonds at Amphipolis-Kastas, a circle at Karytsa. The painted decoration on tomb walls and façades are all-important monuments of Hellenistic art, commonly showing wreaths and

Fig. 61 *The Macedonian tomb at Lefkadia (see Plate 75)*

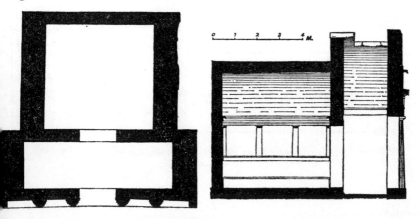

domestic objects, or suits of armour. Sometimes there is a fine
battle scene (as at Niausta) or the exceptional Judgment in Hades
on the façade of the great tomb at Lefkadia. At Dion the artist
carefully copied a Persian rug like those found in Siberian tombs.

Some simpler Macedonian tombs with flat roofs, rock-cut or
of slabs, may be mentioned here. At Sedes near Salonika one has
a gable ceiling and façade. At Edessa short stepped *dromoi* lead to
rock-cut chambers with pits for burials, while at Verroia the
rock-cut tombs include the antechambers of their finer kin,
have simple benches and niches, side chambers and rock-cut doors
with moulded jambs. At Potidaia, Vergina and Sedes there is a
central bench to serve as *kline*. At Sedes the bench is brick-built
and there were planks below the flat slab roof on which it
appears that decorated textiles were fastened. At Vergina small
chambers built of mud-brick are reported.

Outside Macedonia tombs of exactly the Macedonian type with
vaulted ceilings but lacking the architectural façades are found at
Larisa in Thessaly, where there was only the stone receptacle for
an ash urn in the chamber; at Kassope in Epirus, with a vaulted
dromos, while at the same site there are small 'temple-shaped'
tombs with engaged Corinthian columns; at Elaia near Pergamon, with antechamber and three sarcophagi; and at Vathia in
Euboea where there was an antechamber and two *klinai* (Fig. 62).
There is no positive evidence for the construction of any of the
typical Macedonian tombs before the period of Alexander, but it
is a tomb of exactly this type, with tumulus, vault and *klinai*, that
Plato prescribes for the Examiners in his *Laws*, written towards
the middle of the fourth century.

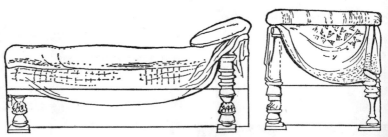

Fig. 62   A painted funeral kline *from a tomb at Vathia in Euboea*

Some features common to all or most of the Macedonian tombs are worth considering on their own. The vaulting belongs to architectural history. The plan, with antechamber and columnar façade, is that of the basic Greek house unit or *megaron*, at its most ornate. The idea of the tomb as a house is implicit even in the earliest Greek epitaphs (p. 261) and influenced the decoration of sarcophagi (p. 268). We shall meet other examples of it in this chapter. The use of stone *klinai* for the bodies was probably the result of a number of different traditions. Earlier Greek chamber tombs had low benches on which the dead were laid out, sometimes in sarcophagi, and in sixth-century Cumae such a bench, presumably, is referred to as '*kline*'. The *prothesis* required a *kline*, and often the body was brought to burial upon it, sometimes buried with it. The house-tomb plan suggests the bedroom or symposium arrangement with *klinai* set around the walls (the Roman *triclinium*). Food had regularly been brought to or buried with the dead, and this had been a normal practice in hero cults, where the hero is shown at a feast. In an age which heroized its dead the provision of *klinai* for both their last sleep and heroic sustenance came naturally. It is analogous to and contemporary with the first use of death-feast reliefs as gravestones (p. 234) while before they had been votive, for hero cults. But in the hero reliefs, as in everyday life, women do not recline on couches: they are seated. This may explain the throne in the Vergina tomb and two at Eretria (see below). The idea of a 'sleep of death' implicit in the use of the word *koimeterion*, 'cemetery', is a late one.

THE MACEDONIAN TOMBS: PREDECESSORS AND KIN

The early Greek chamber tombs of Aegina and Rhodes were underground, without tumuli, and we have to look closer to Macedonia to find more relevant predecessors. In Thessaly round *tholos* tombs broadly resembling the Mycenaean were still being built and used in the Archaic and Classical periods. There are examples at Pharsalos and Krannon (Fig. 63). They are set in tumuli, with *dromoi*, and corbelled vaults like the Mycenaean, not true domes. There are also some with square chambers and

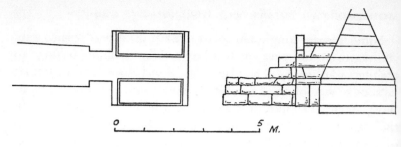

Fig. 63 A pyramid-vaulted tomb chamber from a tumulus at Krannon in Thessaly

pyramidal ceilings, built in the same way. Burials were in sarcophagi or, in one of the Pharsalos tombs, cremation with the ashes
deposited in small stone boxes, one with the lid labelled *agapa*.

Tholos tombs within tumuli were also to be seen in Thrace.
They had long built *dromoi* leading to one or even two rectangular
antechambers before the circular tomb chamber roofed by an
oddly corbelled vault with courses of slabs laid in diminishing
polygons. One on the island of Tenedos is apparently Archaic,
but examples on the mainland are not demonstrably earlier than
the fourth or third century. One at Kazanlik (Bulgaria) had a
gable-roofed *dromos*, and fine Hellenistic wall and ceiling paintings. The type persists, but with rectangular chambers, into the
first century for royal tombs at Karalar in Galatia (one for
Deiotaros II).

In Asia Minor there was a considerable variety of tumulus
burials, and these may be briefly reviewed, although it is unlikely
that many could have had any influence on the Macedonian. We
have also to remember that tumuli over sarcophagi or cremations
are common in East Greece. The eighth- to sixth-century tumuli
of Phrygia, notably in the royal cemetery at Gordion, had
wooden tomb chambers without *dromoi*. In Lydia, at Sardis,
there are finely revetted tumuli with *dromoi* (some vaulted) to
rectangular chambers. Some of these contained elaborate stone
klinai which look no later than fifth-century in date. In Caria
there are tumuli with *dromoi* to rectangular chambers with tall
corbelled roofs from quite early in the Iron Age through the
Classical period. In Lycia and Paphlagonia the only relevant

features are the simple *klinai* in rock-cut tombs, at Xanthos and Kalekapi, some of which seem at least as early as the first half of the fourth century, and the *klinai* in the Nereid Monument at Xanthos of about 400 BC (see below). The recent discovery of a Late Archaic tomb chamber at Elmali in Lycia, with figure painting on its walls, is a further indication of the range of tomb decoration in Asia Minor which could have inspired Greek practice. It too contained *klinai* of stone. These, with the Lydian examples just mentioned, are the only stone burial *klinai* in the east which are clearly pre-Macedonian. Real beds in tombs, had, however, appeared earlier in Asia Minor, at Gordion, and in Cyprus where also there were stone benches in seventh-century tombs.

While the chamber tombs within tumuli, survivors of Bronze Age practice or derived from Anatolian tradition, may have contributed something to the development of the Macedonian tomb, they had nothing to do with its final form, especially in its detailed resemblance to a house. The general type had been familiar to Greeks and their neighbours on the northern and eastern shores of the Aegean for a long time and in places Greek funeral *klinai* had already been translated into stone. We have still much to learn about the beginnings of the Macedonian series, and it may be that we should look rather to simpler Greek chamber tombs in the vicinity, like that at Olynthus (Fig. 40), which should be no later than the mid-fourth century, with its stepped *dromos*, well-built door and rectangular chamber with painted walls.

We may look now to central and southern Greece for tombs which may be related, even if remotely, to the Macedonian. Simple chambers in tumuli are found in Thessaly (Larisa), Thebes (of miserable rubble), Oineona in Locris (with stepped approach and three *klinai*), Trichonion in Aetolia (with a richly appointed cist), and Stymphalos in Arcadia (with a stone ash cist). At Delphi a marble door resembles those to Macedonian tombs. In Aegina, with a long tradition in chamber tombs, the transition was easily made to vaulted roofs and painted walls, but not beneath tumuli. The purely Macedonian tomb at Vathia in

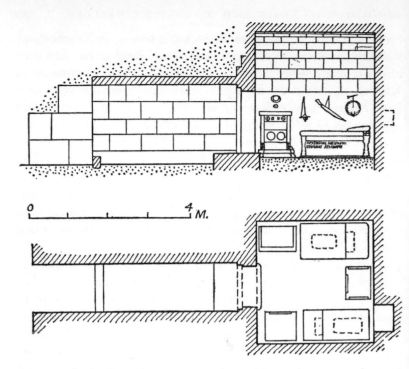

Fig. 64 The chamber tomb at Eretria showing in section the decorated chest and kline
and the objects painted on the wall

Euboea has been noticed: there was another at Eretria, but without a vaulted roof (Fig. 64). At the crown of its tumulus was a
massive brick base for some crowning monument. The chamber
is the best appointed of all in this period (mid-third century). It
held two *klinai*, two thrones and a standed chest, all in marble,
all richly painted, and all two-piece, hollowed for the remains of
the dead. The inscriptions show that the feminine furniture—
thrones and chest—was for the female dead of the family. The
walls were painted with wreaths and armour, and there had
been pegs for hanging other objects, such as have been observed
in the Macedonian tombs. If the stone *kline* is to be taken as
indicative of Macedonian influence we may add a late fourth-
century grave at Corinth—a rectangular pit entered from above
and containing a fine marble *kline*.

At Tanagra a finely fitted cist had paintings on the interior faces of the slabs (a horse and armour; a loom; a landscape; still life) like a miniature painted chamber tomb, and a robbed tomb like that at Eretria has been reported. On Melos rectangular rock-cut chamber tombs, single or in a series of three, have benches for the dead, or, more often, boxes (*thekai*) cut in the walls for the bodies, sometimes two deep. Unfortunately, the date of the tombs is not certain. Hellenistic tombs at Alipheira in Arcadia have monumental façades with pediments, like the Macedonian, but visible, with broad forecourts, and there the resemblance ends (Fig. 65). Behind and between the pillars of the façade stretch long narrow and separate *thekai* for family burials, with a low, flat, slab roof. A tomb with six smaller stone *thekai* for ash urns (a bronze *hydria* with ashes was found in one of them) may be a joint burial for six brothers who had died in battle away from home. There is a rather similar arrangement of *thekai* set over a row of vaulted chambers in late Hellenistic Rhodes.

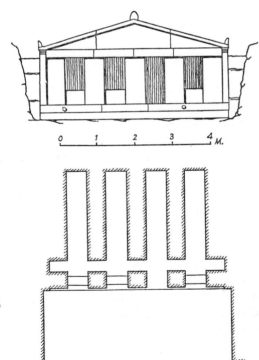

Fig. 65 A multiple tomb with architectural façade in Arcadia

In Asia Minor there are more Hellenistic chamber tombs in tumuli, but generally simpler than the Macedonian. The most canonical is a late fourth-century tomb at Mylasa with double chamber and stone *klinai*. We shall see that the chamber in the Belevi tomb was fitted out in a proper Macedonian manner, and there is near by a finely revetted tumulus with antechamber and corbelled tomb (Fig. 66). A tumulus at Pergamon, probably Hellenistic, had a cross-vaulted chamber. At Lindos in Rhodes there is a small stone tumulus (A. Milianos) with rectangular chamber and a plain *kline*.

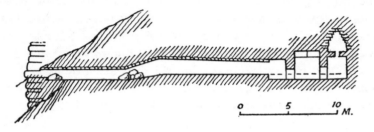

Fig. 66   *The tumulus and chamber tomb at Belevi near Ephesus*

OTHER TUMULI

There were many other Hellenistic tumuli in Greece which did not cover built chamber tombs, and some are worth mentioning. The old practice of covering a group of cists or tile graves with a low mound was continued, even in Macedonia, as at Nikesiani and Vergina. In the Thessalian tumulus at Pilaf Tepe there was a rectangular pit containing a cist grave with the skeleton of a ram, and beneath it a smaller marble-lined pit with a fine silver bucket as ash urn and other offerings including a lamp in a storm lantern. This is a very odd burial and one is tempted to recall the witch Medea's successful rejuvenation of a ram in a cauldron at nearby Iolkos. While her demonstration proved fatal for King Pelias, the ram may have remained a symbol of rebirth or new life. In another Thessalian tumulus (Gremnos) there were remains of wooden coffins within the stone sarcophagi and the dead had been laid in purple and white cloth on a straw-filled pillow. In

Messenia at Tsopani Rachi a tumulus covered a pyre, a strew of complete vases, and below them three sarcophagi containing many burials. This sounds rather like a burial of war dead; and at Megalopolis a tumulus covered only a stone ash urn, like a hat box. At Pergamon the older East Greek practice was followed and tumuli cover sarcophagi, the bodies being bedded on leaves with a sand-filled pillow.

BUILT TOMBS

A quite different type of fourth-century and Hellenistic tomb, at home principally in Asia Minor, is an above-ground structure with architectural pretensions, containing or covering the burial chamber. Whatever the scale the basic features are similar—a massive podium below, then a colonnaded centrepiece which, if it takes the form of a temple or sarcophagus, has a gabled roof, but may otherwise have a pyramidal roof, like a petrified tumulus. At its simplest the type is represented by a raised sarcophagus; at its most ornate, for the Carian dynast Mausolus, it stood over 40 m. high and gave its name to all 'mausolea'.

For the antecedents to these buildings we have to turn to the tombs of Lycian dynasts of the Persian period, many of them decorated by Greek artists. These we know best from the cemetery of Xanthos. Most of the sculptures are in London but the site has been closely studied recently by French archaeologists. The monumental tombs lie within the city walls beside similar constructions which appear to be cult buildings or *heroa*. The earliest type, beginning in the mid-sixth century with the Lion Tomb, has a box-like chamber, usually decorated with reliefs, set at the top of a rectangular pillar. A century later Lycian sarcophagi appear on the pillars, and the type persists into the Roman period. The supports for the sarcophagi may take the appearance of wooden Lycian buildings and also be decorated with reliefs, both at Xanthos and elsewhere in Lycia (notably Kadyanda, Fig. 67). At Trysa (Gjolbashi) a Lycian house-grave is set in a walled enclosure decorated with fine relief friezes in a purely Greek style of about 400 BC (now in Vienna). It is called a *heroon* but there are no specifically cult structures.

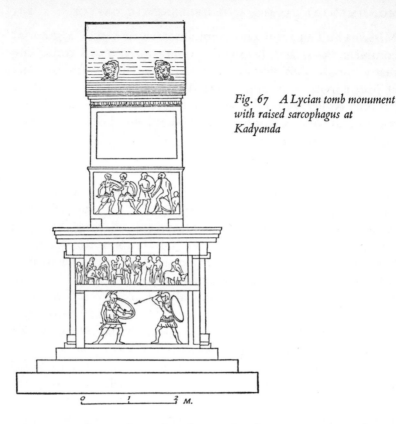

Fig. 67 A Lycian tomb monument with raised sarcophagus at Kadyanda

We may observe here that the tomb of Cyrus at Pasargadai in Persia takes the form of a small house with pitched roof on a stepped podium. Cyrus died in 529 BC, but another Persian tomb of this type has been found recently, and the form may have been evolved in Persia. Although the tomb of Cyrus has some Greek architectural features, it is not possible to argue from it that exposed house-tombs were already known in Greek Asia Minor by this date. Indeed we may wonder whether the influence could not have travelled in the opposite direction since we read in Arrian (*Anabasis* vi 29) that Cyrus' golden coffin lay in his tomb upon a couch, and the funeral couch within the tomb becomes, as we have seen, a feature of burials in the native kingdoms within the western Persian satrapies.

In about 400 BC the 'Nereid Monument', recently reassembled

in the British Museum (*Pl. 76*), was built at Xanthos, and for the first time in Asia Minor the raised part takes the form of a colonnaded Greek temple, but with funeral *klinai* in its *cella*. This helped set the pattern for later monumental tombs in East Greece, but in these the roof is not normally a pitched roof, as for a temple or sarcophagus, but a stepped pyramid. All-stone tumuli were also familiar in Asia Minor—the 'Tomb of Tantalus' near Smyrna was a massive stone-built cone over a low cylindrical base, containing a rectangular tomb chamber with corbelled roof. Its date may be around 600 BC. The 'pyramid tomb' of the Persian period at Sardis may also be relevant but it is much smaller.

The Nereid Monument had a number of successors. Earliest is what may be the tomb of the Lycian king Perikles at Limyra, where the temple-like upper part has Caryatids for columns and the frieze includes a representation of the *ekphora*. The most distinguished successor was also the most famous of all ancient tombs, one of the Seven Wonders of the World, which gave its name to all later monumental tombs. It was built at Halicarnassus for King Mausolus of Caria by his widow Artemisia, but finished only after her death in the middle of the fourth century. The architects Pytheos and Satyros wrote a book about it and four leading Greek sculptors were invited to execute its sculpture. What is left of these is largely in London but the plundered site has been closely studied and, with the help of Pliny's description, the reconstruction of the whole monument has become a favourite exercise for classical archaeologists. What we can be sure of is a massive base or podium, a colonnaded centrepiece, and a pyramidal roof topped by a chariot group, the whole being some 40 m. high (Fig. 68a). The placing of much of the sculpture which has survived—friezes, free-standing figures and lions—remains under discussion. The Mausoleum was built partly over a number of Classical rock-cut chamber tombs but it is not certain whether the burial chamber found below it was for the king, or if there was some chamber higher in the structure.

In apparent imitation of the Mausoleum is the Lion Tomb at Cnidus, some 20 m. high (Fig. 68b). The pyramidal roof is topped by a recumbent lion and the centre section has engaged Doric columns, not an open colonnade. Inside is a tall corbelled *tholos*. While this is clearly a funerary monument of some sort it is not wholly clear whether it should be regarded as a tomb, multiple grave or cenotaph. It used to be associated with the Athenian naval victory at Cnidus in 394 BC but more probably belongs to the middle of the fourth century or later.

The tomb at Belevi near Ephesus was probably built for Antiochos II who died in 246 BC. The general scheme was that of the Mausoleum, although details of the roof are not certain (Fig. 68c), but the tomb chamber was appointed like a Macedonian tomb—appropriately for a Macedonian prince. The tomb chamber is vaulted and contains a *kline*-sarcophagus, distinguished from others we have noted by having a statue of the deceased reclining upon it (*Pl. 82*). The roof or upper parts were decorated with relief friezes and sculpture in the round—Persian lion-griffins, horses and vases. Other tower tombs in different parts of the late Hellenistic world may all owe something to the example of the Mausoleum. Examples are in Syria (notably that at Suweida), Sicily (the so-called 'Tomb of Theron' and 'Oratory of Phalaris' at Acragas), Numidia, and the great second-century mausoleum for two Ptolemies in Libya at Tolmeita.

Finally, there are some minor echoes of these great tombs in the Aegean world, such as the sarcophagi raised on rectangular bases in second-century Paros (Fig. 69); and on the mainland opposite Rhodes the small square tower with pyramid roof, converted to a Turkish tomb, which yielded a grave epitaph indicating that a statue of Diagoras and two lions once adorned it (*GV* 1178). Similar, rather grander tombs in Cilicia seem still Hellenistic, and this is certainly true of rather smaller monuments at Alexandria. A rock-cut tomb at Phocaea looks rather like a free-standing tomb chamber surmounted by a sarcophagus.

ROCK-CUT TOMBS WITH ARCHITECTURAL FAÇADES

The Macedonian tombs were buried below ground, and beneath a tumulus, despite their fine architectural façades. In Asia Minor similar tomb façades are always exposed, cut in the rock face and

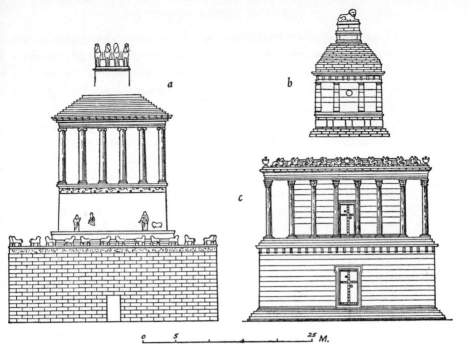

Fig. 68 Three reconstructions of mausolea in Asia Minor, shown to approximate scale: (a) the Mausoleum at Halicarnassus; (b) the Lion Tomb at Cnidus; and (c) the tomb of Antiochos II at Belevi

Fig. 69 A raised sarcophagus burial on Paros

often at a considerable height. We have alluded to them already, since some contain stone *klinai*, and it is possible that their façades played some part in determining this feature in Macedonia. The rock-cut tombs of Asia Minor are, in their earliest phase, wholly non-Greek, but their contribution to the story of Greek tomb construction is so important that they must be described and discussed here. Rock-cut monuments have a long history in Asia Minor, notably in the Hittite empire of the Bronze Age, but not in the form of house façades before tomb chambers. Their successors have often been given early dates in the Iron Age but it is becoming clear that none is necessarily earlier than the sixth century, and there is a strong possibility that they begin only with the arrival of the Persians (Sardis was taken in 546 BC). It would be surprising if the Persians were responsible for introducing or even encouraging the practice, but the finest rock-cut tomb façades of the Near East are those of the Persian kings at Naqsh-i-Rustem, and the Medes favoured far simpler tombs of this type. We have already remarked the earliest exposed house-tombs in Persia (as for Cyrus) and the use of a *kline* in the tomb. It is at about this time too that the Persians reached Cyrene and tomb façades were first cut in the rock there (p. 325).

We may consider the rock-cut tomb façades of Asia Minor in geographical order, starting in the north. In Paphlagonia they have dumpy non-Greek columns, with Achaemenid and Greco-Persian decorative reliefs and there is a fine funeral *kline* at Kalekapi. More Greek in appearance are the Galatian tombs of Hellenistic kings at Amaseia. In Phrygia the mainly sixth-century façades owe little to Greece but the 'Broken Tomb', decorated with a very Persian relief lion, contained *klinai* (Fig. 70). The Lydian tombs, again with *klinai*, do not have elaborate façades, and we have to pass farther south before more of this type are encountered. Some Carian examples of the fourth century and later have Greek columnar façades. In Lycia we meet the local timber construction translated into stone, either strictly rectangular or with the high swelling roof familiar from the Lycian sarcophagi. None seems earlier than the fourth century at Xanthos, where there is only one with a Greek columnar façade.

75 The painted façade of the Macedonian tomb at Lefkadia. The four figures between the columns represent the dead warrior, Hermes, and two judges of the dead, Aiakos and Rhadamanthys. In the metopes above are centauromachies imitating relief sculpture, and in the frieze a fight with warriors and cavalry. The façade was buried below ground, which helped preserve the painting.

76 The façade of the 'Nereid Monument' at Xanthos as recently restored in the British Museum.

77 Rock-cut tomb façades in the cliff at Telmessos in Lycia.

78 Model of the interior of a courtyard tomb at Alexandria (*above*).

79 The court of a rock-cut tomb at Paphos in Cyprus, presumably for the dead of a Ptolemaic garrison.

80–2 Three burial *klinai*: *above*, a relief decorated example from Pydna in Macedonia; *centre*, a painted *kline* from Tarentum; and (*below*) the *kline*-sarcophagus of Antiochos II from his tomb near Ephesus. The reclining figure on the sarcophagus is rare in the east common in Italy.

83 A stone relief from a tomb monument at Tarentum, showing a mourning warrior and a woman making offerings at an altar. Armour is hanging on the wall behind.

84 A fourth-century
Campanian vase (*left*)
showing a grave
monument in the form of
a pillar bearing a vase, to
which offerings are
brought and placed on
a three-legged table
before it.

85 A fourth-century
Apulian vase (*right*)
showing a grave *naiskos*
with a seated youth and
figures carrying offerings.

86, 87 The excavation of the great tumulus at Bliznitza in South Russia (*above*) and the bust of a goddess painted on the ceiling of the tomb chamber (*below*, *left*).

88 The painted plaster slab closing a grave *loculus* in the cemetery at Alexandria (*right*).

89 A stone relief sarcophagus from Amathus in Cyprus (*above*) with scenes in a mixed Greco-Phoenician style.

90 A Cypriot gravestone imitating a Classical Greek style and composition.

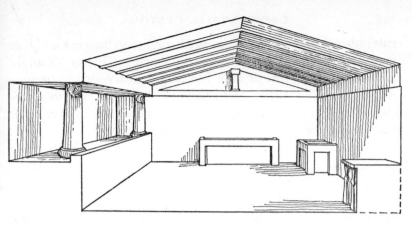

Fig. 70 The interior of the Broken Tomb at Ayazin in Phrygia showing burial klinai

These are, however, common later elsewhere in Lycia, as at Telmessos (*Pl. 77*). The Lycian type is seen also to the east, in Pisidia, but here the most important rock-cut tomb is wholly Greek and Hellenistic. It is at Termessos, and has been plausibly identified as the tomb of Alketas, one of Alexander's generals who committed suicide there after some treacherous dealings between the Termessians and his enemy Antigonos. The tomb façade is gone, but some reliefs on the walls show a horseman and armour. At the back of the chamber is a *kline* with a form of baldacchino above and behind it, and above that a relief showing an eagle holding a snake. This seems to reconcile many of the more decorative elements of Macedonian tombs with the Anatolian tradition of rock-cut façades and chambers.

THE DEAD HEROIZED

Ordinary burials of the Hellenistic period give no indication of a change in attitude to the dead or his aspirations to an after life or immortality. We have to look rather to the finer grave monuments and to the evidence of authors and inscriptions, but first we may consider what earlier evidence there is for worship of the recently dead as a divinity or hero. The *recently* dead, we stress, since the respect shown to the long dead, as at Bronze Age tombs which were discovered in later days, belongs to a study of hero cult rather than burial customs. We have also to bear in mind that many of the offerings to the dead considered in Chapter XI imply a belief in some form of after life which, in favourable circumstances, could be regarded as a form of deification, and to whatever extent the dead were believed to be able to work for good or bad from the grave, so the offerings to them might be taken as propitiatory. From their mythology the Greeks had the example of a Herakles and the cautionary tale of a Tithonos to counsel them on the relative merits of life after death and immortality; and some poets and philosophers promised an after life fit for heroes, like Pindar's English Elysium of gardens, sport and music (fr. 131).

The obvious examples of Classical dead heroized by the state are those killed in war, and we have clear evidence for rites performed at the tombs at Plataea and Marathon. Otherwise a few classes of privileged people might be accorded burial or some form of *mnema* within a city's walls, or be allowed heroic status. Such might be legislators and statesmen—Lykourgos or Aratos at Sparta; founders—the elder Miltiades in the Chersonese, Glaukos on Thasos, Brasidas as 'second founder' at Amphipolis; benefactors—Harmodios and Aristogeiton; Spartan kings. A special case was for the Phocaeans murdered at Agylla, for whom Delphi prescribed offerings and games. The dispersal of the ashes of Phalanthos in the agora at Tarentum (he died in exile), and of Solon over Salamis, has been thought to imply acknowledgement of their semi-divinity. A fifth-century *lekythos* from Sicyon, possibly from a grave, is inscribed 'of the hero'.

There are a few excavated examples of what might be early *heroa* in towns, or incorporated in the expanding circuits of towns. The complex by the West Gate at Eretria (Fig. 36) had a large pit for burnt offerings near by, just after the last grave was dug, a triangular structure immediately over the graves themselves, and later a small shrine over the pit. This might be a founder's family plot. In the Athenian Agora a seventh-century oval structure covered Geometric graves and the finds include votive material. And in Corinth, in the later agora, a partly underground sixth-century shrine and 'altar' may have been occasioned by an adjacent group of graves which range from Geometric to sixth-century in date. We may also cite one example of a cenotaph *heroon*. At Paestum a partly underground tomb chamber was constructed within a walled enclosure in the late sixth century. In the enclosure the fragmentary pot dedication to 'the nymph' may be earlier and so irrelevant. In the chamber were eight bronze vases full of honey and an Athenian clay amphora. At the centre were two blocks on which were laid spits and a mattress making an odd form of bed. Why they and the blocks were required for the mattress rather than a *kline* is a matter for conjecture, but this is basically a cenotaph, marked off as a sacred place, and within the city walls. These are all isolated instances of cult for the specially favoured, and they indicate that there could be, in certain circumstances, a cult of the recent dead in pre-Hellenistic Greece.

In epitaphs immortality is claimed for the dead rarely in the fourth century, and more often in the Hellenistic period. By this time the title 'hero' was more a matter of politeness than admission of positive heroization. A first-century epitaph from Itanos in Crete (*GV* 1157) celebrates three brothers, to be worshipped as heroes, provided with a shrine and grove by their city, and it bids their parents bring offerings of honeycomb and incense as if to Minos and the other heroes. This is the pattern of other Hellenistic epitaphs, and there are other documents of similar import. One set up by the state, rather than by a private person, is from second-century Amorgos (*IG* xii, 7.515) prescribing the sacrifice of a ram by the image of the heroized Aleximachos, and allotting the offerings for prizes in commemorative games and for the priests. A private document is the testament of Epikteta of Thera (*IG* xii, 3.330), of the years around 200 BC, which left instructions for the decoration of a shrine to the Muses with statues of herself and her kin, who were to be honoured as heroes, and which provided for annual sacrifices. On the grave *stelai* themselves heroization is implied in the death-feast reliefs which appear on a number of stones in the Hellenistic period (p. 234).

There are few surviving Hellenistic *heroa* for the recent dead— that is to say, burial monuments combined with some provision for cult. A basic arrangement is to enclose the tomb within a

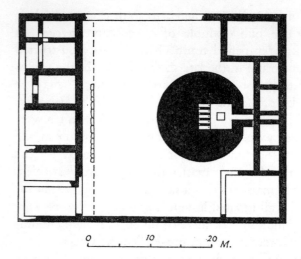

temenos, like a sanctuary. In Miletus town a Hellenistic tumulus is set in a court, with rooms along either wall (Fig. 71). The mound contains a vaulted chamber with five *thekai* in its back wall. In Thessaly there are some rectangular one-roomed structures beside burials, or a tumulus, and these may be *heroa*. In Rhodes, both at Lindos and by the city of Rhodes (at Rhodine) there are rock-cut tombs with Doric colonnades at the façade. That at Lindos is of about 200 BC and was built for Archikrates and his family. The row of four altars over the façade indicates the status of the dead.

Another type of *heroon* construction places a cult chamber over the tomb. In Kos Charmylos and his family were honoured by a two-story building, colonnade above and two rooms below, over a vaulted crypt with side *thekai* for burials (Fig. 72). An inscription mentions a garden and other buildings for the Twelve Gods, and the date may be as early as 300 BC. A simpler *heroon* of similar date near Serrai in Macedonia rose as a stepped superstructure over two sarcophagi, one of them with a painted lid, and it was decorated with statuary. At Kalydon the tomb is a vaulted Macedonian chamber with two *kline*-sarcophagi for ash urns. Over it is a cult room where statues of the family were apparently displayed, and this is combined with a *palaistra* court. The date is about 100 BC. The association of *palaistra* with *heroon* is easily explained in terms of the games regularly celebrated for hero cults. There are also explicitly temple-like structures over tombs in Greece, but most are probably of the Roman period (mainly in East Greece and one on Thera).

The clearest indication of a claim to hero cult was an altar either at the tomb or as a tomb monument. The '*trapezai*' and cubical grave markers discussed in Chapter XII may carry some such connotation, and these appear already in the seventh century. Monuments which resemble ordinary block altars are extremely rare, but there is a Classical example from Thrace. In the late Hellenistic period there are a number from Rhodes and the islands, usually cylindrical with relief swags and bucrania. One from Kyme in Aeolis has a hollowed top for an ash urn (Fig. 73). There were altars too in the larger tombs of Alexandria but the use of grave altars becomes common only with the Roman period. At Alyzia in Acarnania an early Hellenistic sarcophagus was placed in an above-ground structure very like a monumental

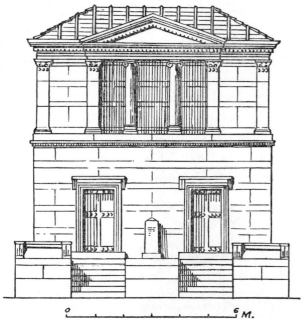

Fig. 72 A reconstruction of the façade of the heroon *of Charmylos on Kos. The basement was a family vault*

0 _____ 5 M.

block altar (Fig. 74). This is unique, and serves to show that the new status for the dead allowed of some originality in the design of tombs and monuments.

ALEXANDRIA

Alexandria is the only Hellenistic Greek capital whose cemeteries have been both productive and extensively explored. Its grave-yards were the first to be called a true City of the Dead, *Nekropolis*. There were separate cemetery areas for Egyptians and non-Egyptians, and within the cemeteries there seem to have been some further distinctions drawn. Thus, to judge from the inscriptions on ash urns (Hadra vases, *Pl. 47*) one tomb was reserved for Greek mercenaries and another for visitors on special missions (sacred embassies). Cremation and inhumation were practised side by side, the simplest burials being in slab-covered pits. A slightly more elaborate type had a pit or stepped entrance to a small chamber with one or more *loculi* cut in its walls. These are long thin cavities for a body or ash urns—the Greek *thekai*.

The above-ground monuments were mainly Greek in type—stepped bases carrying *stelai* painted with conventional Greek funerary scenes, and rarely statues. The tower monuments which may be related to tombs in southern Asia Minor have been noted already (p. 286) and only at the end of the Ptolemaic period were there any Egyptianizing monuments (cube altars, *naiskoi*, small pyramids).

Fig. 73   A grave altar from Kyme in Asia Minor with a hollow top for the ash urn

Fig. 74   A tomb monument in Acarnania in the form of an altar. On the steps at the corners are figures of sphinxes

The finest tombs were wholly underground and seem to combine features of the far simpler Macedonian tombs with the Asia Minor rock-cut tombs. While the latter, however, display a monumental façade, the Alexandrian display a far more involved plan below ground, are approached by stairways, and often have a court or light well open to the sky. Their plans are very like those of Hellenistic houses. One type has a series of rooms on one axis—a court, a 'cult room' and the funeral chamber with a *kline* or *kline*-sarcophagus in the Macedonian manner. The second type has a central peristyle court with rooms grouped around it (Fig. 75). Some rooms may be reserved for sarcophagus burials, but most have their walls lined with *loculi* for burials or ash urns. Each *loculus* is normally closed by a plaster slab (Pl. 88), with a door painted upon it, and the name of the dead above. Some rare examples have circular centre courts with radiating *loculi*. All forms of architectural and painted elaboration are admitted (Pl. 78), though there is far less in the way of fine figure painting than

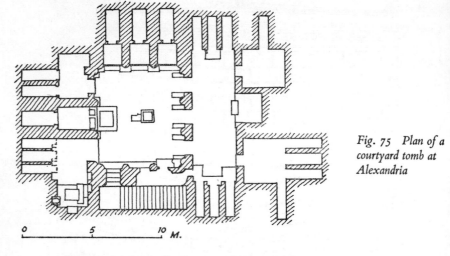

Fig. 75 Plan of a courtyard tomb at Alexandria

0   5   10 M.

there is in Macedonia. In one tomb the approach to the burial chamber was constructed as a raised theatre stage with pillars and five doors, the centre one opening on to the funeral *kline*.

These complicated underground tombs are the prototype for Roman and Christian catacombs. In Greece some chamber tombs on Melos, with a succession of chambers, somewhat resemble them, but there the sarcophagi are arranged uneconomically parallel to the walls. The long slim *loculi* appear in a different arrangement in Hellenistic Arcadia (Alipheira; Fig. 65) and Rhodes, where, at Lindos, the *heroon* was later equipped with *loculi* like the Alexandrian. In Palestine, at Marissa, some Hellenistic tombs with engagingly provincial paintings look like simple versions of the peristyle tombs. More explicit rock-cut versions of the peristyle tombs are seen at Nea Paphos in Cyprus (*Pl. 79*), and may have been intended for Ptolemaic governors in the island.

ALEXANDER THE GREAT

We have remarked the burials of a Hellenistic prince and general at Belevi and Termessos. Alexander's own funeral and burial should provide us with a good idea of Hellenistic ritual at its grandest, but we are to be disappointed. A year before his own death Alexander saw to the burial of his favourite Hephaistion. A funeral monument (rather than a pyre) was designed by Stasikrates and is described by Diodorus (xvii 115). It stood 130 cubits high, and a stadium square, like a stepped pyramid with figures set on each tier—gilt prows, bowmen and warriors, a centauromachy, animals, Macedonian and enemy arms, and to crown all figures of sirens hollowed so that professional mourners could sing their dirges from within them.

Alexander died in Babylon. His body was embalmed, but only two years later did it start its journey to its final resting place in a magnificent hearse prepared by Arrhidaios. Diodorus describes it (xviii 26–8). It took the form of an elaborate eastern covered wagon with a vaulted ceiling carried by Ionic columns over a cubicle hung around with nets and embroidered pictures (Fig. 76). Within, the body lay packed around with spices in a golden anthropoid sarcophagus. It was bound for Libya and the shrine of Zeus Ammon, with whom Alexander was identified, but Ptolemy I interrupted the progress at Memphis and buried him temporarily

Fig. 76   A reconstruction by Bulle of the hearse of Alexander the Great, following Diodorus' description

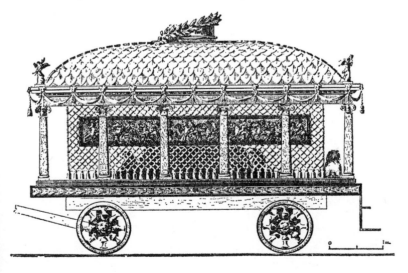

there, 'in the Macedonian manner' (Pausanias i 6.3) until a fitting tomb had been prepared in Alexandria, the foundation which bore his name. Of this we know only that the sarcophagus lay in a *cella* with a temple building above. Ptolemy IV constructed a finer mausoleum which left Alexander at the centre, with the tombs of the Ptolemies around it. He and his wife were cremated, and the last of the Ptolemies were mummified in the Egyptian manner. By this time Alexander's golden coffin had been replaced by one of crystal. All this we learn from ancient authors only and the royal cemetery has completely eluded the spade.

CHAPTER XVII

COLONIES AND NEIGHBOURS

THE WEST

THERE HAS BEEN OCCASION to mention various aspects of the burial customs in the Greek cities of South Italy and Sicily in earlier chapters, but a general appraisal of their types of burial is best kept apart since there are a number of distinctive local features, and they may have something to tell us of relations with neighbours and mother cities: an approach generally ignored in historical studies.

We would expect the burials in colonies to follow the custom of the mother city in the early years, and to some degree this expectation is borne out. In the earliest colony, sent by Euboeans to the island of Ischia (Pithekoussai) before the mid-eighth century, the cemetery contains cremations, apparently secondary, with the ashes collected below small earth tumuli or stone cairns. Children were buried, some in coffins and wearing eastern amulets round their necks. In the slightly later foundation at Cumae on the mainland there are also cremations, the bronze ash urns sometimes being set in stone boxes (about 700 BC). Back home in Geometric Eretria cremation had been preferred and stone receptacles for the bronze urns are found there earlier than anywhere else in Greece, except at Athens. The rites broadly correspond, but in Eretria no tumuli or cairns were noticed, and in Cumae there were also slab-covered pit graves resembling the immediately preceding native graves on the same site except that the Greeks used wooden coffins. Of the other Euboean colonies, Mylai in Sicily (founded about 717 BC) has early cremation graves also. The natives had also cremated since they, unlike the rest of Sicily at this time, shared the Ausonian culture of the Lipari islands, but in the circumstances we need not, as some do, relate the Greek to the native practice. The Euboeans seem to have been alone among the colonizers in their interest in cremation, but early cemeteries in their other colonies have yet to be explored. On their way to the west they had settled Corcyra (Corfu) and were followed there by the Corinthians. The seventh-century cremations on the island hardly match the Corinthian practice and rather recall Crete, with ash urns placed in *pithoi*, while the sixth-century inhumations (with some cremations) in upright *pithoi* seem an individual and local phenomenon.

The Corinthians founded Syracuse in 733 BC. In the early cemetery inhumations outnumber cremations by ten to one, and apart from the pot burials monolithic sarcophagi were generally used. These were also a feature of Geometric and later Corinth—more there than in other parts of Greece—but in Corinth the bodies were buried contracted, at Syracuse they are almost all extended. Contracted burials are a feature of native Sicel graves, so perhaps the colonists deliberately changed their habits in this respect. Isolated examples of contracted burials at Syracuse and Gela might be of Sicel slaves or residents. As at Corinth there are also slab-covered pits or shafts, and some at Syracuse have rectangular sinkings at the corners as though for a footed bier or coffin standing in them. We do not know the early cemeteries of homeland Megara but Megara Hyblaea (founded in 728 BC) also uses stone sarcophagi in the seventh century, apart from the usual pot burials, although it has a higher incidence of cremation, about one in five.

Rhodians and Cretans founded Gela in 688 BC. Of the Archaic graves about one in seven are cremations and the majority of the inhumations are in large clay vases (*pithoi*) with a number of monolithic sarcophagi also. In both Rhodes and Crete decorated *pithoi* were especially common as funeral vases, but usually for cremation burials.

In the Achaean colonies of South Italy we have some early stone sarcophagi and cists from Metapontum and Posidonia (Paestum) which are likely to tally with the inhumation habits of the homeland Peloponnese. Spartans founded Tarentum in 706 BC and early graves there and in nearby towns which were infiltrated are slab-covered pits or cists with an occasional cremation. Polybius (viii 30.6–8) says that the Tarentines buried dead within their city and this, of course, would probably derive from the Spartan custom (p. 181) rather than the local native Apulian. From the fifth century on there is some evidence for burials within the area of occupation but earlier graves may simply have been overtaken by the city limits expanding along the peninsula.

Of the new foundations resulting from expansion within Sicily, Selinus, founded from Megara Hyblaea in 627 BC, used stone sarcophagi as well as pots and some cremation urns. Acragas, founded from Gela in 580 BC, is said to follow its mother city's practice and there is evidence for a pre-foundation disaster (p. 257).

From this it can be judged that there is a broad correspondence between the burial rites in colonies and their mother cities in the Archaic period, but some distinctive local habits were developed, to which we shall return in a moment. Native practices had no influence at all, and where they do correspond in some details (Cumae, Mylai, Tarentum) these can be better explained in terms of the homeland practice of the colonizers even when they do not match the practice in other Greek colonies near by. The Sicels of South Italy and Sicily buried their dead in small chamber tombs, the bodies contracted, but already in the seventh century they were learning cremation from the Greeks, as at Butera near Gela. In the Phoenician cities of west Sicily there are chamber tombs, sarcophagi and some cremations. At Panormus (Palermo) in the Archaic period Greek and Phoenician graves lay side by side. In native Apulia and the south-east generally sarcophagi and cists were used but the bodies were contracted. In Etruria cremation was preferred but not exclusively, and simple inhumations appear beside cremations in south Etruria and Latium, including Rome, in the Geometric and Archaic periods. The distinctive tombs of Etruria are strongly reminiscent of the tumulus graves of Asia Minor—tumuli with stone revetments, chamber tombs, *klinai*, or groups of cremations covered by a single tumulus (as at Vetulonia). In the Late Archaic period fine clay *kline*-sarcophagi are being made.

We have still to review briefly the later or specific local customs of the western colonies, and here we can move from the general

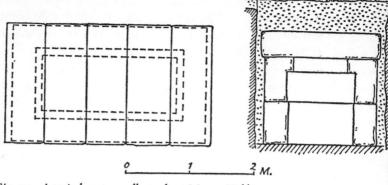

Fig. 77 *A typical western* cella *tomb, at Megara Hyblaea*

to the particular. The special incidence of stone sarcophagi has been noted. Some are quite well fashioned, notably at Syracuse, and an exceptional sarcophagus at Tarentum was elaborately painted, set in a heavy cist within a chamber, with a Panathenaic vase at each corner (see below). Otherwise burial in pots or in slab-covered pits, rather than cists, is the common practice. There are examples, however, of a special type of cist built of massive blocks (Fig. 77), called *celle* by Italian archaeologists, which appear in most Sicilian sites, and in some as early as the seventh century (Gela, Megara Hyblaea). A special type of slab sarcophagus with pitched roof, like a small chamber tomb, is seen at Paestum in the fifth to third centuries. These were decorated with paintings on the inner faces, at first in an accomplished Greek style which became more crudely provincial as the years passed. The subjects of the paintings are games, fights, horsemen and mourning, with one *prothesis* accompanied by a pipes player (Fig. 78). Some Classical chamber tombs with wall paintings at Paestum may have been built above ground. There are rather similar rectangular tombs in Apulia with painted decoration within, notably the fourth-century tomb at Ruvo (a hellenized Peucetian town) with a frieze of dancing women, hands linked, around its upper walls, and there is painting within some of the Tarentine chamber tombs (see below).

Plain, but carefully fashioned clay sarcophagi were used in

Fig. 78 The painted decoration on the inner faces of two sides of a tomb at Paestum. They show a cavalier and prothesis

Fig. 79 A burial at Gela in a clay sarcophagus with architectural relief decoration within

0   1 M.

several Sicilian cemeteries but special mention must be made of the fifth-century sarcophagi of Gela which carry architectural relief decoration inside and out, including on occasion interior corner columns (Fig. 79). Other unusual clay objects used in Sicilian tombs are broad tubes (Archaic Megara Hyblaea and Gela) and broad, oval, shallow containers with flat rectangular rims, laid over child burials (Fig. 80).

There is the usual range of construction for Classical and Hellenistic tile graves which we met in Greece (Fig. 81), but very large semi-cylindrical tiles, not from roofs, it seems, are sometimes used (as at Locri), while in fourth-century and later Rhegion flat tiles are plastered together to make thick roofs for pits or *celle*, either in the form of slabs or blocks (Fig. 82). This seems to anticipate later construction in small fired bricks, not the usual large Greek mud bricks. In fifth-century Gela some cists are lined or roofed with a thick concrete-like layer of clay. In South Italy in the fourth century, when the grave furniture often included large red-figure vases of local make, a separate square container (ripostoglio) for such offerings was constructed at the end of a sarcophagus.

Chamber tombs are found in some of the Greek cities of South Italy, rather than in Sicily. There are some small built examples in sixth- and fifth-century Cumae and Paestum (see above) and one only in Sicilian Camarina. In the Cumae tombs the names of the dead are inscribed on the walls, once referring to the *kline* (p. 277) and in the fifth century one tomb is reserved for initiates of

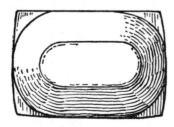

Fig. 80 Clay bins used for a burial at Locri

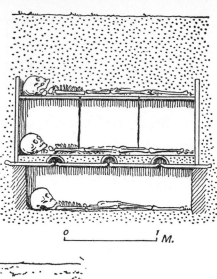

Fig. 81 Typical tile graves at Locri: (a) multi-story; and (b) a group including one with decorated vase offerings on and beside it

a

b

Dionysos. The finest examples are in Tarentum and the earliest are seen already in the late sixth century. They are approached down steps and their ceilings are supported by between one to four Doric columns (Fig. 83). Burials are in sarcophagi. A remarkable group, with which the fine sarcophagus burial already described may be associated, is particularly well stocked with Panathenaic prize vases of the late sixth and fifth centuries (Fig. 84). Tarentum is known to have had several victors in the Olympic Games in these years and successful athletes in the Greek national games were generally treated with some respect by their home cities. These could be their graves. With the fourth and third centuries the column supports in the tombs are omitted and the burials are in fine *kline*-sarcophagi of stone (cf. Pl. 81). There is also a third-century chamber tomb with *kline* at Metapontum, and at Rhegion some small vaulted tombs of the same date.

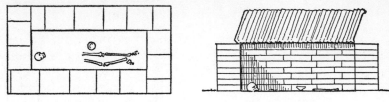

Fig. 82   A cella tomb at Rhegion with tiles plastered together as its roof

Western Greek grave markers have little in common with those of the Aegean world. The locally made red-figure vases, of which so many show scenes at a tomb that it seems likely that they were made as tomb furniture, depict palmette *stelai*, pillars and columns topped by various objects in Campania (*Pl. 84*), and similar pillars and *naiskoi* with figures in Apulia (*Pl. 85*). The Apulian at least can be matched by the monuments. Tarentine tomb sculpture in high relief or in the round is of the highest quality, showing strong Attic influence in around 400 BC (*Pl. 83*) and continuing for two centuries at least in a distinguished style. The monuments are columnar *naiskoi, stelai* or friezes on the tomb buildings. The subjects are often mythological.

The only other site with important grave monuments is Megara Hyblaea—all of them Archaic since the city was destroyed by Syracuse in 483 BC. There are *kouroi*—one inscribed with the epitaph of a doctor, another installed in an elaborate Doric *naiskos*; a stone group of two horsemen; the extraordinary statue of a woman nursing twins, erected over a *cella* tomb; and an inscribed Doric capital. The relief of a horseman, with a pediment decorated with triglyphs, may also be funerary.

Fig. 83   A tomb at Tarentum with stairs to a chamber containing rock-cut sarcophagi and a central Doric column

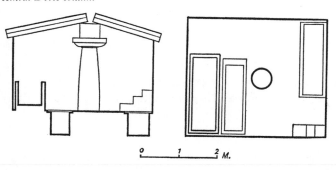

Simpler monuments in the form of short pillars on square bases are found in Megara Hyblaea and Syracuse, and truncated pyramids at these two sites and at Locri (Fig. 85a, b). For such markers the Latin term *cippus* is regularly employed by Italian and other archaeologists. A low pyramid at Megara Hyblaea over a *cella* tomb was crowned by a stone sphere (Fig. 85c). Fifth-century Camarina has some stranger monuments—a block *cippus* with a niche in it; Ionic capitals; a stone *loutrophoros* vase; what appear to be round stone tumuli and other built superstructures of various forms, seen also at Gela. Fourth-century Leontinoi yields three-stepped bases, one of them crowned by a small altar. Simpler block *cippi* of roughly square section are ubiquitous, many of them inscribed or painted—one at Syracuse with fine flying swans.

Of the cemeteries in the farther flung western colonies of the Archaic and Classical periods we know virtually nothing, but Valerius Maximus (*Facta* ii 6.7) is probably recording a much earlier practice at Massilia when he describes the custom of burying slaves and children in two separate pits outside the city gates, and alludes to provision for state-aided euthanasia. In the Etrusco-Greek city of Spina at the head of the Adriatic there was a high incidence of cremation in the fifth century (two in five) with fine Athenian vases as urns. Inhumations were in the bare ground or wooden coffins.

Fig. 84   An athlete's tomb at Tarentum. Four Panathenaic prize vases stand at the corners of his painted sarcophagus

THE NORTH

In Illyria, Macedonia and Thrace, Greece's northern neighbours, much the same variety of burial customs can be observed as in Greece itself. The Dorian Greeks came from the north and boundaries were linguistic rather than cultural. Macedonians were acceptable as Greeks, especially with an Alexander to put their case; Illyrians and Thracians were not. The Illyrians were in touch with the Hallstatt and La Tène cultures of Europe; the Thracians with the Scythians and related tribes of the Black Sea shores. It is not surprising that no clear pattern of funeral practice emerges, and we confine ourselves to examples of burials related to Greece as much as anything by their contents.

The Late Archaic warrior graves at Trebenishte, near Lake Ochrid, were well stocked with Greek metal vases. They were inhumations in large pits, without wood or stone construction or, it is said, tumuli. A feature of the burials are the gold sheet masks and other ornaments. Farther east the fifth-century graves at Duvanlij in Bulgaria were similarly furnished, but covered with tumuli, containing large cist graves of stone and wood or, for some men, secondary cremation. One stone sarcophagus contained remains of a low-legged wooden bed. These correspond well enough with tumulus burials in adjacent Greek areas, but show a preference for one-burial tumuli. Farther west, at Demir Kapu, a tumulus covered a large cremation chamber where the offerings included two Athenian white-ground *lekythoi*, possibly indicating the burial of an Athenian immigrant.

Fig. 85 Sicilian stone grave markers from Syracuse (a, b) and Megara Hyblaea (c, a unique shape)

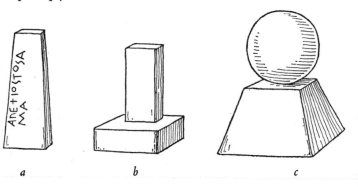

We know little of the early cemeteries of the Greek colonies on the north shores of the Aegean. At Oisyme which, with Neapolis (Kavalla), had been settled by Parians from their colony on Thasos, the early graves are dominantly cremations in urns. These are not incompatible with Parian practice but are as readily matched by Greek and native usage in other North Aegean islands (Samothrace, Lemnos). The East Greek colony (from Clazomenae, then Teos) at Abdera also preferred cremation, but the tumuli and sarcophagi of clay and stone recall home. At Elaeus on the Dardanelles, settled from Athens, there are no cremations: the burials are in stone sarcophagi or *pithoi*.

The cemeteries of the Black Sea colonies are far more informative, productive and interesting. Some of the cities were as rich as any in the homeland or the western colonies, and the example of the lavish burial customs of the Scythians might be expected to have had some influence on Greek practice. The main colonizing state was Miletus, of whose early graves we still know nothing.

At Istros, the colony set near the mouth of the Danube, the earliest graves have yet to be found. A Late Archaic and later tumulus cemetery opposite the town presents many non-Greek features. The early graves have the buried remains of men, women and horses near the main primary cremations—pyres set on platforms of a type found in Thracian burials. These blood sacrifices are not Greek, yet later graves in the cemetery have more Greek features and no other major cemetery for the Greek city has been identified. A stone-ringed tumulus at Kallatis, south of Istros, covered a cist containing the body of a man holding a papyrus roll. At the same site there are primary cremations, three of which were enclosed in a rectangular stone structure, and massive cists built like the Italian *celle*. These burials at Kallatis are fourth-century.

The earliest Greek settlement on the north shores of the Black Sea was on the island of Berezan, outside the Bug-Dniepr estuary, at the end of the seventh century. The earliest burials are secondary cremations, the urns sometimes being set in slab-lined compartments. A large burning pit has been identified, provided with

Fig. 86 A painted stele from Apollonia on the Black Sea

what was described as a 'chimney'. The settlement was eclipsed by Olbia in the Late Archaic period, by which time some simple inhumation was practised, once accompanied by a pet bird as an offering.

Once established in their new cities in South Russia the Greeks had to deal with the Royal Scythians who had also lately moved into that area. The native population was related, and they buried their dead beneath tumuli, often in a contracted position and smeared with red pigment. A few contracted 'native' burials are found in many of the Greek cemeteries. The Scythian tombs are altogether grander, with a built chamber or chambers within a large tumulus, and accompanying burials of sacrificed men and horses. Herodotus (iv 71–3) gives a graphic account of a Scythian tomb and burial. Many of the tombs were well stocked with goods made for Scythians by Greeks, but the only Greek influence on tomb construction is seen in the massive stone corbelling of some of the chambers in tombs near the Greek cities in the east Crimea and the Kuban peninsula.

The Greeks themselves, mainly from the coastal cities of Asia Minor, were familiar with chamber tombs in tumuli, and in South Russia the finer tombs were similarly constructed, often with circular revetting walls. Since these include some of the richest Classical Greek burials to have survived unplundered until recent times it is a pity that the details of their digging are so often obscure or incompletely recorded. There are no elaborate architectural façades in the Macedonian manner, nor vaulted chambers until the Roman period. Burials are in wooden coffins (Pl. 71) with the bodies bedded on seaweed, on *klinai* or occasionally in stone sarcophagi within the chambers, and there are ash urns. The Classical and Hellenistic *stelai* are generally simple with flat, pediment or palmette tops, and some of the later ones are painted with ribbons (cf. Fig. 86), offerings (as recent finds at Chersonesos) or exceptionally with figures (Kerch, the gravestone of Apphe). Some chambers have wall paintings and the bust of a goddess is painted on the roof of a chamber in the Great Bliznitza tumulus (Pls. 86, 87) in the Taman peninsula (late fourth-century) like a Byzantine Pantokrator. Most of these

Fig. 87   A pit grave at Kerch in South Russia

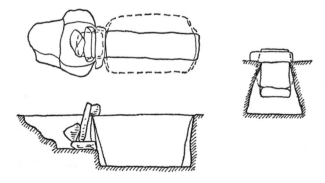

lavish South Russian tombs belong to the fourth and third centuries and they are distinguished by the number and richness of the offerings and jewellery which accompany both inhumations and cremations. Primary cremation burial is not uncommon, covered by a tumulus or a tile grave of the sort reserved in Greece for inhumation. Small rock-cut chambers for single burials at Kerch and Olbia are entered from pits (Fig. 87), like graves at Myrina in Asia Minor. At Olbia an unusual covering for pit graves is a roof of empty wine amphorae, and an ash urn was surrounded by a ring of amphorae.

According to Apollonius Rhodius (*Argonautica* iii 203ff.) the Colchians, to the east of the Black Sea in an area lightly colonized by Greeks, buried their dead in trees—a practice not allowing archaeological demonstration.

THE EAST

The burial customs of the native inhabitants of Asia Minor have been adequately discussed already and seen to have some bearing on Greek practice from the fourth century on, while Greek artists had a hand in the decoration of their tombs as early as the sixth century.

Cyprus presents a special case. There was a strong continuity of culture with the Bronze Age, and the years around 1200 BC and afterwards saw the influx of many Mycenaean Greeks. The Late Bronze Age rock-cut chamber tombs approached by *dromoi* or shafts remain the basic type of tomb construction right into the Roman period. Some of the finer Late Geometric and Archaic tombs are distinguished by having broad sloping *dromoi* and built chambers with flat or vaulted stone roofs. Striking examples of such tombs have been excavated at Salamis in recent years with chariots and horses buried on their broad *dromoi* (Fig. 88). Some of the later Archaic tombs have relief-decorated façades or architectural features, but none very elaborate, and a few have benches for the dead. One at Salamis has a painted interior in the Egyptian style. At Marion a *kouros* of Greek type was found in a *dromos* and it seems that *stelai* were often set within the chamber tombs marking the individual burial rather than the whole tomb.

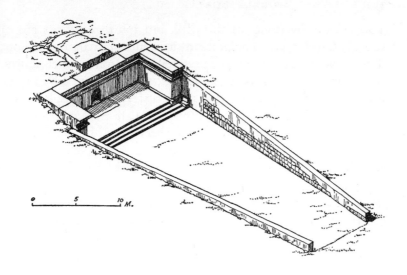

Fig. 88 Plan of a seventh-century tomb at Salamis in Cyprus. A two-horse chariot was buried on the broad dromos

Fig. 89 A Cypriot gravestone surmounted by a lion and showing a death-feast

The relief gravestones of the fifth and fourth centuries are of broadly Greek type, some of them surmounted by figures of lions (Fig. 89) or sphinxes, and with a preference for frontal relief figures. A few are so Attic in type and style that they may be by immigrant artists. Others copy Attic models slavishly or display some provincial originality (Pl. 90). From the Late Archaic period on in Cyprus the number of tomb chambers served by one entrance is sometimes increased and the approach is stepped. There are two fine relief sarcophagi of fifth-century date, from Golgoi and Amathus, mixed Greek and Phoenician in subjects and style (Pl. 89). The exceptional royal cenotaph at Salamis has been described on p. 258, and the Nea Paphos rock-cut tombs with central peristyle in the Alexandrian manner on p. 304.

The evidence for burial customs in the countries of the eastern Mediterranean seaboard and Mesopotamia is patchy and deserves fuller study. Excavators have been generally even more concerned with architecture, architectural sculpture and artefacts than they have in Greece and Italy. In the period surveyed in this book inhumation was the normal practice, sometimes within a town's limits, as even in the Greek trading post at Al Mina, and often with very few offerings of a personal nature, rather as the Greek. Cremation was, however, practised in some places, even beside inhumation, as at Babylon, while there are some important cremation cemeteries with ash urns in North Syrian sites (as Hama) whose relations with Greece in the Early Iron Age and orientalizing periods seem to have been of great importance. The close similarity of cremations in Carchemish and Cretan Afrati has been remarked (p. 173). At Carchemish, too, relief slabs with seated figures may have been gravestones, and the many relief slabs from this 'neo-Hittite' area, in series dating down to the seventh century BC, show seated and standing figures, but there is no demonstrable connection with the later Greek gravestones. At Tell Sukas, a port just south of Al Mina, the Early Iron Age cremations give place to burials by the seventh century or soon after close contact with Greek merchants was established. Elsewhere cremation is rare, and the Israelites regarded it as an outrage. Phoenician cemeteries at either end of the Mediterranean present some variety, but favour inhumation in chamber tombs approached by a shaft, or simpler pits, and some relief or anthropoid sarcophagi. Child sacrifices in the *topheths* were by cremation. The royal tombs at Sidon (p. 270) with their fine relief sarcophagi of Greek workmanship, indicate the degree of hellenization in the Persian period. In the Hellenistic period the models for the finer tombs were taken from Asia Minor or Egypt, and at the same time there are some distinctive monumental grave markers of cylindrical or conical form (Amrit).

Persia has been often mentioned in these pages especially for possible influence on the Greeks in the western satrapies of the Achaemenid empire. As the Greeks knew (Strabo xv 735) Persian religion prescribed the exposure of bodies so that the unclean and corrupting flesh should be consumed by birds and animals. Herodotus (i 140) writes of the remains being waxed before burial, but possibly this was after exposure. The Medes had rock-cut tombs and royal Persian burials presented a monumental setting although it is not always clear what happened to the body, which some scholars believe to have been exposed on a tower like a 'fire altar'. Cyrus had a gold coffin in a raised house-tomb (p. 284) while other royal tombs are rock-cut behind colossal architectural façades with colonnades like the palaces, and reliefs showing offerings brought to the king. The pious Persian slave's attitude to fire and water has been noticed already (p. 199) but Achaemenid officials far from home were not worried by cremation—as Boges at Eion (Herodotus vii 107); or by ordinary burial—as Artachaees, architect of Xerxes' canal, buried by the King beneath a tumulus and subsequently worshipped as a hero by the Greeks of Acanthus (Herodotus vii 117).

THE SOUTH

The burial customs of Egypt—the massive tomb chambers, mummification and the elaborate ritual preparation for the after life—held nothing for the Greeks until the last of the Ptolemies who, assured of their divinity, were mummified. The cemeteries of Greeks in Egypt become of interest only with the foundation of Alexandria and these have been described already (p. 302).

For the earlier period we know nothing of the Archaic and Classical cemeteries of Naucratis, the Greek trading city in the Delta, and the later graves there are poor and purely Greek in type, including some clay appliqués from wooden coffins. Although there were small Greek communities in other Egyptian cities there is only one funeral monument worth noticing. This is a relief from Abusir, apparently the gravestone of a Milesian. The execution is Egyptian, as is the winged disc crowning the *stele*, but the scene is a typical Greek *prothesis*, probably Late Archaic in Greek terms.

To the west Cyrenaica was an important Greek colonizing area in the later seventh century. The founders of Cyrene came from Thera and were reinforced from Rhodes and probably Crete. By the time we learn anything of their graves any clear connection with practice in the founding cities had been broken. Cyrene is our main source and offers a variety of monumental tombs. Some are round, with stout supporting walls and covering cists. It is not certain that any are as early as the sixth century. The round tombs continue into the Roman period and include two built in the Agora (the so-called Tomb of Battus and another).

Some monumental rectangular tombs of the fourth century and later take the form of massive sarcophagi but enclose compartments for separate burials (Fig. 90). There may be some connection here with the above-ground house-tombs of Asia Minor,

Fig. 90   A grave monument at Cyrene in the form of a large sarcophagus containing several burials

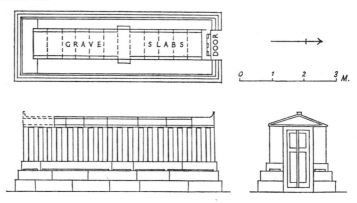

rather than with the Egyptian *mastaba*. Stepped monuments supporting pillars or *stelai* and marking ash urn burials resemble the monuments in cemeteries of Alexandria and are Hellenistic in date. Many Hellenistic inhumations are in sarcophagi whose boxes are cut in the rock and provided with separate lids. The lids carry a central plinth for a finial of some sort, possibly statuary. These sarcophagi are sometimes grouped around a court forming an enclosure, with a stone offering table at the centre (Fig. 91), like simplified open-air versions of the Alexandrian peristyle tombs.

The tombs with architectural rock-cut façades begin in the second half of the sixth century at about the time that Achaemenid Persian domination spread this far west. We have suggested that

Fig. 91   Lidded rock-cut sarcophagi at Cyrene, arranged in the open air around a sunken courtyard with an offering table

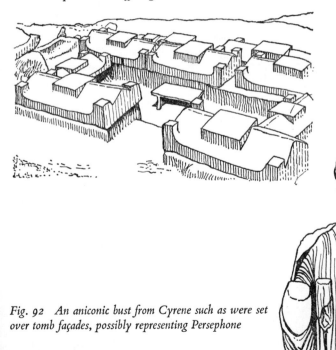

Fig. 92   An aniconic bust from Cyrene such as were set over tomb façades, possibly representing Persephone

Persian influence might have encouraged the cutting of tombs with columnar façades in Asia Minor and it may be that the case is the same here. Later rock-cut tombs take various forms: with pedimental façades; with an arrangement of parallel *loculi* most closely resembling the tombs at Alipheira in Arcadia (Fig. 65); and with false columnar façades which are built over the tomb chamber and not cut in the rock. Above the entrances to some tombs there are rock-cut shelves which apparently supported female marble busts, some of them 'aniconic'—with the facial features wholly omitted (Fig. 92). These are Hellenistic, possibly beginning in the fourth century. They are clearly not ordinary sculptural tomb markers and current opinion favours the identification of a Persephone.

Uniformity of practice throughout Cyrenaica cannot be assumed. At Messa, near Cyrene, there is a simple tumulus over a primary cremation, which seems Archaic, and near Barce a fine mid-fifth-century grave has recently been found which resembles the South Italian *celle* in construction, but with the roof slabs gabled. It contained a wooden coffin, a Panathenaic amphora, two wine amphorae, a large stone *alabastron*, a strigil and a glass bowl, with other vases.

CHAPTER XVIII

CONCLUSION

What Song the Syrens sang, or what
name Achilles assumed when he hid
himself among women, though puzling
Questions are not beyond all conjecture.
What time the persons of these Ossuaries
entred the famous Nations of the dead,
and slept with Princes and Counsellours,
might admit a wide solution. But who
were the proprietaries of these bones, of
what bodies these ashes made up, were a
question above Antiquarism.

IN THE PRECEDING CHAPTERS we have surveyed Greek burial
customs over approximately one thousand years. Only in the last
two centuries of this period did Greece become a 'world power'
and the Greek way of life become dominant far beyond the
shores of the Mediterranean; and by that time the rival world
power of Rome was ready to eclipse her. For the four centuries
before Alexander the Great Greece had spread knowledge of her
tongue and ways, through trade and colonization, to remote
parts of the inland seas, but although the effect was profound,
occupation was limited and only in the south of the Italian peninsula and in Sicily did a new Great Greece arise. So in terms of
territory and rule we should not exaggerate the part Greece
played in the early history of the Mediterranean countries. Her
art and thought were to dominate the development of the western
world, but in this thousand years the Greeks were but one of
many peoples whom we have come to know from texts and
excavation, and beside the peoples of the Near East and Egypt
the achievements of the Greeks are outstanding for their quality
and type rather than in terms of empires built or conquered. This
difference in the quality of their civilization may easily blind us

to those more basic features of their life and behaviour which they shared with their contemporaries. The subject we have been studying is in many respects farthest from those special achievements which occupy the attention of most classical scholars. And it is fitting that a Conclusion should be devoted not to a summary but to an evaluation of Greek burials in terms of what is understood from other places and periods of man's ideas about the disposal of his dead. Then, perhaps, we may discern whatever there is of distinction or rarity in Greek practice.

In 1945 Gordon Childe published an article called 'Directional Changes in Funerary Practice during 50,000 years'. It summarized the archaeology of burial in the western world, and his basic conclusions can serve as text for some aspects of our attempt to compare Greek burials with others of antiquity. He took note of Iron Age Greece, naturally, but its evidence played a small part in his study. Of the change from burying the dead in a contracted position to an extended one he remarks that it 'seems quite unconnected with ethnic changes but may perhaps be correlated with increasing wealth, a rising standard of living, and warmer bedding'. In Greece contracted burial persisted in Corinthia and the Argolid, the most clearly new-settled areas of mainland Greece and by no means the poorest. Cremation, he observed, argued no inferiority. Certainly in Greece cremation burials may be as richly furnished as any inhumations, and in a country where wood was scarce or valuable it was the more expensive operation. 'In a stable society the grave goods tend to grow relatively and even absolutely fewer and poorer as time goes on. In other words, less and less of the deceased's real wealth, fewer and fewer of the goods that he or she had used, worn or habitually consumed in life were deposited in the grave or consumed on the pyre.' This is broadly true of the period we have surveyed but there is a striking proportion of exceptions, and with Greek offerings we seldom note any particular effort to equip the dead fully either with his life possessions or with possessions for the after life. 'With progress in civilization a dwindling proportion of society's growing wealth has been devoted to the preparation of tombs and their furnishing.' Of Greece this is quite untrue, even excepting royal or princely tombs. The Greeks' concern with what was disposed below ground was never great, but barely flagged; their concern with tomb architecture and memorials was considerable; their burial rites were carefully defined and, throughout our period, there seems to have been no lapse in their observance. If the history of their attitude to death differs from that of the majority of ancient peoples, it is likely that we should seek the explanation in their different attitude to life.

Childe was generalizing. We must now turn to the particular in considering Greek burials in the light of what went before in Greece and in the conduct of her neighbours. Iron Age burials present no positive innovations, but what had before been isolated in occurrence—cist burial in individual graves, and particularly cremation—became normal. But the idea of communal burial or the family vault was not wholly forgotten and a case can be made for regarding the change as one of emphasis, suggesting a changed society rather than a significantly new population. It is understandable that the new practices should have most in common with the northern Balkans whence the new Greeks came. There is no clear evidence that pre-burial rites in the Bronze Age were as those of Classical Greece although this is very likely for Mycenaean Greece, and the offerings in the graves are of roughly the same character as the later ones. Cremation was nothing special, and although it was long dominant on Thera, in most places cremation and inhumation were practised side by side. In the Near East the few cremation cemeteries are rather more exclusive but the ordinary burials are far more poorly appointed than the Greek. Egyptian burials, the *reductio ad absurdum* of man's belief in an after life, could hold nothing to interest or influence the Greeks. In the advanced Archaic and Classical period Greek tomb architecture is influenced by Anatolian or farther eastern house-tombs, massive tumuli and rock-cut façades, but the influence is superficial and effected as much as anything by Greek artists' participation in the construction and decoration of tombs for their neighbours.

We can make little progress with purely archaeological comparisons of this sort, and when texts and representations are available they describe and illustrate, they do not usually explain. When the anthropologist or ethnographer studies burial rites he is often able to record explanations given for particular practices, and it would be wrong not to take note of the observations of these other disciplines in trying to understand the Greek. At the same time consideration of Greek burial can itself be instructive, and it is a tragic symptom of the modern attitude to Classical studies that a recent archaeological-ethnographical study of the interpretation of funeral remains should completely ignore Greece, where the archaeological and textual evidence is incomparably richer than for any other ancient culture with the exception of Dynastic Egypt.

In many respects the Greeks' attitude to their dead is at one with that of many other 'primitive' peoples who have been studied, and we should not expect otherwise. Obvious instances are the recognition that the body and house are impure, and that the kin of the dead, for the period of impurity, are in a sense cut off from the community, distinguished from their neighbours in dress and behaviour and requiring special rites before they return to society.

There is a common tendency to regard death as a slow and difficult transition to another form of life, which in some cultures meant temporary or delayed burial, or exposure sometimes for quite a long time after death. In Greece the period of *prothesis* may correspond to this, but by the time we can study it, it seems rather to have been used for family mourning, and Plato explains it as a demonstration that the body is truly dead. The ninth-day rites and those attending the end of the period of mourning may also have been thought to correspond with stages in the passage of the dead to the other world. There may have been the feeling that the process of death was not complete until the flesh had rotted from the bones. Cremation accelerates the process, the very name *sarkophagos* means carnivorous, and the red-painted inner walls of coffins might be a substitute for the more expensive fire. There was certainly no sustained interest in the remains of the dead, which could on occasion be bundled aside for new interments, and exceptions were made only for mythical heroes like

Theseus, whose bones had to be sought and returned home. To judge from epitaphs rather more notice was taken of safeguarding the remains from disturbance in the Hellenistic period, when the ordinary Greek was more selfconscious about his hopes of an after life.

The death of a child could be treated lightly, at least so far as ritual went, and they could be buried at home. The practice of exposure of unwanted children may argue some lack of sentiment too. Certain types of death were singled out for special honour or treatment—death in war, in childbed or by violence. And the funeral was a time for feasts and possibly for competitions. These are practices and attitudes recorded in many other societies.

From the material evidence we can deduce no strong feeling about reincarnation in any other human or animal body, unless there is something of this in the common practice of naming a child after his grandfather. In Greek epitaphs, where the dead often address the living from beyond the grave, they speak as though still alive, and there is no mention of them as a soul, ghost or shade. They are purely a projection of the living, who talk with them man to man, and have no clear conception of their different state in death. In art the dead are shown as alive, or, if as 'souls', as small winged humans, the wings being the simplest indication of super-humanity.

The only magical property attached to the grave itself was its efficacy as a post box for curses for the attention of and action by nether deities. Lip service only was paid to the mythology of death, in the occasional provision of Charon's Fee, a lamp or shoes. The notion that the land of the dead lay in the west, to which cemeteries and graves should be oriented, was generally ignored. Oddly enough it was the more 'advanced' religious sects of the Classical period, like the Orphics or the Pythagoreans, who insisted most on the mythological paraphernalia of death as a journey (p. 210). These too are the ones which preached reincarnation in animal, plant or human form—concepts which appealed to Plato and other philosophers but which were probably not widely entertained and which had no effect on funerary art. They preserved by dogma many of the more superstitious traits in the Greek view of death in their formulation of rules for entry to Elysium.

In some communities a man's possessions are destroyed at his death or buried with him since they cannot be used by others. In Greece there was no regular depositing of even basic personal possessions, and certainly no serious attempt to equip him fully for a journey or sojourn elsewhere. Many offerings are clearly determined by sentiment and sometimes, we may suspect, by the desire of the kin to display the measure of their grief. The commonest articles in graves provide food and drink, which may be regarded as provision for a journey, but may as readily reflect the reluctance of the living to acknowledge that the departed has in fact passed beyond all earthly needs and comforts. In all this there is a contradiction in motive and act, but why should we look for logic in the face of death?

Although most Greek burial customs can be related to those practised by other peoples at other times, we have the impression that by the Classical period their significance has been largely forgotten. Yet the rites and provision for the tomb remain important and occupy considerable time and expense. When man disposes of his dead he is usually trying to satisfy the emotional and even physical needs of the living, faced by a puzzling sense of loss or even danger, haunted by memories or dreams of the dead as still alive. By the Classical period Greek burials seem to have developed as far as they possibly could to satisfying the living, within a sequence of rites which preserved traditional practice, yet which gave scope to expression of human grief, admiration, even hope. Many features described in this book illustrate this, even if they are not universally true for all periods or places in the Greek world: in the funerary art the suppression of myth and divinity in favour of the expression of grief or the depiction of the dead as in life, and an increasing reluctance to illustrate extreme grief even in periods when the artists' skill and interest in representing emotion were at their height; the dominant concern with funeral rites and tomb monuments rather than with the disposal of the physical remains; the advertisement of the names of the dead and his family, and of his virtues, in what was for this period an exceptionally literate society; the thoroughly practical character of all funerary legislation. In these and many other respects the Greek way of death differs profoundly from that of other ancient societies, and reflects those characteristics which we most admire in the Greek way of life.

SOURCES OF PLATES

1, 2, 6–9, 22, 40, Agora; 3, 10–18, 21, 23, 24, 25, 28, 30, 31 (Hege), 39, 41, 43, 46, 49, 54, 56, 60, 65, 69, German Institute; 4, 33, 80, Chuzeville; 5, 32, 59, 67, 72–4, Hirmer; 19, 20, 58, Alison Frantz; 26, 27, 36, 44, Ioannidou and Barziote; 29, National Museum, Athens; 34, 35, Bibliothèque Nationale, Paris; 42, Berlin Museum; 45, 47, 61, Ashmolean Museum, Oxford; 48, Museum of Fine Arts, Boston (Francis Bartlett Fund); 50, 66, after Akurgal; 51, after Brunn-Bruckmann; 52, 63, 64, Berlin (East) Museum; 55, after Saraphianos; 57, after Frazer and Rönne; 62, after Arvanitopoulos; 68, 90, Cyprus Dept. of Antiquities; 71, Hermitage Museum, Leningrad; 75, after Petsas; 76, 85, British Museum; 77, after Benndorf and Niemann; 78, J. Anthony James, by courtesy of Mrs Bickerdike; 79, Courtauld Institute; 81, Taranto Museum; 82, Vienna Institute; 83, 89, Metropolitan Museum, New York; 84, Toronto Museum; 86, 87, after Artamonov; 88, after Pagenstecher

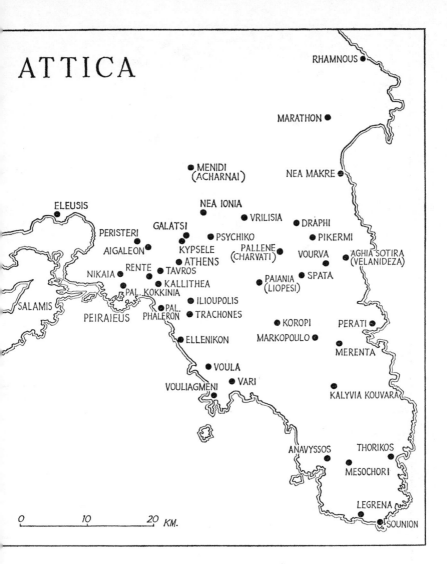

ATTICA

RHAMNOUS

MARATHON

MENIDI
(ACHARNAI)

NEA MAKRE

ELEUSIS

NEA IONIA

VRILISIA

DRAPHI

GALATSI

PERISTERI

PSYCHIKO

PIKERMI

AIGALEON

KYPSELE

PALLENE
(CHARVATI)

VOURVA

AGHIA SOTIRA
(VELANIDEZA)

NIKAIA

RENTE

ATHENS

TAVROS

PAIANIA
(LIOPESI)

SPATA

KALLITHEA

PAL. KOKKINIA

ILIOUPOLIS

SALAMIS

PEIRAIEUS

PAL.
PHALERON

TRACHONES

KOROPI

PERATI

ELLENIKON

MARKOPOULO

MERENTA

VOULA

VOULIAGMENI

VARI

KALYVIA KOUVARA

ANAVYSSOS

THORIKOS

MESOCHORI

LEGRENA

SOUNION

0   10   20   KM.

Map 1   Attica

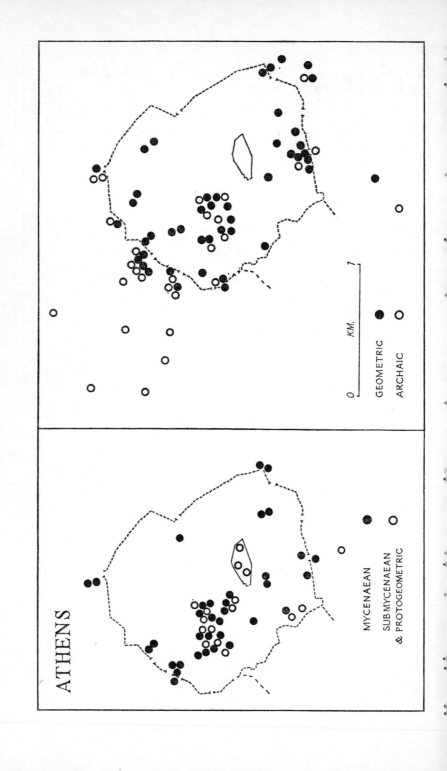

ATHENS

MYCENAEAN ●

SUBMYCENAEAN ○
& PROTOGEOMETRIC

GEOMETRIC ●

ARCHAIC ○

0   1
KM.

Classical and Hellenistic

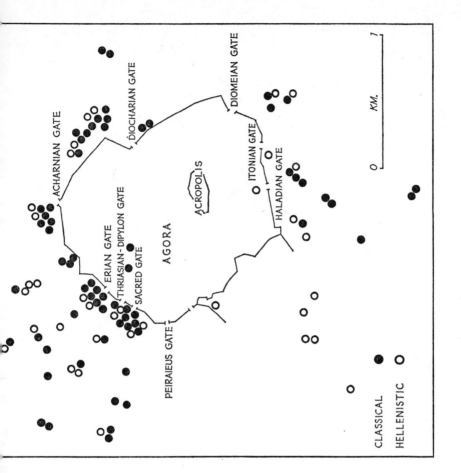

ACHARNIAN GATE

DIOCHARIAN GATE

DIOMEIAN GATE

ITONIAN GATE

HALADIAN GATE

ACROPOLIS

AGORA

ERIAN GATE

THRIASIAN - DIPYLON GATE

SACRED GATE

PEIRAIEUS GATE

CLASSICAL ●
HELLENISTIC ○

0   KM.   1

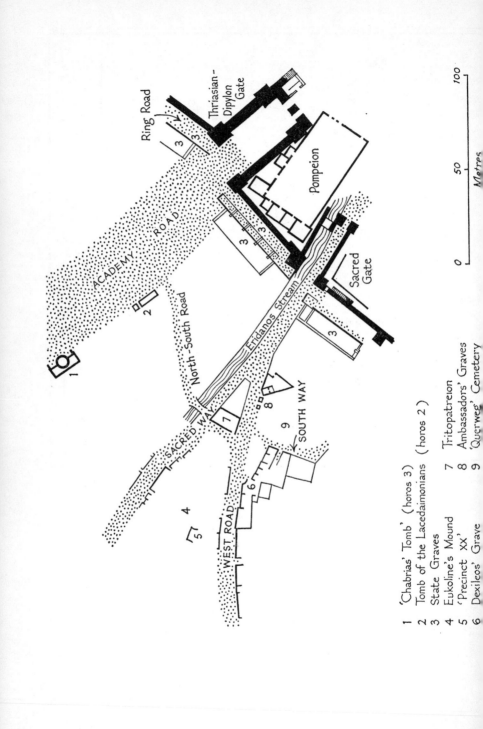

Thriasian-Dipylon Gate

Ring Road

Pompeion

ACADEMY ROAD

Sacred Gate

Eridanos Stream

North-South Road

2

1

SACRED WAY

7

8

9

SOUTH WAY

Tritopatreion

4

5

6

WEST ROAD

100

Metres

50

0

1 'Chabrias' Tomb' (horos 3)
2 Tomb of the Lacedaimonians (horos 2)
3 State Graves
4 Eukoline's Mound
5 'Precinct XX'
6 Dexileos' Grave
7 Tritopatreion
8 Ambassadors' Graves
9 'Querweg' Cemetery

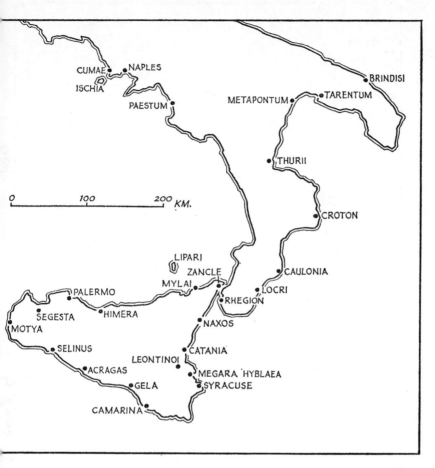

Map 6 South Italy and Sicily

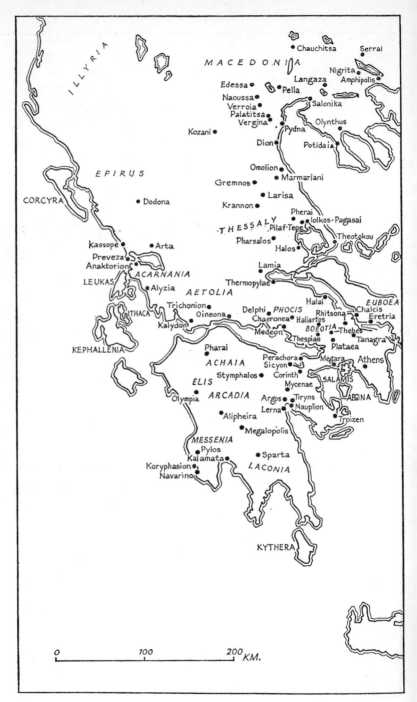

Map 7   Greece

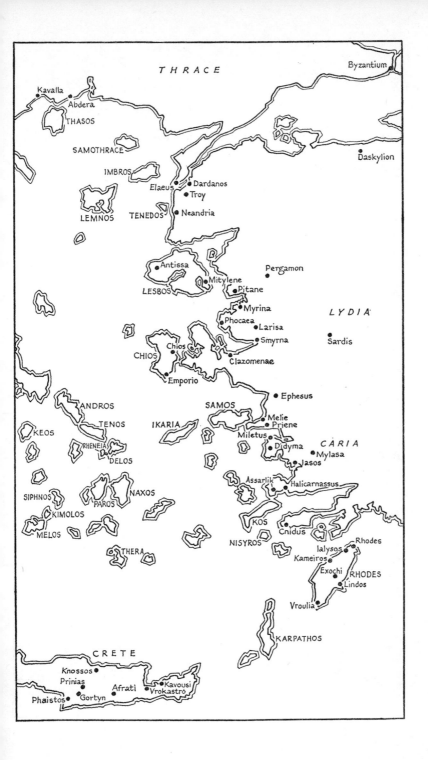

THRACE

Byzantium

Kavalla
Abdera
THASOS

Daskylion

SAMOTHRACE

IMBROS

Elaeus
Dardanos
Troy

LEMNOS
TENEDOS
Neandria

Antissa

Pergamon

Mitylene
Pitane

LESBOS

Myrina

LYDIA

Phocaea
Larisa

Smyrna

Sardis

Chios

CHIOS

Clazomenae

Emporio

Ephesus

ANDROS

SAMOS

TENOS

IKARIA

Melie

KEOS

Priene
Miletus
Didyma

CARIA

RHENEIA

Mylasa

DELOS

Jasos

Assarlik

Halicarnassus

SIPHNOS

PAROS

NAXOS

KOS

NISYROS

Cnidus

KIMOLOS

Ialysos
Rhodes

MELOS

Kameiros

THERA

Exochi
RHODES

Lindos

Vroulia

KARPATHOS

CRETE

Knossos
Prinias
Afrati
Kavousi
Vrokastro
Phaistos
Gortyn

NOTES

The Notes are mainly bibliographical, concentrating on topography and the subjects discussed in the text. References to general works cited for each chapter are not usually repeated in the later sections within it.

ABBREVIATIONS

AA	*Archäologischer Anzeiger*
AAA	*Athenian Annals of Archaeology*
ADelt	*Archaiologikon Deltion*
AE	*Archaiologike Ephemeris*
AJA	*American Journal of Archaeology*
AM	*Athenische Mitteilungen*
Andronikos	M. Andronikos, *Totenkult* (Archaeologia Homerica, W, 1968)
Annuario	*Annuario della Scuola Archaeologica di Atene*
ARV	J. D. Beazley, *Attic Red-Figure Vase-Painters*² (1963)
BCH	*Bulletin de Correspondance Hellénique*
Blümel	C. Blümel, *Katalog der Sammlung antiker Skulpturen, Berlin* iii (1928)
Brückner	A. Brückner, *Der Friedhof am Eridanos* (1909)
BSA	*Annual of the British School at Athens*
BSR	*Papers of the British School at Rome*
Coldstream	N. Coldstream, *Greek Geometric Pottery* (1968)
Collignon	M. Collignon, *Les statues funéraires dans l'art grec* (1911)
Conze	E. Conze, *Die attischen Grabreliefs* (1890–4)
Desborough, *PGP*	V. R. d'A. Desborough, *Protogeometric Pottery* (1952)
Desborough, *LMS*	idem, *The Last Mycenaeans and their Successors* (1964)
Ergon	*To ergon tes en Athenais Archaiologikes Etaireias*
GGA	*Göttingische gelehrte Anzeigen*
GV	W. Peek, *Griechische Versinschriften* i (1955)
Helbig⁴	W. Helbig, *Führer durch die Sammlungen klassischer Altertümer in Rom*⁴ (1963–)
Hesp	*Hesperia*
JdI	*Jahrbuch des deutschen archäologischen Instituts*
Jeffery	L. H. Jeffery, *The Local Scripts of Archaic Greece* (1961)
JHS	*Journal of Hellenic Studies*
Johansen	K. F. Johansen, *The Attic Grave-Reliefs of the classical period* (1951)

Karouzou, *NM* *Coll.Sc.*	S. Karouzou, *National Museum, Collection of Sculpture, a catalogue* (1968)
Ker.	*Kerameikos: Ergebnisse der Ausgrabungen* (K. Kübler et al.).
LSJ	Liddell and Scott, *Greek-English Lexicon,* revised by H. Stuart Jones
Mon. Ant.	*Monumenti antichi: Accademia Nazionale dei Lincei*
Nilsson	M. P. Nilsson, *Geschichte der griechischen Religion* (1950)
NSc	*Notizie degli Scavi di Antichitá*
ÖJh	*Jahreshefte des österreichischen archäologischen Institutes in Wien*
PAE	*Praktika tes Archaiologikes Etaireias*
RE	*Paulys Real-Encyclopädie der classischen Altertumswissenschaft*
Richter, *AGA*	G. M. A. Richter, *The Archaic Gravestones of Attica* (1961)
RM	*Römische Mitteilungen*

References to verse epitaphs are, where possible, given to A. S. F. Gow and D. L. Page, *The Greek Anthology: Hellenistic Epigrams* (1965), naming the poet and the editors' number for the epigram. Other references are to Peek's corpus, *GV.*

References to ancient authors which occur in the text are given in full; those in the Notes are abbreviated as in *LSJ.*

NOTES TO CHAPTER I

FROM BRONZE AGE TO IRON AGE

GENERAL

V. Desborough, *The Last Mycenaeans and their Successors* (1964); F. Stubbings, *The Recession of Mycenaean Civilization* (*Cambridge Ancient History,* revised edition, vol. 2, ch. 27; 1965); E. Vermeule, *Greece in the Bronze Age* (1964), especially ch. 9.

'CULT OF THE DEAD'

General: M. Andronikos, *Totenkult* (1968); C. Blegen, *AE* 1937. i, 377ff.; G. Mylonas, *Mycenae and the Mycenaean Age* (1966) 176ff.

Reuse of Tombs, Offerings to earlier graves: Enclosures: J. Deshayes, *Argos: les Fouilles de la Deiras* i (1966) 45f., 252; H. Mussche *et al., Thorikos* i, 1963 (1968) 37; *ADelt* xxi (1966) B. 85ff. (Geom. sherds in Myc. tomb); xx (1965) B. 80 (Geom. enclosures); *BCH* lxxx (1956) 244f. (PG and Geom. burials in earlier graves at Eleusis), 246 (Geom. burial in Myc. Tomb at Aliki); *PAE* 1955, 44 (enclosure); *Hesp* xxiii (1954) 58, xxiv (1955) 200, xxix (1960) 412 (PG and Geom. burials in Myc. tombs); *JdI* xiv (1899) 103ff. (Myc. tomb with later vases at Menidi).

INHUMATION

ADelt xix (1964) B. 223f. (Medeon); Deshayes, *op. cit.*, 240ff. (Argos); N. G. L. Hammond, *Epirus* (1967) 202ff., 362; *AE* 1969, 179ff.; *AAA* iii (1970) 198ff. (Iolkos).

Skeletal analysis: E. Breitinger in *Ker.* i, 223ff.; L. Angel, *Hesp* xiv (1945) 279ff., 323.

CREMATION

Middle Bronze Age: *BCH* xcii (1968) 1038f. (Argos); Hammond, *op. cit.*, 229.

Late Bronze Age: Desborough, *LMS* 71, 115, 157; G. Styrenius, *Submycenaean Studies* (1967) 154f.; Vermeule, *op. cit.*, 301ff., 349f.

Sites: Deshayes, *op. cit.*, 69(?), 246, 249 (Argos); *Boll. d'Arte* 1950, 324 (Kos); Hammond, *op. cit.*, 202ff., 362; *PAE* 1955, 252 (Pylos); *ADelt* xix (1964) B. 224 (Medeon): *Annuario* vi/vii (1923–4) 240, xiii/xiv (1930–1) 254, 285, 329 (Ialysos).

For Athens and Salamis see Notes to Chapter II.

LAMENT FOR THE DEAD

Desborough, *LMS* 115; Vermeule, *op. cit.*, 210, 342f. and *JHS* lxxxv (1965) 123ff.; S. Iakovides, *AJA* lxx (1966) 43ff.; S. Marinatos, *AAA* iii (1970) 61f., 184ff.; *Ergon* 1969, 5ff.

ATHENS AND ATTICA

TOPOGRAPHY

In the Text references to sites in Athens are by modern street names and ancient monuments. In the Notes a different procedure is followed, largely for economy of space: graves near the site of a gate in the Themistoclean Wall, or along the road which passed through it, are listed under the name of the gate. For the course of the Themistoclean Wall we follow in the main the work of Judeich and Travlos, with corrections necessitated by recent excavation, and the names of the gates (which are indicated on the map of Classical Athens, Map 4) are those used by Travlos in *Poleodomike*.

Generally only the latest excavation reports are cited, and these are drawn primarily from the last ten years of the *Chronika* (B) of *Archaiologikon Deltion*. For earlier excavations the *Archäologischer Anzeiger* of the *Jahrbuch des Deutschen Archäologischen Instituts* is the major source. A convenient source for references to eighteenth- and early nineteenth-century excavations is L. Ross, *Archäologische Aufsätze* i (1855), who quotes from Fauvel's *Letters*.

Since the Kerameikos finds are extensively used, the following volumes of the excavation publication should be consulted:

Kerameikos i: Die Nekropolen des 12. bis 10. Jahrhunderts (1939): W. Kraiker, K. Kübler, and E. Breitinger.

Kerameikos ii: Die Skulpturen (1940): H. Riemann.

Kerameikos iv: Neufunde aus der Nekropole des 11. und 10. Jahrhunderts (1943): K. Kübler.

Kerameikos v.1: Die Nekropole des 10. bis 8. Jahrhunderts (1954): K. Kübler.

Kerameikos vi.1: Die Nekropole des Späten 8. bis Frühen 6. Jahrhunderts (1959): K. Kübler.

Kerameikos vi.2: Die Nekropole des Späten 8. bis Frühen 6. Jahrhunderts (1970): K. Kübler.

The following general works may be found useful:

I. T. Hill, *The Ancient City of Athens* (1953).

W. Judeich, *Topographie von Athen* (1931).

G. Karo, *An Attic Cemetery* (1943).

E. Kirsten and W. Kraiker, *Griechenlandkunde* i (1967); ii, 865ff.

(H. Thompson), *The Athenian Agora, A Guide* (1962).

I. Travlos, *Poleodomike Exelixis ton Athenon* (1960).

W. Wrede, *Attika* (1934).

GRAVE NUMBERS

The numbers of specific graves have not been given in the text. They appear in the Notes where it would otherwise be difficult to find the objects mentioned. Each excavation has produced its conventions for numbering and most are straightforward, requiring no comment. That of the Kerameikos is more complicated. Generally there is a code for the area, such as hS for Sacred Way (*heilige Strasse*), followed by the grave number. The convention for the Archaic burials is the most complex; *Ker.* vi. 1, 10ff. should be consulted.

GRAVE RELIEFS

Grave reliefs mentioned in the text are cited by their number in E. Conze, *Die Attischen Grabreliefs*. References to those not included by Conze may be found in the Notes, either under the type of monument or the name of the dead.

NOTES TO CHAPTER II

THE END OF THE BRONZE AGE

GENERAL

C. Blegen, *Harvard Studies in Classical Philology* Suppl. 1 (1940) 1ff.; O. Broneer,

Antiquity xxx (1956) 9ff.; Desborough, *LMS* 112ff., 264, 281, and the index of sites; R. Hope-Simpson, *A Gazetteer and Atlas of Mycenaean Sites* (1965) 101ff.; Vermeule, *op. cit.*, 297ff., 367f., 383f.

ATHENS

Agora: *Hesp* xxiv (1955) 187ff. (188, nn. 3, 4), xxxv (1966) 55ff.; S. Immerwahr, forthcoming volume of the *Agora* series.
Ilissos: *Hesp* xxxv (1966) 55, n.2, 60, n.4.; *ADelt* xxi (1966) B. 85ff.
Mouseion Hill: *AM* xxv (1900) 453.
Hill of Nymphs: *ADelt* xxiii (1968) B. 21ff.; *AAA* i (1968) 18ff.

ATTICA

Hope-Simpson, *op. cit.*, 101ff.
Marathon: *BCH* lxxxiii (1959) 583ff.; Andronikos, 85.
Menidi (Acharnai): *AM* xii (1887) 139f.; *BSA* liii/liv (1958-9) 292ff.
Perati: *PAE* 1963, 32ff.
Thorikos: H. Mussche *et al.*, *Thorikos* i, 27ff.

NOTES TO CHAPTER III

THE EARLY IRON AGE

I. SUB-MYCENAEAN

GENERAL

Desborough, *Protogeometric Pottery* (1952) 1ff.; *LMS*; G. Styrenius, *Submycenaean Studies* (1967), reviewed by Desborough, *JHS* lxxxviii (1968) 228f., and by Kraiker, *Gnomon* xli (1969) 599ff.; A. M. Snodgrass, *The Dark Ages of Greece* (1971).

SALAMIS

C. Tsountas and I. Manatt, *The Mycenaean Age* (1897), appendix C; *AM* xxxv (1910) 17ff.; *Opusc. Ath.* iv (1962) 103ff.

ATHENS

Kerameikos (Thriasian and Sacred Gates): *Ker.* i; *GGA* ccxv (1963) 47ff.; *Hesp* xxx (1961) 174ff.; *AA* 1942, 203; 1938, 605f.
Erian Gate: *AAA* i (1968) 20ff.; *ADelt* xxii (1967) B. 92ff.; xxiii (1968) B. 67.
Acharnian Gate: *Ker.* i, 132; *AM* xviii (1893) 77ff.
Diomeian Gate: *BCH* lxiv/lxv (1940-1) 237f.; *ADelt* xvii (1961-2) B. 10.
Itonian Gate(?): *ADelt* xxiii (1968) B. 73ff.
Haladian Gate: *PAE* 1955, 43; *ADelt* xxi (1966) B. 71; xxiii (1968) B. 55f.
Agora: Volume in preparation; Styrenius, *op. cit.*, 31.
Acropolis: Styrenius, *op. cit.*, 22f.; *AJA* lxix (1965) 176.

MARKERS

Andronikos, 110; *ADelt* xvii (1961–2) A. 176ff.; *Ker.* i, 9, 11, 45; Styrenius, *op. cit.*, 33, 78.

CREMATION

Styrenius, *op. cit.*, 30ff., 65f., 73ff.

OFFERINGS

General: Styrenius, *op. cit.*, 38ff., 68ff., 80ff.

Metal: H. Müller-Karpe, *JdI* lxxvii (1962) 59ff.; P. Jacobsthal, *Greek Pins* (1956) 1f.; R. Higgins, *Greek and Roman Jewellery* (1961) 90ff., 205, and *BSA* lxiv (1969) 144.

II. PROTOGEOMETRIC

GENERAL

Desborough, *PGP*, and site index, 315f.; *LMS* 264; N. Coldstream, *Greek Geometric Pottery* (1968) 9ff., 335f., 399ff. (site index).

ATHENS

Kerameikos (Thriasian and Sacred Gates): *Ker.* i, 89ff. ('Precinct XX'), 180ff. ('South Cemetery'); *Ker.* iv; *AM* lxxxi (1966) 4ff.; lxxviii (1963) 148ff.; *GGA* ccxv (1963) 47ff.

Erian Gate: *AAA* i (1968) 20ff.; *ADelt* xxii (1967) B. 92ff.; xxiii (1968) B. 67.

Acharnian Gate: *ADelt* xviii (1963) B. 36.

Diocharian Gate: *AE* 1953/4 iii, 89ff.; 1958, 2ff.

Diomeian Gate: *BCH* lxiv/lxv (1940–1) 238.

Itonian Gate: *ADelt* xxiii (1968) B. 73ff.

Haladian Gate: *ADelt* xviii (1963) B. 41; xxi (1966) B. 71.

Mouseion Hill: *AE* 1911, 251.

'Heidelberg Graves' (Between the Areiopagos and the Amyneion): *CVA* Heidelberg iii, 33ff., pls. 101f.; cf. *AJA* lxxiv (1970) 203f.

Odeion of Herodes Atticus: *PAE* 1955, 44; *Ergon* 1957, 7.

Agora: Volume in preparation; Styrenius, *op. cit.*, 89ff.; *Hesp* xxiii (1954) 58; xxiv (1955) 200f.

ATTICA

General: Desborough, *PGP* 316f. (site index).

Eleusis: *AE* 1885, 169ff.; 1898, 76ff.; *BCH* lxxx (1956) 244.

Marathon: *PAE* 1939, 27ff.; *AA* 1940, 178ff.

Nea Ionia: *Hesp* xxx (1961) 147ff.

MARKERS

Mounds: *Ker.* i, 181; iv, 3; *Hesp* xxx (1961) 149ff.; Andronikos, 110f.
Vases: *Ker.* iv, 3, 38f., 39, pl. 2; *Hesp* xxx (1961) 152; Andronikos, 94.
Stone: *Ker.* iv, 3, 39, pl. 2; Andronikos, 118f.; *ADelt* xvii (1961–2) A. 177.

OFFERINGS

Vases: *Ker.* i, 109ff., 195ff.; iv, 5ff.; Styrenius, *op. cit.*, 99ff.
Coarse Ware with incised decoration: *Ker.* iv, 19f., pls. 29–32; *Hesp* xxx (1961)
170ff., pl. 30; xxxvii (1968) 103ff.; J. Bouzek, *Acta Universitatis Carolinae*
(1966) 65ff.
Clay Figures: *Ker.* iv, 39ff., pl. 26 (stag); *ADelt* xxii (1967) B. 49, pl. 70b (horse
on wheels).
Metal: *JdI* lxxvii (1962) 120ff.
Jewellery: *Ker.* i, 220f.; iv, 25f.; *Hesp* xxiii (1954) 58, pl. 16a (child with shoulder
pins); Jacobsthal, *op. cit.*, 2f.; Higgins, *op. cit.*, 90ff., 205 (site index), and
BSA lxiv (1969) 144.
Weapons: *Ker.* i, 220f.; iv, 26ff.; A. Snodgrass, *Early Greek Armour and Weapons*
(1964). Swords around ash urns: *Ker.* i, 183; iv, 34. Sword lying beside
inhumed dead: *Ker.* iv, 47. Shield-boss on belly-handled amphora: *Ker.* iv,
32f., pl. 37.
Food and Drink: *Ker.* i, 258 (goat); iv, 4f.; Styrenius, *op. cit.*, 110ff.; Andronikos, 88f., 92ff.

NOTES TO CHAPTER IV

THE GEOMETRIC PERIOD

ATHENS

General: Coldstream, chs. 2 and 14; 399ff. (site index); Wrede, *Attika* 27f.
Kerameikos (Thriasian and Sacred Gates): *Ker.* v. 1; 'South Cemetery' 209ff.,
'North Cemetery' 256ff.; reviewed by E. Homann-Wedeking, *Gnomon*
xxx (1958) 335ff., and by R. Hachmann, *GGA* ccxv (1963) 47ff.; *ADelt* xx
(1965) B. 40; xxi (1966) B. 51; *AM* lxxxi (1966) 4ff., 112ff.
Erian Gate: *AM* xviii (1893) 73ff.; *ADelt* xvii (1961–2) B. 23; xxi (1966)
B. 61ff.; xxii (1967) B. 92ff.; xxiii (1968) B. 67ff., 79ff.
Between Erian and Acharnian Gates: *ADelt* xxiii (1968) B. 89ff.
Acharnian Gate: *BCH* lxxxvi (1962) 644.
Diomeian Gate: *ADelt* xvii (1961–2) B. 10; xviii (1963) B. 37f.; xxiii (1968)
B. 61; British School at Athens, Notebooks of the Kynosarges Excavation.
Itonian Gate: *ADelt* xxi (1966) B. 85; xxiii (1968) B. 73ff.
Haladian Gate: *ADelt* xi (1927–8) B. 2; xviii (1963) B. 41; xix (1964) B. 60;
xx (1965) B. 75ff., 80, 87; xxii (1967) B. 106; xxiii (1968) B. 48ff., 55ff., 88;
PAE 1955, 43f.

Pnyx: *AM* xviii (1893) 414.

Piraeus Gate: *ADelt* xxii (1967) B. 79ff., 110ff.

Agora: Volume in preparation; Coldstream, 399f., adding *ADelt* xx (1965) B. 47ff.; *AJA* lxxiv (1970) 203f.

ATTICA

Academy: *PAE* 1956, 49ff.; 1959, 9; 1961, 5ff.; *BCH* lxxxi (1957) 507f.; lxxxiv (1960) 644f.

Anavyssos: *ADelt* xxi (1966) B. 97f.

Eleusis: *ADelt* xxii (1967) B. 122f.

Kallithea: *ADelt* xix (1964) B. 65ff.

Marathon: *AA* 1935, 179ff.; 1940, 178ff.

Merenta: *Ergon* 1960, 30ff.; *AAA* i (1968) 30ff.

Thorikos: *ADelt* xxii (1967) B. 138; *Thorikos* ii, 1964 (1967) 27ff.; iii, 1965 (1967) 31ff.; iv, 1966–7 (1969) 70ff.

Trachones: *AA* 1940, 175.

Vari (Anagyrous): *ADelt* xx (1965) B. 112ff.

CREMATION

General: *Ker.* v. 1, 7ff.; *GGA* ccxv (1963) 52ff.; *AJA* lxxiv (1970) 203f.

Divided Pits: *Ker.* v. 1, 218, 239; *PAE* 1955, 76.

Phoenician Bowl: *Ker.* v. 1, 201ff., 236ff.

Metal Ash urns: *Ker.* v. 1, 205ff.; *AM* xviii (1893) 414f. (Pnyx, on tripod).

Cloth around urns: *Ker.* v. 1, 24, n. 59; 237; *Ker.* vi. 2, 405; *AE* 1898, 114, and 1912, 38.

INHUMATION

General: *Ker.* v. 1, 11ff.; *GGA* ccxv (1963) 55ff.

Open-ended cists: *ADelt* ii (1916) 16; xx (1965) B. 112.

'Isis Grave': Coldstream, 402; *Hesp* Suppl. 2, appendix 2, 234ff.

Coffins and Biers: *Ker.* v. 1, 10f., 21f.; *AM* lxxxi (1966) 7 (no. 7), 10 (no. 14).

Vase Pillow: *AA* 1935, 182.

Pithos burial of adult: *AM* xviii (1893) 133f.; *ADelt* xxii (1967) B. 138.

Children: *Hesp* ii (1933) 552f. (with piglet); *Ker.* v. 1, 13; *AM* lxxxi (1966) 115 (no. 208).

CEMETERY PLANS

Athens: *Ker.* v. 1, 6f., 14ff.; *GGA* ccxv (1963) 59ff.; *Gnomon* xxx (1958) 337; *Hesp* Suppl. 2, 14; *ADelt* xx (1965) B. 75ff.

Attica: *AA* 1935, 179ff.; 1940, 178f.; *PAE* 1939, 27f. (Marathon); *PAE* 1951, 116ff. (Pal. Kokkinia); *ADelt* xxi (1966) B. 97f. (Anavyssos).

Enclosures: *Ker.* v. 1, 17ff., and n. 50 on page 17; *PAE* 1955, 44f.; *ADelt* xx (1965) B. 80; *Hesp* Suppl. 2, 6ff.; *PAE* 1953, 81ff., and 1954, 50.

MARKERS

General: *Ker.* v. 1, 7ff., 33ff.; *ADelt* xvii (1961–2) A. 176ff.

Mounds: *Ker.* v. 1, 10 and n. 35, 13, 35; Andronikos, 111f.; *AE* 1898, 78f.; *PAE* 1911, 110ff.

Stone: Andronikos, 118f.; K. Johansen, *The Attic Grave-Reliefs* (1951) 65ff.; *Ker.* v. 1, 7f., 34ff.; vi. 2, 407; *ADelt* xx (1965) B. 40; xxi (1966) B. 51; *AE* 1898, 86ff.; *ADelt* xxi (1966) B. 97; *AM* lxxxi (1966) 5, 112, 114.

VASE SCENES

Ker. v. 1, 19ff., 33f.; F. Poulsen, *Die Dipylongräber und die Dipylonvasen* (1905); W. Hahland, *Festschrift F. Zucker* (1954) 177ff. (musicians); J. Boardman, *JHS* lxxxvi (1966) 1ff. (chariot processions, food, musicians); W. Zschietzmann, *AM* liii (1928) 17ff. (*prothesis, ekphora*); S. Laser, *Hausrat* (1968) 17ff. (biers); *AA* 1963, 215 (warrior *prothesis*); *Gnomon* xlii (1970) 163f. (*ekphora*); J. Davison, *Yale Classical Studies* xvi (1961); Coldstream, 71f. (musicians); *AJA* lxxiii (1969) 459ff. (musicians); G. Ahlberg, *Opusc. Ath.* vii (1967) 177ff. (musicians); H. Marwitz, *Antike und Abendland* x (1961) 7ff.; K. Fittschen, *Untersuchungen zum Beginn der Sagendarstellungen bei den Griechen* (1969) 18ff.; R. Tölle, *Frühgriechische Reigentanze* (1964) 88ff. (list of scenes). Vase with multiple *prothesis*: BM 1912. 5–22.1, *Yale Classical Studies* xvi (1961) fig. 29.

OFFERINGS

General: *Ker.* v. 1, 19ff.; *JdI* lxxvii (1962) 124ff. (metal).

Jewellery: *Ker.* v. 1, 183ff.; *Hesp* xxxvii (1968) 77ff.; Higgins, *Greek and Roman Jewellery* 93f., 95ff., 205f. and *BSA* lxiv (1969) 144ff.

Gold Bands: Andronikos, 41ff.; *Ker.* vi. 2, 403, 559; Ross, *Arch. Auf.* 25; J. Cook, *BSA* xlvi (1951) 45ff.; D. Ohly, *Griechische Goldbleche* (1953), especially 68ff.; *ADelt* xviii (1963) B. 29f., 37; xx (1965) B. 40; xxii (1967) B. 80, 95; *AM* lxxxi (1966) 7f.

Ivory Inlay: *AM* xviii (1893) 120ff., 127ff.

'Rich Graves': *ADelt* vi (1920–1) 136ff. (Spata); *AE* 1898, pl. 6 (Eleusis); *ADelt* xx (1965) B. 78 (Kavalotti Street); xxi (1966) B. 98 (Anavyssos); *Hesp* xxxvii (1968) 77ff.; Higgins, *BSA* lxiv (1969) 144ff.

Weapons: Snodgrass, *op. cit.*; *Ker.* v. 1, 197ff., 234 (sword folded over); *Hesp* xxi (1952) 279ff.; *JdI* lxxvii (1967) 124ff.; *BSA* xii (1905–6) 91f. (shield boss); *ADelt* xxi (1966) B. 36ff. (greaves).

Boots: *AE* 1898, 103f. (Eleusis); *Hesp* xviii (1949) 296f.; *ADelt* xix (1964) B. 54f. Cf. Mycenaean and Hittite clay boots with pointed toes, S. Marinatos, *Kleidung, Haar- und Barttracht* (1967) 32ff., 50f.

'Granaries': *Hesp* Suppl. 2, 186f.; *Hesp* xxxvii (1968) 92ff.; *Expedition* xii (1969) 8 (coarse ware); H. Drerup, *Griechische Baukunst* (1969) 75f.; J. Perrot, *Atiquot* iii (1961) 16ff. (Azor); F. Behn, *Hausurnen* (1924).

Clay Figures: *AE* 1911, 250; *ADelt* xix (1964) B. 60 (centaur and chariot); *Hesp* Suppl. 2, 53f. (mourner), 65 (woman on throne).

Food and Drink: *Ker.* v. 1, 29ff., 222f., 228f., 236, 267f.; *Hesp* Suppl. 2, 19ff.; *Hesp* xviii (1949) 275ff.; xxi (1952) 279ff.; Andronikos, 89ff., 92, 94.

Burnt Deposits: *Ker.* v. 1, 29ff., 233, 245f.; *Hesp* Suppl. 2, 44ff., 55ff.; *ADelt* xx (1965) B. 78; *AM* lxxxi (1966) 112, 114.

Offering Ditches: *Ker.* v. 1, 29ff., 240ff., 250ff. and see Notes to Chapter V.

'Grave 3': *Ker.* v. 1, 212f.; *GGA* ccxv (1963) 51.

NOTES TO CHAPTER V

THE ARCHAIC PERIOD

ATHENS

Sites published before 1958 are listed in *Ker.* vi. 1, 95ff. with nn. 32ff.

Kerameikos (Thriasian and Sacred Gates): *ADelt* xvi (1960) B. 19ff.; xvii (1961–2) B. 16ff.; xviii (1963) B. 22ff.; xix (1964) B. 38ff., 60f.; xx (1965) B. 39ff.; xxi (1966) B. 74ff., 77; xxii (1967) B. 114; *AA* 1965, 277ff.; 1964, 434ff.; *AM* lxxxi (1966) 16ff., 116ff.

Erian Gate: *ADelt* xvii (1961–2) B. 22ff.; xxi (1966) B. 61ff.; xxii (1967) B. 92ff., 97f.; xxiii (1968) B. 79ff.; *AAA* i (1968) 26f.

Between Erian and Acharnian Gates: *ADelt* xxiii (1968) B. 89ff.

Acharnian Gate: *JHS* lxxx (1960) 52; *BCH* lxxxvi (1962) 644; *ADelt* xviii (1963) B. 33f. For the account of Fauvel's excavation of 1812, Ross, *Arch. Auf.* 31.

Diomeian Gate: *BCH* lxxxiv (1960) 631f.; *ADelt* xxiii (1968) B. 61.

Haladian Gate: *ADelt* xx (1965) B. 78f.; xxii (1967) B. 76ff.; xxiii (1968) B. 50ff.

Piraeus Gate: *ADelt* xxiii (1968) B. 36.

Agora: Volume in preparation; *Hesp* xx (1951) 67ff.

ATTICA

General: *Ker.* vi. 1, 95ff. and nn. 32ff.; Coldstream, 401ff.

Academy: *PAE* 1958, 10f.; 1959, 9; 1961, 5; 1963, 12ff.; *BCH* lxxxv (1961) 618; lxxxiv (1960) 644f.

Aigaleon: *ADelt* xix (1964) B. 70.

Anavyssos: *PAE* 1911, 110ff.

Draphi: *BCH* lxxx (1956) 246f.; lxxxi (1957) 516ff.

Eleusis: *PAE* 1954, 58f., 60ff.; *ADelt* xxii (1967) B. 122; *AAA* ii (1969) 89ff.

Hymettos: *JdI* ii (1887) 52.

Kalyvia Kouvara: *AE* 1903, 43.

Marathon: *AM* xviii (1893) 46ff.; *JHS* lxxxviii (1968) 12ff.; C. Haspels, *Attic Black-Figured Lekythoi* (1936) 91ff.

Menidi: *JdI* xiii (1898) 13ff.; xiv (1899) 103ff.; D. Feytmans, *Les Louteria Attiques* (1965) 43ff.

Merenta: *AAA* i (1968) 31ff.

Phaleron: *BCH* xvii (1893) 25ff.; *AE* 1911, 246ff.; *ADelt* ii (1916) 13ff.; *AA* 1916, 139f.; *PAE* 1951, 122ff.

Spata: *ADelt* xix (1964) B. 72.

Thorikos: *Thorikos* i, 47ff.; ii, 34ff.

Vari: *AA* 1936, 124; 1937, 121; 1940, 175; *BCH* lxi (1937) 451; S. Karouzou, *Angeia tou Anagyrountos* (1963); *ADelt* xvii (1961–2) B. 37ff.; xviii (1963) A. 115ff.; xx (1965) B. 112ff.

INTRA-MURAL BURIALS

The 'pre-Themistoclean wall': Judeich, *Topographie* 120f.; *Hesp* xx (1951) 131ff.; Travlos, *Poleodomike* 33ff.

INHUMATION

General: *Ker.* vi. 1, 80ff.; *Hesp* xx (1951) 80f.

Coffins and biers: *Ker.* vi. 1, 82; *Hesp* xx (1951) 80f.; *AM* lxxxi (1966) 13f., 17.

Kline with ivory inlay: *ADelt* xix (1964) B. 44.

Adult in *Pithos*: *Ker.* vi. 1, 75.

Pot burials of children: *Ker.* vi. 1, 81; *AM* lxxxi (1966) 11ff.; *PAE* 1954, 60.

Inscribed Pot: *AAA* i (1968) 26f., 29, fig. 13.

Pot of offerings: *ADelt* xviii (1963) A. 115f.

CREMATION

General: *Ker.* vi. 1, 83f.; *Hesp* xx (1951) 80ff.

Ash urns in stone boxes: *ADelt* ii (1916) 16.

Triple cremation(?): *Ker.* vi. i, 75f.

Children: *PAE* 1951, 123 (Pal. Kokkinia); *PAE* 1961, 5 (Academy); *Hesp* Suppl. 2, 15; *ADelt* xx (1965) B. 40.

POSITION OF OFFERINGS

Offering Places: *Ker.* vi. 1, 87f.; *ADelt* xviii (1963) A. 115ff.; *AM* lxxxi (1966) 11, 16, 17, 21.

Offering Ditches: *Ker.* vi. 1, 87f.; *AA* 1940, 175; R. Hampe, *Ein frühattischer Grabfund* (1960) 71ff.

OFFERINGS

'Rattles': R. Hampe, *Die Stele aus Pharsalos* (1951) 33 n. 22 (list of examples); H. Payne, *Necrocorinthia* (1931) 313f.; R. Ginouvès, *Balaneutiké* (1962) 242ff.; *AA* 1959, 1ff.; *BSA* xliv (1949) 247f.; *NSc* 1913, Suppl. 27 and n.1 (Locri, with references to other sites); *AA* 1912, 354 (Olbia); *AE* 1898, 112 (Geom., Eleusis); cf. *AM* lxxviii (1963) Beil. 17.2 (Geom., Tiryns); *CVA* Mannheim i, pl. 11.9 (Thebes).

Eggs: *Archiv Rel.-wiss.* xi (1908) 530ff.; P. Amandry, *Coll. Helène Stathatos* iii (1963) 160ff. (H. Metzger).

'Tables': *Ker.* vi. 1, 79ff.; *Ker.* vi. 2, 512f.; *ADelt* xviii (1963) A. 123f.; H. Payne and T. Dunbabin, *Perachora* ii (1962) 131ff.

Mourners: Amandry, *op. cit.*, 116ff. (C. Rolley); P. Knoblauch, *Archaisch-griechischen Tonbildnerei* (1937) 173ff.; G. Richter, *Korai* (1968) figs. 31–6; *Ker.* vi. 2, 380ff., 492f.

Vari Cart: *AA* 1937, 123; *Ker.* vi. 2, 380ff., 393f., 426; Andronikos, 51, pl. 4a; Hampe, *Ein frühattischer Grabfund* 74.

Thymiateria: *Ker.* vi. 2, 381ff.; vi. 1, 22ff.; Richter, *Korai*, figs. 33–6; *AA* 1933, 268f.

Pedestalled Vases: *Ker.* vi. 2, 162ff., 461ff.; S. Karouzou, *Angeia tou Anagyroun-tos*; Hampe, *op. cit.*; *CVA* Mainz i, 18ff., pls. 8ff.; cf. fragment from Athens, *AM* xxxii (1907) 563, fig. 37.

MOUNDS AND BUILT TOMBS

Round Mounds: General: H. Herrmann, *Omphalos* (1959); *Ker.* vi. 1, 88ff.; *AM* lxxxi (1966) 17ff.; with vases: *Ker.* vi. 1, 18ff., 22ff., 37ff., 51ff.; vi. 2, 491f.; with *stelai*: *Ker.* vi. 1, 27ff., 30ff., 33ff.; vi. 2, 561f.; cf. *BSA* lvii (1962) 123f.

Rectangular Mounds and Built Tombs: K. Kübler, *Mitt. d. Inst.* ii (1949) 7ff.; *Ker.* vi. 1, 90ff.; *AA* 1964, 434ff.; *ADelt* xviii (1963) B. 22ff.; xix (1964) B. 38ff.; Wrede, *Attika* 20ff., 30ff.

Painted Plaques: *AM* liii (1928) 17ff.; *BSA* l (1955) 51ff.

Marble Slabs: *AM* xxxii (1907) 543ff.; Karouzou, *NM Coll. Sc.* (1968) 30 (nos. 89, 2823, 2826).

'Marathon Runner': *AE* 1953–4 ii, 317ff.

Crowning Vases: *Ker.* vi. 1, 43ff.; 53ff., 72f.; vi. 2, 488f., 492f., 505f.

Crowning Sculpture: Lions: *Ker.* vi. 1, 70f.; vi. 2, 412f., 564f.; H. Gabelmann, *Studien zum frühgriechischen Löwenbild* (1965) 97ff. Sphinxes: *AA* 1936, 125. See also the Notes to Chapter VI.

GRAVESTONES

General: Johansen; Richter, *The Archaic Gravestones of Attica* (1961); E. Harrison, *Agora* xi (1965) 41ff.; L. Jeffery, *BSA* lvii (1962) 116ff.; F. Willemsen, *AM* lxxviii (1963) 104ff.; *AA* 1963, 431ff. For recent bibliography, *Ker.* vi. 2, 407ff., 561ff.

Broad Reliefs: Johansen, 135ff.; Richter, *AGA* 55ff.; Jeffery, *op. cit.*, 149f.; *ADelt* xxi (1966) A. 102ff. (Velanideza).

Discs: P. Jacobsthal, *Diskoi* (1936); Jeffery, *op. cit.*, 147; *Greek, Roman and Byz. Studies* viii (1967) 261ff.

STATUARY

Kouroi: G. Richter, *Kouroi* (1960); C. Karouzos, *Aristodikos* (1961).

Korai: Richter, *Korai*; Brauron Museum, Merenta 1265.

Seated Figures: *Ker.* vi. 2, 411f., 564; *Antike Plastik* vi (1967) 7ff.; Jeffery, *BSA* lvii (1962) 150f., and 127 for base; M. Collignon, *Les Statues Funéraires* (1911) 65ff., and 70ff.; P. Kavvadias, *Katalogos tou Kentrikou Archaiologikou Mouseiou* (1886–7) 17, no. 7, and 18, no. 7a; *AM* lxxviii (1963) 139ff. (bases). Horsemen: Jeffery, *op. cit.*, 151; *AM* lxxviii (1963) 136ff.

NOTES TO CHAPTER VI

THE CLASSICAL PERIOD

ATHENS

Kerameikos (Thriasian and Sacred Gates): A. Brückner, *Der Friedhof am Eridanos* (1909); E. Boehringer, *Neue deutsche Ausgrabungen* (1959) 249ff. (D. Ohly); *ADelt* xviii (1963) B. 31; xix (1964) B. 60ff.; xxi (1966) B. 51f., 74f., 77; xxii (1967) B. 86ff., 96, 114; *AM* lxxix (1964) 85ff.; lxxxi (1966) 21ff., 116ff.

Erian Gate: *AM* xviii (1893) 156ff.; *Hesp* xxxii (1963) 113ff.; *AE* 1968 Chronika 8ff.; *ADelt* xvii (1961–2) B. 22ff.; xxi (1966) B. 61ff.; xxii (1967) B. 92ff., 97ff.; xxiii (1968) B. 31ff., 43ff., 67, 79ff.; *AAA* i (1968) 20ff.; ii (1969) 257ff.

Between Erian and Acharnian Gates: *ADelt* xxii (1967) B. 114ff.; xxiii (1968) B. 34, 89ff.

Acharnian Gate: *BCH* lxxviii (1954) 108ff.; *ADelt* xviii (1963) B. 33ff.; xx (1965) B. 100; xxii (1967) B. 115; xxiii (1968) B. 39ff. Fauvel's Letter of 4 April 1811, Ross, *Arch. Auf.* 31.

Diocharian Gate: *ADelt* ix (1924–5) B. 68ff.; xi (1927–8) B. 91ff.; *AA* 1927, 346f.; 1928, 571; *AE* 1958, 1ff.; *ADelt* xvi (1960) B. 22ff., 27; xvii (1961–2) B. 29; xx (1965) B. 101; xxi (1966) B. 79ff.; xxii (1967) B. 75, 103, 115; *AAA* ii (1969) 329ff.

Diomeian Gate: *ADelt* xxi (1966) B. 65; xxii (1967) B. 84; xxiii (1968) B. 61; British School at Athens, Kynosarges Notebooks.

Itonian and Haladian Gates: *AM* xxv (1900) 453; *BCH* xc (1966) 741f.; *ADelt* xix (1964) B. 57ff.; xxi (1966) B. 85; xxiii (1968) B. 50ff., 97.

Long Walls: *ADelt* xvii (1961–2) B. 26.

Intra-mural: *ADelt* xxiii (1968) B. 65, 71ff.

Demes between Athens and the Piraeus: *ADelt* xvii (1961–2) B. 43; *AAA* ii (1969) 334ff. (Tavros); *ADelt* xviii (1963) B. 46ff. (St John Rente).

ATTICA

Academy; *PAE* 1958, 10f.; 1963, 12ff.

Aigaleon: *ADelt* xix (1964) B. 70; xxi (1966) B. 105.

Anavyssos: *ADelt* xvi (1960) B. 39.

Charvati: *AA* 1926, 400.

Draphi: *BCH* lxxx (1956) 246; lxxxi (1957) 516ff.; lxxxii (1958) 681ff.

Eleusis: *PAE* 1952, 66ff.; 1953, 77ff.; 1954, 55ff.; 1955, 73ff.; 1956, 59ff.;
  BCH lxxviii (1954) 111ff.; lxxix (1955) 220ff.; lxxx (1956) 242ff.; lxxxi (1957)
  512ff.; *ADelt* xxii (1967) B. 122ff.
Galatsi: *ADelt* xix (1964) B. 71.
Helleniko: *ADelt* xvii (1961–2) B. 30ff.
Ilioupolis: *ADelt* x (1926) B. 60.
Kallithea: *ADelt* xix (1964) B. 67.
Legrena: *ADelt* xviii (1963) B. 44f.; *BCH* lxxxvii (1963) 717f.
Liopesi: *AA* 1916, 142.
Marathon: *PAE* 1939, 36ff.; *AA* 1935, 182; 1936, 125f.; 1940, 182f.
Markopoulo: *BCH* lxxv (1951) 111.
Merenta: *Ergon* 1960, 30ff.; *BCH* lxxxv (1961) 626ff.; *AAA* i (1968) 31ff.;
  ADelt xxiii (1968) B. 110f.
Mesochori: *AA* 1963, 455ff.
Nea Makri: *ADelt* xxi (1966) B. 107.
Nikaia: *ADelt* xx (1965) B. 121f.
Psychiko: *ADelt* xix (1964) B. 71.
Rhamnous: *PAE* 1958, 28ff.
Salamis: *ADelt* xxi (1966) B. 107.
Thorikos: *Thorikos* i, 59ff., 74ff.; ii, 36ff., 77ff.; iv, 110ff.
Trachones: *ADelt* xxi (1966) B. 104ff.
Vari: *BCH* lxxxvii (1963) 715ff.; lxxxvi (1962) 658; *ADelt* xvii (1961–2)
  B. 37ff.; xix (1964) B. 72; xx (1965) B. 112ff.; xxi (1966) B. 95ff.
Voula: *ADelt* xx (1965) B. 111.
Vouliagmeni: *ADelt* xxi (1966) B. 103f.
Vrilisia: *ADelt* xix (1964) B. 72.

INHUMATION
'Half Grave': *AE* 1958, 130f.
Adult in tub: *AM* lxxxi (1966) 67f.
Inscribed vases: *Thorikos* ii, 43; *ADelt* xx (1965) B. 115.

CREMATION
Kerameikos Ash urn: *AA* 1936, 188.
Children: *Hesp* xx (1951) 110ff.; *AM* lxxxi (1966) 14f.

CENOTAPHS
AA 1936, 188. See also section on State Graves.

OFFERINGS
Offering Places: *AM* lxxxi (1966) 26, 36, 44ff., 47, 53, 55f., 63f., 71ff., 91f., 95;
  AA 1940, 182; 1927, 346; *ADelt* ix (1922–5) B. 71.
Offering Ditches: *BCH* lxxxi (1957) 518; lxxxii (1958) 681; *AE* 1958, 67ff.; *AA*
  1964, 432ff., 450.

Clay mourners: *AA* 1964, 455.

Dummy *alabastra*: *Hesp* xx (1951) 110ff.

Jewellery: *ADelt* xviii (1963) B. 34; *AM* xxv (1900) 453; lxxxi (1966) 85, 93.

Arms: *AA* 1935, 271ff.; R. Higgins, *Catalogue of the Terracottas—British Museum* i (1954) 172, 183; *Olympiabericht* v (1956) 62 and nn. 62ff.; *ADelt* xxiii (1968) B. 83; *AM* lxxxi (1966) 50.

Lead 'Coffins' and curse tablet: *AM* lxxxi (1966) 38 n. 6, 54.

WHITE-GROUND LEKYTHOI

A. Fairbanks, *Athenian White Lekythoi* (1907, 1914); W. Riezler, *Attische Weissgrundige Lekythen* (1914); E. Buschor, *Attische Lekythen der Parthenonzeit* (1925); J. Beazley, *Attic White Lekythoi* (1938).

MOUNDS AND BUILT TOMBS

Mounds: *AM* lxxxi (1966) 77ff. (Eukoline's Mound); *AE* 1968, B. 44ff.; *ADelt* xxi (1966) B. 96.

Built Tombs and *peribolos* Tombs: Brückner, *op. cit.*; W. Wrede, *Attische Mauern* (1933), nos. 40, 56, 100, 101, 102, 103, and *Attika* 20ff., 30ff.; *Mitt. d. Inst.* ii (1949) 7ff.; *AAA* ii (1969) 334ff. ('mound', but perhaps a Built Tomb).

STATE GRAVES

Excavations: *AM* xxxv (1910) 183ff.; *AA* 1965, 301ff.; 1969, 31ff.

Ancient Literature: Thu. ii 34; Paus. i 29; *Ath. Pol.* 58. 1; D. 40; Lys. 2; Pl. *Menex.*; Diodoros Periegetes (*FGH* no. 372).

Tomb of the Lacedaimonians: *AA* 1915, 111ff.; 1930, 89ff.; 1937, 200; 1965, 314ff.; *ADelt* xvii (1961–2) B. 18f.

Tombs between *horoi* 2 and 3: *AA* 1938, 612ff.; 1940, 344; 1942, 206ff.; 1965, 313f.

Tomb at *horos* 3 ('Chabrias' '): *AA* 1965, 322ff.

Discussions of the archaeological and literary evidence: J. Wenz, *Studien zu attischen Kriegergräbern* (1913); F. Jacoby, *JHS* lxiv (1944) 37ff. (*patrios nomos*), and *Classical Quarterly* xxxviii (1944) 65ff. (*Genesia*); W. Kierdorf, *Erlebnis und Darstellung der Perserkriege* (1966) 83ff.; K. Meuli, *Der griechische Agon* (1968) 62ff.; D. Bradeen, *Classical Quarterly* lxiii (1969) 145ff. (casualty lists).

GRAVESTONES

General: A. Conze, *Die attischen Grabreliefs* (1890–4); M. Collignon, *Les Statues Funéraires*; H. Diepolder, *Die attischen Grabreliefs* (1931); T. Dohrn, *Attische Plastik* (1957); Johansen, *Attic Grave-Reliefs*; S. Karouzou, *AM* lxxi (1956) 124ff. (painted); H. Möbius, *Die Ornamente der griechischen Grabstelen* (1968); Riemann, *Ker.* ii; G. Richter, *Catalogue of Greek Sculpture: Metropolitan Museum*

(1954) 47ff.; M. Bieber, *The Sculpture of the Hellenistic Age* (1961); S. Adam, *The Technique of Greek Sculpture* (1966); C. Clairmont, *Gravestone and Epigram* (1970)—this appeared too late for full account of it to be taken here. Legislation: Cic. *de Leg.* ii 59ff.; F. Eckstein, *JdI* lxxiii (1958) 18ff.; J. Kirchner, *Die Antike* xv (1939) 93ff.; R. S. Young, *AJA* lii (1948) 377ff.; Möbius, *op. cit.*, 101ff.

(The following references include gravestones mentioned in the text which are not in Conze's corpus of Attic grave reliefs.)

Slab *stelai*: *BCH* lxxi/lxxii (1947–8) 389.

Rosette *stelai*: Möbius, *op. cit.*, 108, and *Studia Varia* (1967) 24f., 32; *Ker.* vi. 2, 411 and n. 24 (significance of rosettes); *AA* 1936, 195f. and Möbius, *op. cit.*, 108, n. 113a (Hipparete's rosette). Rosettes on sides of *stelai*: Epigraphical Museum, Athens, no. 10281. Single rosette on principal face: Eretria Museum. Representation on vases: *Anthemion*: *ARV* 1239, 58, cf. Möbius, *op. cit.*, pl. 10a.

Relief *stelai*: Conze no. 763, pl. 120; cf. *ARV* 754, 14 (Tymbos Painter).

Vases: Conze nos. 1690–1734; F. Brommer, *Madrider Mitteilungen* x (1969) 155ff. ('Huge *Lekythoi*'); *AE* 1953–4 ii, 237ff. (stone *lekythoi* with tomb scenes); B. Schmaltz, *Untersuchungen Marmorlekythen* (1970); Bieber, *op. cit.*, 63f.; Richter, *Catalogue* 48f.; *Ker.* ii, inv. 4867, pl. 4.1 (woman with child on *loutrophoros*); Conze no. 1146 (Myrrhine); S. Karouzou, *NM Coll.Sc.* 78 (no. 2584, inscribed *horos mnematos*), 112 (no. 896, vase scene), 112 (no. 4498, base), 114 (no. 815, vase scene).

Columns: Collignon, *op. cit.*, 37ff.; *AM* iv (1879) 299ff.; Conze no. 1740 (Bion); Brückner, *op. cit.*, 108ff.; *ADelt* xix (1964) A. pl. 10 (column with cauldron); cf. *AM* li (1926) 98ff., and Museo Nazionale Romano, Sala I, no. 135980.

Bases: S. Karouzou, *NM Coll.Sc.* 48 (no. 4502, 'Apple-picking'), 109 (nos. 3416–7, Salamis relief slabs), 111 (no. 3640, Piraeus slab). For revetment slabs, cf. *AA* 1932, 189f., and fig. 2; *Illustrated London News* 27 June 1931, 1098 ('Dexileos base', *NM* 3708), and *AA* 1931, 217ff., figs. 1–3.

Gravestones with Figure Decoration: Möbius, *Studia Varia* 61f. (recent bibliography) and *AM* lxxxi (1966) 136ff.; lxxix (1964) Beil. 48 (Eupheros); *AAA* i (1968) 85ff.; *Hesp* Suppl. viii (1949) pl. 17a (Athenian decree relief of about 430 BC); Diepolder, *op. cit.*, pl. 16 (Chairedemos and Lykeas) and pl. 23 (Hippomachos and Kallias); *AM* xlix (1934) pl. 5 (Ampharete).

Architectural Frames: *Mus. Helveticum* viii (1951) 147ff.; Adams, *op. cit.*, 17, 38.

STATUARY

Seated Figures: Collignon, 118ff.; Helbig[4] no. 123; *JdI* lxxiv (1959) 137ff.; lxxvi (1961) 72ff.; Helbig[4] no. 341; P. Herrmann, *Das Gräberfeld von Marion auf Cypern* (1888) 40ff.; Collignon, 185; P. Dikaios, *A Guide to the Cyprus Museum* (1961) 140, no. 4 (inv. no. C 240). Relief decoration: Collignon,

107ff.; Blümel, K 55; Karouzou, *NM Coll. Sc.* 108 (no. 1688, Doric frieze); H. Bloesch, *Antike Kunst in der Schweiz* (1943) 74f. (pediment). Servant girls: Blümel, K 13 a, b; Collignon, 210ff.; Bieber, *op. cit.*, 64; *AM* x (1885) 404f. (Diocharian Gate); Karouzou, *NM Coll. Sc.* 120 (no. 825, Menidi/Acharnai). Scythian Bowmen: Collignon, 200ff. and Karouzou, *NM Coll. Sc.* 116 (nos. 823–4).

'Herculaneum Maidens': Collignon, 165ff.; Bieber, *op. cit.*, 22f.; Karouzou, *NM Coll. Sc.* 86 (no. 3622), 126 (no. 1005).

Sphinxes: Collignon, 214ff.; Conze nos. 1680–2, and no. 1005, pl. 195 (supporting vase); *Ker.* ii, inv. 4119, pl. 3.1; J. Pollard, *Seers, Shrines and Sirens* (1965) 137ff.; A. Furtwängler, *Mün. Jb. Bild. Kunst* i (1906) 1ff.; *AM* lxxxi (1966) 137; Blümel, K 40 (Silenis' gravestone); *ARV* 755, 40 (*lekythos* with sphinx).

Sirens: Collignon, 216ff.; Bieber, *op. cit.*, 29; Conze nos. 1663–77; Pollard, *op. cit.*, 137ff. and 141ff. (summary of earlier studies); Conze nos. 1666 and 1666a (mourning women); Brückner, *op. cit.*, 57ff.

Men: Collignon, 144ff.; G. Richter, *The Portraits of the Greeks* (1965) 3ff.

Children: Collignon, 188ff.

Animals: General: Collignon, 226ff.; Bieber, *op. cit.*, 63.

Lions: Brückner, *op. cit.*, 74ff.; Karouzou, *NM Coll. Sc.* 126f.; *ADelt* xix (1964) B. 67; xx (1965) B. 123; *AAA* ii (1969) 263ff.; *AJA* lxxii (1968) 99ff.; *The Museum Year*—Boston Fine Arts Museum (1965) 66; *Olympische Forschungen* iv (1959) 48ff.; *Arch. Class.* i (1949) 113ff.; iv (1952) 1ff.; xx (1968) 321ff. Panthers: Käppeli Collection, *Kunstwerke der Antike* (E. Berger) A 16; *AA* 1912, 121f.; 1914, 455; Möbius, *op. cit.*, 105.

Dogs: Collignon, 240ff.; Bieber, *op. cit.*, 63; *AA* 1965, 322ff.; *ADelt* ix (1924–5) B. 31f.; *AJA* lxxii (1968) 95ff.; Brückner, *op. cit.*, 83ff.; *Ker.* ii, 100f.; cf. *stele* with dog in relief, *Antike Kunst* xiii (1970) 95ff.

Bull: Brückner, *op. cit.*, 74ff.; W. Riezler, *op. cit.*, 122f. pl. 57 (NM 1938); *Olymp. Forsch.* iv, 46.

REUSE AND REPRODUCTION OF GRAVE MONUMENTS

Karouzou, *NM Coll. Sc.* 110 (no. 1022; names of sons added); ibid., 107 (no. 818, figures chiselled away); Epigraphical Museum no. 10432 (record relief recut); P. Zanker, *AA* 1965, 145ff. (Cretan 'Atticizing' grave relief). See also Chapter XII.

ICONOGRAPHY OF GRAVE RELIEFS

See general notes under 'gravestones', adding: J. Thimme, *Antike Kunst* vii (1964) 16ff., and *AA* 1967, 199ff.; N. Himmelmann-Wildschutz, *Studien zum Ilissos-Relief* (1956); C. Karouzos, *Münchener Jb. Bild. Kunst* xx (1969) 1ff.

Gestures: Johansen, ch. 2; G. Neumann, *Gesten und Gebärden* (1965) 151ff.

NOTES TO CHAPTER VII

FUNERAL RITES

GENERAL

L. Deubner, *Attische Feste* (1932), especially 93ff. and 229ff.; S. Eitrem, *Opferritus und Voropfer* (1914); K. Hermann, *Lehrbuch der griechischen Privatalterthümer* iv³ (1882), sections 39f.; K. Meuli in *Phyllobolia für Peter von der Mühll* (1946) 185ff.; P. Stengel, *Die griechische Kultusaltertümer* (1920), and *Opferbrauche der Griechen* (1910); U. von Wilamowitz-Moellendorf, *Der Glaube der Hellenen* (1926, 1932); E. Evans-Pritchard, *Theories of Primitive Religion* (1965).

LEGISLATION

See Notes to Chapters VI and VIII, adding A. Martina, *Solon* (1968) frr. 465–76; E. Ruschenbusch, *Solonos Nomoi* (1966).

ANNUAL RITES

C. Hignett, *History of the Athenian Constitution* (1952) 61ff. (*gene*); F. Jacoby, *Classical Quarterly* xxxviii (1944) 56ff.; *FGH* IIIb Suppl. (1954) i, 544f.; ii, 439f. (Philochorus, no. 168); N. Wyse, *The Speeches of Isaeus* (1904) 269ff.

WATER IN FUNERARY RITES

A. B. Cook, *Zeus* iii (1940) 354ff., 370ff.; R. Ginouvès, *Balaneutiké*, 239ff.; D. Lucas, *Proc. Camb. Phil. Soc.* 1969, 60ff.; M. Nink, *Die Bedeutung des Wassers im Kult und Leben der Alten* (1960 reprint of *Philologus* Suppl. xiv (1921)); L. Mouliner, *Le Pur et l'Impur dans la Pensée des Grecs* (1952) 76ff.

VESSELS

Spouted vessel with low foot: Feytmans, *Les Louteria Attiques*; H. Kenner, *ÖJh* xxix (1935) 109ff.

'Louteria': *JdI* xiv (1899) 103ff. (Menidi); D. Amyx, *Hesp* xxvii (1958) 221ff.; B. Shefton, *Hesp* xxxi (1962) 330ff.; Karouzou, *Ta Angeia tou Anagyrountos*.

Lebetes gamikoi: R. Lullies, *JdI* lxi/lxii (1946–7) 74; J. Boardman, *BSA* xlvii (1952) 30ff.; *AM* lxxxi (1966) 72ff.

Loutrophoros: Cook, *op. cit.*, 354ff., 370ff.; J. Frazer, *Pausanias' Description of Greece* v (1898) 388ff.; L. Kahil in *Gestalt und Geschichte* (1967) 146ff.; K. Johansen in *Poulsen Festschrift* (1941) 67ff.; E. Karydi, *AM* lxxviii (1963) 90ff.; H. Rose, *Class. Philology* xx (1925) 238ff.

Hydria: E. Diehl, *Die Hydria* (1964) 128ff., pl. 33 (Corinthian *prothesis*) and pl. 44 (South Italian *prothesis*); *AM* lxxxi (1966) 21, 42, 63; Laval University, Quebec, red-figure *hydria* with *prothesis* on shoulder (H. Giroux).

SELECTED LITERARY REFERENCES AND COMMENTARIES

Miasma: E. *Hipp.* 1437–9; W. Barrett, *Euripides Hippolytos* (1964) 414; E. *Alc.* 22.

Legislation: Cic. *de Leg.* ii 59ff.; *FGH* no. 228; F. Wehrli, *Demetrios von Phaleron* (1949); Plu. *Solon* 21; D. 43.62; Pl. *de Leg.* 12.958D–960B.

Burial: Ael. *V. H.* v 14 (written laws); E. *Ph.* 1447–50, *Suppl.* 524–7; A. *Th.* 1013ff.; S. *Aj.* 1381ff.; S. *Ant.* 1072ff. Denial of burial: S. *Ant.* 255f., *Aj.* 1332f.; X. *H.G.* i 7.22; Thu. i 138.6 (Themistocles). Duty of the family: A. *Ag.* 1551–9; E. Fraenkel, *Aeschylus Agamemnon* (1950) 735f.; cf. A. *Ch.* 8f.; D. 43.58ff.; Is. 4.19; Lys. 19.59(family, friends and *demarch*). Burial of parents: Is. 2.36; 6.64f., and Wyse, *op. cit.*, 263f.; cf. E. *Alc.* 664ff., *Med.* 1032ff.; Pl. *Hp. Ma.* 291D/E; Din. 2.8.

Expense: Is. 2.35f.; 8.25f.; and Wyse, *op. cit.*, 263, 605f.; Pl. *de Leg.* 12.959D.

Prothesis: Antiphon 6.34; Ar. *Ec.* 1030ff., *Lys.* 599ff.; D. 43.62; E. *El.* 148f., *Hec.* 653f., 1089, *Supp.* 826; Is. 8.22f.; Men. *Asp.* 344ff., 3 59ff.; Pl. *de Leg.* 12.959A; J. Denniston, *Euripides Electra* (1939) 67 (gestures of grief); Eustathius on *Iliad* xix 212 (face turned towards the door).

Third Day rites at the grave and at home: For the traditional interpretation, E. Rohde, *Psyche* (1894) ch. 5, n. 83; A. *Ch.* 8f., *Pers.* 610; Antiphon 6.34; Ar. *Lys.* 611ff.; D. 43.62; E. *I.T.* 166; *Or.* 115, 1187; Is. 2.37; Pl. *de Leg.* 12. 959E–960B; Plu. *Solon* 21; Wyse, *op. cit.*, 264f.; Cic. *de Leg.* ii 59, 64; E. *Alc.* 98ff. (vessel outside the door); cf. Ar. *Ec.* 1033 and perhaps also Men. *Asp.* 467. For later references to the practice: Pollux viii 65; Hesychius and Suidas, s.v. *ardanion*.

Meal: Hegesippos, T. Kock, *Comicorum Atticorum Fragmenta* iii (1888) 312, fr. 1, v. 11–16; Men. *Asp.* 232f.; Aen. Tact. 10.5; A. *Ch.* 483ff.; Artem. O. i 14; v 82; D. 18.288; Plu. *Arist.* 21; cf. Lucian *de Luct.* 24; Cic. *de Leg.* ii 59; D. 43.58 (purification of the house); cf. E. *Her.* 922ff., 1145; Meuli, *op. cit.*, 199 (festival to mark end of mourning).

Ninth Day: Aeschines 3.226; Is. 2.36; 8.39; Wyse, *op. cit.*, 264f., 619f.

End of Mourning: Aeschines 3.77; Lys. 1.14; Harpokration and Suidas, s.v. *triakas*; cf. Pollux i 66 (30 days); Plu. *Lyc.* 27 (11 days). For *ta nomizomena*: E. Bruck, *Totenteil und Seelgerät* (1926) 177ff.

Annual (selected): *AB* i, 75ff.; D. 43.65; 57.28; Hdt. iv 26; Is. 2.10, 46; 6.51, 65; 7.30, 32; 8.15; 9.7, 36; Pl. *de Leg.* 717E; Philochorus, *FGH* no. 328; Wyse, *op. cit.*, 269ff.; *Ath. Pol.* 55.3; Din. 2.17; Is. 2.46; 9.7; Lykourgos 25.60; Pl. *de Leg.* 717B (ancestral objects).

Water (references only to passages cited in the text): Pl. *Ph.* 115a, 116 (Socrates); E. *Alc.* 158ff. (Alcestis); S. *O.C.* 1598ff. (Oedipus); E. *Alc.* 74ff. (preparation of the body); E. *Ph.* 1667 and S. *El.* 84 (drink offerings); E. *Alc.* 424 (Thanatos); E. *Hec.* 495f. and cf. *Suppl.* 826 (ashes poured over the head); E. *Or.* 42 (Orestes); Athenaeus 409F–410A (Kleidemos, *aponimma*).

THE HELLENISTIC PERIOD

ATHENS

Kerameikos (Thriasian/Dipylon and Sacred Gates): See Notes to Chapter VI; *ADelt* xix (1964) B. 60ff.; xxii (1967) B. 86ff.; xxiii (1968) B. 66; *AM* lxxxi (1966) 75ff., 108ff., 122ff.; *AA* 1932, 192ff.; 1933, 282; 1935, 272ff.; 1942, 224ff.

Erian Gate: See Notes to Chapter VI; *AE* 1968 B. 48; *Hesp* xxxii (1963) 125ff.; *ADelt* xxiii (1968) B. 43ff., 79.

Between Erian and Acharnian Gates: *ADelt* xxiii (1968) B. 35ff., 75.

Acharnian Gate: *BCH* lxxxvi (1962) 644; *ADelt* xviii (1963) B. 35; xxiii (1968) B. 39ff.

Diocharian Gate: See Notes to Chapter VI; *ADelt* xvi (1960) B. 27.

Diomeian, Itonian and Haladian Gates: *ADelt* xix (1964) B. 58; xxi (1966) B. 65, 68f.; xxii (1967) B. 73.

Long Walls: *ADelt* xvii (1961–2) B. 25f.; xx (1965) B. 98; xxii (1967) B. 70; xxiii (1968) B. 39.

Intra-mural: *ADelt* xxiii (1968) B. 57.

CEMETERY PLANS

AM lxxxi (1966) 75ff.; *ADelt* xxiii (1968) B. 43ff.

ASH URNS

Hesp xxxii (1963) 126ff. (marble urn with lead liner); *AA* 1942, 243.

Griffin urn: H. B. Walters, *Catalogue of Terracottas* (1903) 186, C12; cf. *NSc* 1897, 479 and 1924, 100.

OFFERING PLACES

AM lxxxi (1966) 78, 98, 91f.

OFFERINGS

Fusiform *unguentaria: Hesp* iii (1934) 311ff., 472ff.; *AM* lxxxi (1966) 81, 108.

Gold: *ADelt* xxiii (1968) B. 88 (band); *AA* 1942, 239f. (jewellery); *AA* 1942, 238; *Hesp* xxxii (1963) 126; *ADelt* xxiii (1968) B. 88 (wreaths and leaves).

Silver mirror: *AE* 1968, B. 48.

Ivory handle and inlay; *AA* 1942, 240.

'Charon's Fee': *AA* 1942, 243; *Hesp* xxxii (1963) 126f.; *ADelt* xx (1965) B. 98.

LEGISLATION

See Notes to Chapter VI, adding: *FGH* no. 228 (Demetrios of Phaleron); Dio. Laert. v 75ff.; J. Kirchner, *Die Antike* xv (1939) 93ff.; H. Süsserott, *Griechische Plastik des IV. Jhr. v.C.* (1938) 120f., and n. 136; Möbius, *op. cit.*, 113, n. 178.

GRAVESTONES

Kioniskos: Conze iv, 5f., 10ff., 21; *Olympiabericht* v, 62, nn. 62f.

Labellum: Conze iv, 6f.; Feytmans, *op. cit.*, 41ff.; *BCH* vi (1882) 500ff. (invocation to the gods); Diehl, *Hydria* 65ff.; Ginouvès, *op. cit.*, 251ff.; Kenner, *ÖJh* xxix (1935) 109ff.

Trapeza: Conze, iv, 7f., 13ff.; Plu. *Vit. X. Or.* 838B–D (Isokrates) and 842E (Lykourgos); *AM* lxxxi (1966) 155f.; *AE* 1963, 46ff.; Brückner, 66, 76, 100, 102.

Gravestones with figure decoration, third to second centuries: Möbius, *op. cit.*, 113, n. 180; *AM* lxxi (1956) 119ff.

NOTES TO CHAPTER IX

THE EARLY PERIOD

See the Gazetteer for references to sites named.
For the Early Iron Age see especially Desborough, *PGP*, and A. M. Snodgrass, *The Dark Ages of Greece* (1971).
Homer: Andronikos; G. S. Kirk, *Museum Helveticum* xvii (1960) 195.

NOTES TO CHAPTER X

EVERYMAN'S GRAVE

See the Gazetteer for references to sites named.
Trees: C. Boetticher, *Der Baumkultus der Hellenen* (1856) 276f.; Pl. *de Leg.* 947.
Sacred areas: W. Vollgraff, 'Inhumation en terre sacrée dans l'antiquité grecque', *Mém. prés. a l'Acad. des Inscr.* xiv. 2 (1951) 315ff.
Cremation: H. L. Lorimer, 'Pulvis et Umbra', *JHS* liii (1933) 161ff.; D. Mustilli, *Annuario* xv/xvi (1932–3) 267ff.
Orientation: H. J. Rose, *Classical Review* xxxiv (1920) 141ff.
Disturbed burial: Athens, *Hesp* xxiv (1955) 187ff.; A. Parrot, *Malédictions et Violations de Tombes* (1939); *ADelt* xx (1965) pl. 284a (Thebes, reused *stelai*).
Criminals: *RE* Suppl. vii, s.v. 'Todestrafe' (K. Latte); Phaleron, *ADelt* ii (1916) 49ff.
Slaves: E. F. Bruck, *Totenteil und Seelgerät* (1926) 32, 128; F. Bömer, *Untersuchungen über die Religion der Sklaven in Griechenland und Rom* (1958–63) 88, 994ff.

NOTES TO CHAPTER XI

RITES AND OFFERINGS

GENERAL

Nilsson, especially 40–2, 174ff., 374ff., 714f.; K. F. Hermann, *Lehrbuch der griechischen Privataltertümer* iv³ (1882) sections 39, 40, for evidence in ancient authors.

LEGISLATION

Nilsson, 714f. Keos: F. Sokolowski, *Lois sacrées des Cités grecques* (1969) no. 97. Delphi: ibid., no. 77. Crete: *Insc. Creticae* iv, 22, 46, 76. Gambreion: F. Sokolowski, *Lois sacrées d'Asie Mineure* no. 16. Thasos: F. Sokolowski, *Lois sacrées: Suppl.* no. 64. Nisyros: G. Dittenberger, *Sylloge³* no. 1220. Pautalia: *BCH* xciv (1970) 113ff. Pl. *de Leg.* 947, 958–60. Sparta: Plu. *Lyk.* 27. Thessaly: Schol. Homer, *Iliad* xxii 397; xxiv 15.

DIRGES

E. Reiner, *Die rituelle Totenklage der Griechen* (1938).

GAMES

K. Meuli, *Der griechische Agon* (1968).

GEOMETRIC PROTHESIS SCENES

AM liv (1929) pl. 2 (Samos); E. Pfuhl, *Malerei und Zeichnung der Griechen* iii, fig. 17 (Thebes).

OFFERINGS: GENERAL

S. Eitrem, *Opferritus und Voropfer der Griechen und Römer* (1915); P. Stengel, *Opferbräucher der Griechen* (1910); D. M. Robinson, *Excavations at Olynthus* xi (1942) 174ff.; J. Thimme, *AA* 1967, 199ff.
Strigils: Argos strigil on forehead, *ADelt* xv (1938) 40ff. Sickles: *ADelt* xii (1929) 212ff. (Rheneia); R. M. Dawkins, *Artemis Orthia* (1929) 285ff. (Sparta). Used by children: Aristophanes fr. 139.
Astragals: R. Hampe, *Die Stele aus Pharsalos* (1951) 15f.; *NSc* 1913, Suppl. 9, grave 587 (Locri); *AA* 1956, 215, 218, fig. 14 (Tarentum, whip).
Hydriai: E. Diehl, *Die Hydria* (1964); B. F. Cook, *Inscribed Hadra Vases* (1966).
Orphic plaques: A. Olivieri, *Lamellae aureae Orphicae* (1915); W. K. C. Guthrie, *Orpheus and Greek Religion* (1935) 171ff.; *AE* 1950–1, 80ff. (Pharsalos).
Coins: E. F. Bruck, *Totenteil und Seelgerät* (1926) 145; in flask, *Opusc. Athen.* vii (1967) 187f. Ghost money: *Hesp* xxxii (1963) 125f. (Athens); *NSc* 1956, 386f. (Rhegion); *NSc* 1907, 743, 747 (Syracuse); E. A. Gardner, *Megalopolis* (1892) 9f.; *ADelt* xxii (1967) B. 164ff. (Sicyon).

Spits and firedogs: P. Courbin, *Annales* xiv (1959) 211f.; *BCH* lxxxi (1957) 370ff. (Argos); lxxxvii (1963) 292ff. (Kouklia); xci (1967) 343f. (Salamis); Kavousi, unpublished.

Shoes: E. Samter, *Geburt, Hochzeit, Tod* (1911) 206ff.; C. M. Robertson, *Greek Painting* (1959) 157 (painted *stele*); S. Marinatos, *Kleidung* (1967) pl. 6 (clay, Geometric); R. Naumann-B. Neutsch, *Palinuro* ii (1960) 159; *NSc* 1957, 388 (Rhegion, sarcophagus); *BCH* xci (1967) 827 (Argos).

False jewellery: R. Lullies, *Vergoldete Terrakotta-Appliken aus Tarent* (1962) 43f.

Head bands and masks: Andronikos, 41ff.; D. Ohly, *Griechische Goldbleche* (1953) 68f.; K. F. Johansen, *Exochi* (1958) 177f.; *BSA* xxiv (1919–21) 21; xxvi (1923–5) 23, pl. 3a (Macedonia, early); B. Hrouda, *Tell Halaf* iv (1962) pls. 1.8, 2.9; P. Wolters, *AM* xxi (1896) 367ff. (head piece from Athens); P. Amandry, *Coll. Helène Stathatos* i (1953) 36ff., 49f., iii (1963) 191; A. von Salis, *Museum Helveticum* xiv (1957) 68f. (in situ, late); E. Minns, *Scythians and Greeks* (1913) 507; *Materials and Researches* (Moscow) lxix (1959) 203; P. Jacobsthal, *Greek Pins* (1956) 201 (Trebenishte).

Vase decoration: *Expl. Délos* xvii, pl. 8, Bb 1; *PAE* 1952, 159, fig. 4 (Eretria); *Annuario* x/xii (1927/9) 605–7 (Kavousi), 402 (Afrati); *Corinth* xiii, 121 (white-ground *lekythoi*); H. Hoffmann, *Tarentine Rhyta* (1966) 111f.; K. P. Stähler, *Grab und Psyche des Patroklos* (1967, b.f. and r.f. scenes); S. Ferri, *Parola del Passato* xvi (1961) 174ff. (*kalos* inscriptions).

Clay figures: M. Collignon, *Les statues funéraires* (1911) 17f.; *Thera* ii, 24; *AM* lxxiii (1958) Beil. 83 (Thera); G. M. A. Richter, *Korai* (1968) figs. 86–102; *Annuario* x/xii (1927/9) 184, 196 (Afrati), 455 (Lato); *Clara Rhodos* vi/vii, 72 and *BM Cat. Terracottas* i, pls. 1.6, 2.14 (Kameiros); F. Winter, *Die Typen der figürlichen Terrakotten* (1903) 60 (Boeotia); *Apollo* 1969, 468 (Boeotia); *Coll. Stathatos* iii (1963) 117; *ADelt* xxi (1966) B.pl. 163d (Navarino); *Clara Rhodos* viii, 191, fig. 182 (Ialysos, bier); V. Karageorghis, *Exc. Salamis* i, 119f. (Cypriot death carts); *JdI* xxvi (1911) 90 (Tanagra *kline*); *AM* lxxix (1964) Beil. 55 (Athens *kline*).

Inscribed vases in Thera tombs: *PAE* 1961, 201ff.; *Ergon* 1969, 165f.

Food offerings: cf. *JHS* lxxxvi (1966) 2f.

Nails: *NSc* 1932, 145 (strigil); *Mon. Ant.* ix (1899) 256 (Camarina); *Olynthus* xi, 159f. (tile grave 304, cremations 300, 571).

OTHER SUBJECTS

Curses: Nilsson, 800ff.; *RE* s.v. 'Nekydaimon' (K. Preisendanz); *AM* lxxiii (1958) 94ff., lxxxi (1966) Beil. 51.1 (Athens); A. Audollent, *Defixionum Tabellae* (1904).

Red: F. von Duhn, *Archiv für Religionswissenschaft* ix (1906) 1ff., cf. 525ff.; 'Rote Farbe in Totenkult' in M. Ebert, *Reallexikon* xi (1927–8); *Opusc. Ath.* vi (1965) 137.

GRAVE MARKERS AND MONUMENTS

GENERAL

RE s.v. '*Stele*' (H. Möbius); Jeffery, for inscribed *stelai* and columns; Johansen, for a detailed summary; G. M. A. Hanfmann, review of von Hall, *AJA* lvii (1953) 230ff.
See the Gazetteer for further references.

EARLY STELAI

Andronikos, 107ff.; *ADelt* xvii (1961–2) A. 152ff. (Kymisala, pl. 88); *Theoria* (Festschrift Schuchhardt, 1960) 129ff. (Kimolos); R. Koldewey, *Neandria* (1891) 16f.

ARCHAIC STELAI

Samos, etc.: *AM* lviii (1933) 22ff., lxxiv (1959) 6ff.; *Antiquaries Journal* xxxix (1959) 188f. (Chios), 201f.
Daskylion: *Rev. Arch.* 1969, 17ff.; *Iranica Antiqua* vi (1966) 147ff.; *Istanbul Arch. Mus.* xiii/xiv (1967) 19ff.; *Istanbul Mitt.* xviii (1968) 161ff.
Corinth xiii, pl. 82.X.120. Aegina: *AA* 1938, 30. Chalcedon: *BSA* l (1955) 81ff. Kos: *AM* lxxi (1956) 121ff. Phanagoria: *Arch. Repts. 1962–3* 49, fig. 35.

NOT CERTAINLY GRAVESTONES

Laconian hero reliefs: M. Andronikos, *Peloponnesiaka* i (1956) 253ff. Paros: *ADelt* (1960) pl. 215. Prinias, Crete: Johansen, 80ff.; *BCH* lxxxiv (1960) 840.

EARLY CLASSICAL

Johansen, 120ff.; Richter, *AGA* 53ff.; E. Akurgal, *Zwei Grabstelen vorklassischer Zeit aus Sinope* (1955); H. Biesantz, *Die thessalischen Grabreliefs* (1965) 59ff.; G. Bakalakis, *Hellenika Amphiglypha* (1946); *Arch. Ereunes ste Thrake 1959–60* 13ff. Borgia stele: *AA* 1936, 65. Thrace: *AE* 1956, 199ff. Islands: G. Despinis, *Antike Plastik* vii (1967) 77ff.

CLASSICAL

Anthemion stelai: H. Möbius, *Die Ornamente der griechischen Grabstelen*[2] (1968). Thessaly: Biesantz, *op. cit.*
Boeotia: *JdI* xxviii (1913) 309ff. (Thespiae); *AE* 1920, 1ff. (painted); *ADelt* xxi (1966) B. pls. 189a, 203, 209; xxii (1967) A. 1ff., B. 234; *AAA* i (1968) 92ff.; ii (1969) 80f.; P. M. Fraser and T. Rönne, *Boeotian and West Greek Tombstones* (1957).
Thrace: *AM* lxxvii (1962) 197ff.

Rhodes: *Clara Rhodos* iv (1929–30) 37ff. (Krito and Timarista); *Marburger Winckelmannsprogramm* 1968, 74ff.

Crete: ibid., 39f.

HELLENISTIC

H. Möbius, *AA* 1969, 507ff.

East Greek: E. Pfuhl, *JdI* xx (1905) 47ff., 123ff.; l (1935) 9ff.

Rhodes: *AE* 1958, 208ff.

Alexandria: *AM* xxvi (1901) 258ff.

N. Firatli, *Les stèles funéraires de Byzance* (1964).

Demetrias: A. S. Arvanitopoulos, *AE* 1908, 1ff. and *Graptai Stelai Demetriados-Pagason* (1928); M. Andronikos, *Balkan Studies* v, 287ff.

Death-feast reliefs: N. Thönges-Stringaris, *AM* lxxx (1965) 1ff.; J. M. Dentzer, *Rev. Arch.* 1969, 195ff. (Asia Minor).

BLOCK MONUMENTS

General: G. Despinis, *AE* 1963, 46ff.; H. Möbius, *AM* lxxxi (1966) 154ff.; and see the Gazetteer.

Tanagra: *AM* xxviii (1903) 331ff. Chios: *BCH* lxxi/ii (1947–8) 273ff., lxxiii (1949) 384ff.; *BSA* lviii (1963) 63ff. Thrace: *ADelt* xviii (1963) A. 161.

Altars: See Notes to Chapter XVI.

STATUARY

General: M. Collignon, *Les statues funéraires* (1911).

Kouroi: G. M. A. Richter, *Kouroi*[3] (1970); *PAE* 1965, 183 (Thera; feet in situ); J. Boehlau, *Aus ionischen und italischen Nekropolen* (1898) 33f. (Samos); *AJA* lxv (1961) 51 (Pitane); G. Kleiner, *Ruinen von Milet* (1968) 127; *AE* 1937, 692f. (Keos).

Korai: Antike Plastik i (1962) 43ff. (Chios, Samos); *AM* lxxiii (1958) 117 (Thera).

Others: Seated women at Miletus: Kleiner, *op. cit.*, 127. Sphinxes on *tymboi* (Attic r.f.): *Mon. Piot* xxix (1927–8) pls. 5, 6. Sirens: E. Buschor, *Die Musen des Jenseits* (1944).

COLUMNS

Collignon, *op. cit.*; Jeffery. Ankara: E. Akurgal, *Die Kunst Anatoliens* (1961) fig. 249. Urns on columns: C. W. Vollgraff, *Compte-Rendu Acad. Ins.* 1946, 281ff.

HERMS AND PHALLOI

Nilsson, 504ff.; Collignon, *op. cit.*, 46; *RE* s.v. 'Phallos' 1728ff. (H. Herter); *JdI* xx (1905) 88ff.; cf. H. V. Herrmann, *Omphalos* (1959) 39ff.; L. Curtius in *Festschrift Klages* (1932) 19ff. (Ergili). Thera: *ADelt* xix (1964) 409, pl. 479a. Corinth: *Hesp* xxxviii (1969) 5f., 21f. *Athenian Agora* xi, 141. Verroia relief: *BCH* lxxxix (1965) 793. H. von Gall, *Die paphlagonischen Felsgräber* (1966) 114f.

NOTES TO CHAPTER XIII

COMMUNAL GRAVES AND CENOTAPHS

See the Gazetteer for references to sites outside Attica.

Marathon: Paus. i 32 (with Frazer's commentary); *Insc. Graecae* ii² 1006, lines 26, 69; *Hesp* v (1936) 225, xxxv (1966) 93ff.; *JHS* lxxxviii (1968) 14ff.; *AAA* iii (1970) 164ff.

Thermopylae: Hdt. vii 228.

Plataea: Hdt. ix 85; Thu. iii 58; Paus. ix 2.5, 6; Plu. *Arist.* 21.

Artemisium: Plu. *Them.* 8.

Gravestones of Corinthians and Argives: Jeffery, 119, 164.

Thasos: F. Sokolowski, *Lois sacrées: Suppl.* no. 64.

Salamis, Cyprus: *BCH* xci (1967) 328ff.; *AA* 1966, 242ff.; Karageorghis, *Salamis* (1969) ch. 4.

Athens: *AA* 1936, 186f.

J. Schäfer, 'Eidolon of Leonidas' in *Charites* (Festschrift Langlotz, 1957) 223ff.

Treatment of enemies: R. Lonis, *Les usages de la guerre entre grecs et barbares* (1969) 56ff.

Ecbatana lion: *Arch. Mitt. aus Iran* i (1968) pls. 45–7.

NOTES TO CHAPTER XIV

EPITAPHS

W. Peek, *Griechische Versinschriften* i (1955), a corpus of texts classified by subjects; here *GV*.

W. Peek, *Griechische Grabgedichte* (1960), a general introduction and selection with German translations.

R. Lattimore, *Themes in Greek and Latin Epitaphs* (1942).

G. Pfohl, *Greek Poems on Stones* i (1967).

C. Clairmont, *Gravestone and Epigram* (1970).

Chios, Heropytho: H. T. Wade-Gery, *The Poet of the Iliad* (1952) 8f.

Use of dative: *AM* xxxi (1906) 416.

Demetrias, childbed *stele*: Arvanitopoulos, *Graptai Stelai*, pl. 2.

Gravestone of Phoenician Antipatros in Athens: *GV* 1601; Conze no. 1175; *Corpus Ins. Semit.* i, pl. 23; *Ins. Graecae* ii/iii² 8388; *AM* xiii (1888) 310ff.; S. Karouzou, *National Archaeological Museum, Coll. of Sculpture* (1958) 117; *AJA* lxxiii (1969) 233; C. Clairmont, *Gravestone and Epigram* (1970) no. 38.

Sparta, 'with shield or on it': Plu. *Mor.* 241f.

See Abbreviations on references to epigrammatists.

NOTES TO CHAPTER XV

DECORATED SARCOPHAGI

General: C. Rodenwaldt, *Röm. Mitt.* lviii (1943) 2ff.

Chios: *PAE* 1952, 520ff.; *ADelt* i (1915) 67ff., fig. 5 (relief clay).

Samos: I. Kleemann in *Festschrift Matz* (1962) 44ff.; Boehlau, *op. cit.*, 14ff.

Athens: *Hesp* xx (1951) 75ff., fig. 3.

Taman: *Rev. Arch.* 1952, 89.

Clazomenian clay: R. M. Cook in *Corpus Vasorum Antiquorum, London* viii, 45ff., *Greek Painted Pottery* (1960) 138f.

Wood: C. Watzinger, *Griechische Halzsarkophage* (1905); E. Minns, *Scythians and Greeks* (1913) 322ff.; N. I. Sokolski, *Antichnie Derevyannie Sarkophagi* (1969); P. Jacobsthal, *Die melische Reliefs* (1931) 108f.; R. Lullies, *Vergoldete Terrakotta-Appliken aus Tarent* (1962) (cf. J. Weisner, *JdI* lxxviii (1963) 200ff.).

Sidon, etc.: I. Kleemann, *Die Satrapen-sarkophag aus Sidon* (1958); G. Mendel, *Catalogue des Sculptures, Istanbul* i (1912) 18ff.; E. Kukahn, *Anthropoide Sarkophage in Beyrouth* (1955).

Hellenistic: G. Kleiner, *Istanbuler Mitt.* vii, 1ff.; Vienna 169, Brunn-Bruckmann 493; *Thessalika* iv, 28ff.; *ADelt* xxiii (1968) B. 265; *AA* 1939, 449ff. (painted).

NOTES TO CHAPTER XVI

MONUMENTAL TOMBS, HEROA AND HELLENISTIC GREECE

GENERAL

F. Matz, 'Hellenistische und römische Grabbauten', *Die Antike* iv, 266ff.; G. Kleiner, *Diadochen-Gräber* (1963); G. Mansuelli, 'Monumento Funerario', in *Enc. dell'Arte Antica*.

On the architecture of tombs, see especially A. W. Lawrence, *Greek Architecture* (1957); W. B. Dinsmoor, *The Architecture of Ancient Greece* (1950); P. Petsas, *O Taphos ton Lefkadion* (1966); A. K. Orlandos, *Les matériaux de construction* ii (1969) 194ff. (corbelled tombs).

Klinai: K. G. Vollmoeller, *Griechische Kammergräber mit Totenbetten* (1901).

NON-GREEK AND LATE TOMBS IN ASIA MINOR

Paphlagonia: H. von Gall, *Die paphlagonischen Felsgräber* (1966); *AA* 1967, 585ff.

Galatia: Royal tombs at Karalar: *Türk Tarih* ii (1934) 102ff.; *Rev. Arch.* 1935. ii, 133ff.; *AA* 1967, 518ff.; cf. *AJA* lxxiv (1970) 175f.

Phrygia: E. Akurgal, *Phrygische Kunst* (1955); G. Perrot-C. Chipiez, *L'Histoire de l'Art* v (1890) 110f. and *VIII. Congr. Arch. Class.* (1963) 473 (Broken Tomb,

Ayazin); G. and A. Körte, *Gordion* (1904); R. S. Young, reports on Gordion, *AJA* lix (1955) on.

Lydia: H. C. Butler, *Sardis* i (1922) ch. 8; Perrot-Chipiez, *op. cit.*, 265ff. (tomb of Alyattes); *Rev. Arch.* 1876.ii, 73ff. (*klinai*); E. Akurgal, *Ruins of Turkey* (1969) 127 (pyramid tomb).

Caria: J. M. Cook, *BSA* l (1955) especially 165ff. (general); *BSA* xlvii (1952) 177 (tumuli, Burgaz); *BSA* lii (1957) 71 (chamber tombs, Idyma); *JHS* viii, 66ff. and *AM* xiii (1888) 273ff. (Assarlik); *Annuario* xxxix/xl (1961–2) 557ff., xliii/xliv (1965–6) 479f., 492 (Iasos)

Lycia: O. Benndorf and G. Niemann, *Reisen im südwestlichen Kleinasien* (1884); Perrot-Chipiez, *op. cit.*, 385 (town on Nereid Monument); F. N. Pryce, *British Museum Catalogue of Sculpture* i.1(1928) 117ff.; E. Akurgal, *Griechische Reliefs des VI. Jhr. aus Lykien* (1941); P. Demargne, *Xanthos* i (1958), ii (1963) 60f., iii (1969, Nereid Monument); *Ist. Mitt.* xvii (1967) 151ff. and *AJA* lxxvii (1970) (Limyra); *Rev. Ét. Anc.* 1962, 35ff. (sarcophagus); *AA* 1968, 178ff. (Kadyanda); *JHS* lxiii (1943)· 113ff. (false doors); *AJA* lxxiv (1970) 251–3 (Elmali); P. M. Fraser and G. E. Bean, *The Rhodian Peraea* (1954) 44f. (pyramid tomb); O. Benndorf and G. Niemann, *Das Heroon von Gjolbaschi-Trysa* (1889–91).

Pisidia: G. Kleiner, *Diadochen-Gräber* (1963); G. E. Bean, *Turkey's Southern Shore* (1968) 127f., 134f.; E. Akurgal, *Ruins of Turkey* (1969) 273ff.

Cilicia: *Mon. Asiae Minoris Ant.* iii (1931) 26, 28, 32, 57 (pyramid tombs).

Urartu: *Ist. Mitt.* xviii (1968) 58ff.

For references to other monuments outside Greece, see the Notes to the next Chapter.

THE DEAD HEROIZED

Cult at Bronze Age tombs: see Notes to Chapter I.

L. R. Farnell, *Greek Hero Cults and Ideas of Immortality* (1921) 361ff.; A. D. Nock in W. S. Ferguson, *The Attic Orgeones* (1944) 141ff.; K. Forbes, *Philologus* c (1956) 235ff.; C. Habicht, *Gottmenschtum und griechische Städte* (1956).

Altars: W. Altmann, *Die römischen Grabaltäre* (1905) 1–8; C. G. Yavis, *Greek Altars* (1949) 149ff.; *ADelt* xi (1927–8) B. 19ff. (Lesbos, post-Hellenistic?); *ADelt* xviii (1963) A. 161ff. (Thrace); P. M. Fraser, *BSA* lxvi (1971, Rhodes). Late *heroa*: *AJA* lxxiii (1969) 412ff. and see the Gazetteer.

ALEXANDRIA

R. Pagenstecher, *Nekropolis* (1919); A. Adriani, 'Alessandria' in *Encl. dell'Arte antica*; idem, *La nécropole de Moustafa Pacha* (1936); idem, *Ann. Mus. Gréco-romaine* 1935–9; idem, *Repertorio dell'arte dell'Egitto greco-romano*, Serie C, i-ii (1966); *JdI* lxv/lxvi (1950–1) 231ff.; A. Bernand, *Alexandrie la Grande* (1966) 155ff.; P. M. Fraser, *Ptolemaic Alexandria* (1971) i, 32ff., ii, 102ff.; G. Ville, *Rev. Arch.* 1969, 273ff.

ALEXANDER THE GREAT

Hephaistion's monument: F. R. Wüst, *ÖJh* xliv (1959) 147ff., and cf. the Ecbatana lion, our p. 367.

The hearse: K. Müller, *Der Leichenwagen Alexanders des Grossen* (1905); H. Bulle, *JdI* xxi (1906) 52ff.

Royal tombs of Alexandria: H. Thiersch, *JdI* xxv (1910) 55ff.; F. Jacoby, *Rheinisches Museum* 1903, 461f.; M. L. Bernhard, *Rev. Arch.* 1956, 129ff.

NOTES TO CHAPTER XVII

COLONIES AND NEIGHBOURS

See the Gazetteer for references to sites named. Jeffery, for inscribed monuments.

THE WEST

See the topographical bibliography with J. Bérard, *La colonisation grecque* (1941); T. J. Dunbabin, *The Western Greeks* (1948); recent reports on Sicily and South Italy in *AA* 1954, 465ff.; 1956, 193ff.; 1964, 657ff.; 1966, 255ff.

R. Pagenstecher, *Unteritalische Grabdenkmäler* (1912); H. Klumbach, *Tarentiner Grabkunst* (1937); P. Wuilleumier, *Tarente* (1939); E. Langlotz, *The Art of Magna Graecia* (1965); *AJA* lxxiv (1970) 125ff.; F. T. Bertocchi, *La pittura funeraria apula* (1964); F. von Duhn, *Italische Gräberkunde* (1924–39); D. Randall-MacIver, *Villanovans and Early Etruscans* (1924), *The Iron Age in Italy* (1927); F. Schachermeyr, *Etruskische Frühgeschichte* (1929); P. G. Gierow, *The Iron Age Culture of Latium* i (1964) 47ff.; E. Gjerstad, *Early Rome* iv (1966) 245ff.; M. F. Briguet, *Rev. Arch.* 1968, 49ff. (clay sarcophagi).

THE NORTH

Illyria: *Archaeology* xix (1966) 43ff. (Atenica).

Thrace (see also the Gazetteer for Greek sites): B. D. Filow, *Die archaische Nekropole von Trebenischte* (1927), *Die Grabhügelnekropole bei Duvanlij* (1934); P. Jacobsthal, *Greek Pins* (1956) 201ff. (Trebenishte); *ÖJh* xxvii (1931) 1ff. (Trebenishte); *JdI* xlv (1930) 285ff. (Duvanlij); *Rev. Arch.* 1951.ii, 24ff. (Brezovo); *Starinar* ix/x (1958–9) 281ff. (Demir Kapu).

South Russia: E. Minns, *Scythians and Greeks* (1913); M. Rostovtzeff, *Iranians and Greeks in South Russia* (1922); G. von Kieseritzky and C. Watzinger, *Griechische Grabreliefs aus Südrussland* (1909); C. Watzinger, *Griechische Holzsarkophage* (1905); Olbia graves with amphorae, *AA* 1912, 351; 1913, 194.

CYPRUS

E. Gjerstad, *Swedish Cyprus Expedition* iv. 2 (1948) 29ff. (Archaic and Classical); O. Vessberg and A. Westholm, ibid., iv. 3 (1956) 50ff. (Hellenistic); K. Nikolaou, *Ancient Monuments of Cyprus* (1958).

V. Karageorghis, *Excavations in the Necropolis of Salamis* i (1967); annual reports in *BCH*; *Salamis* (1969).

P. Dikaios, *Guide to the Cyprus Museum* (1961), summary and *stelai*.

V. Wilson, *Rept. Dept. Ant. Cyprus* (1969) 56ff. (*stele*).

K. Nikolaou in *Mélanges K. Michalowski* 600ff. (Nea Paphos Hellenistic).

NEAR EAST

Tell Sukas: *AA* 1962, 374. Al Mina: *JHS* lviii (1938) 13f.

Babylon: L. R. Farnell, *Greece and Babylon* (1911) ch. 12; *AA* 1941, 795 (attributing seventh-century cremation to Greek influence!).

Carchemish: *Liverpool Annals* xxvi, 11ff. Deve Huyuk: *Liverpool Annals* vi, 95ff.

Hama: P. J. Riis, *Hama* ii. 3 (1948) 27ff. (on cremation in the Near East in general).

North Syria: E. Akurgal, *Späthethitische Bildkunst* (1949) 121ff. (*stelai*); *Birth of Greek Art* (1968).

Phoenicia: S. Moscati, *The World of the Phoenicians* (1968).

Marissa: J. D. Peters and H. Thiersch, *Painted Tombs in the Necropolis of Marissa* (1905).

Palestine: P. de Vaux, *Ancient Israel* 56ff.; *Bibl. Arch.* xxxiii (1970) 2ff.

PERSIA

General: *JHS* xlviii (1928) 142ff.; A. T. Olmstead, *History of the Persian Empire* (1948); E. Porada, *The Art of Ancient Iran* (1965) 146ff.

Tomb of Cyrus and related: D. Stronach, *Iran* ii (1964) 21ff.; L. vanden Berghe, *Festschrift Moortgat* (1964) 243ff.; C. Nylander, *Iranica Antiqua* vi (1966) 144ff.; Arrian, *Anabasis* vi 29.

F. Sarre and E. Herzfeld, *Iranische Felsreliefs* (1910).

Median rock-cut tombs: H. von Gall, *AA* 1966, 19ff.

Fire temples or tombs: B. Goldman, *Journal of Near Eastern Studies* xxiv (1965) 305ff.; D. Stronach, ibid., xxvi (1967) 278ff. and *Iran* iii (1965) 14ff.

EGYPT

E. A. Gardner, *Naucratis* ii (1888) 21ff.; J. Boardman, *Greeks Overseas* (1964) pl. 9c (Abusir *stele*).

NOTES TO CHAPTER XVIII

CONCLUSION

G. Childe, 'Directional Changes in Funerary Practices during 50,000 years', *Man* 1945, 13ff.

P. J. Ucko, 'Ethnography and archaeological interpretation of funerary remains', *World Archaeology* i (1969) 262ff., with bibliography.

E. E. Evans-Pritchard, *Theories of Primitive Religion* (1965).

L. Lévy-Bruhl, *The 'Soul' of the Primitive* (translation, 1965) part 2.

R. Hertz, *Death and the Right Hand* (translation, 1960).

SELECT GAZETTEER OF CEMETERIES OUTSIDE ATTICA

These are select references to the more important publications of finds and excavations. Studies of local types of monuments are cited in the Notes to Chapter XII. Indication is given in parenthesis of interesting features remarked in the text.

CRETE

General: I. Pini, *Beiträge zur minoischen Gräberkunde* (1968), includes consideration of PG and bibliography. See also the publications of Afrati and Fortetsa (Knossos).

A. Paraskioi. *AE* 1945/7, 47ff. (Geom. *tholos*).

Afrati. D. Levi in *Annuario* x/xii (1927/9).

Karphi. *BSA* xxxviii (1937–8) 100ff.

Kavousi. *AJA* v (1901) 125ff. (Geom. *tholos*).

Knossos, A. Ioannis. *BSA* lv (1960) 128ff. (PG and on reuse).

Knossos, Hogarth's tombs. *BSA* vi (1899–1900) 82ff.; xxix (1927–8) 224ff.

Knossos, Fortetsa. J. K. Brock, *Fortetsa* (1957); *BSA* lvi (1961) 68ff.

Knossos, Teke. *BSA* xlix (1954) 215ff.; lviii (1963) 34ff. (PG); lxii (1967) 57ff. (goldsmiths' *tholos*).

Knossos, others. *BSA* lviii (1963) 39ff. (PG); lxiii (1968) 133ff. (Geom.).

Kourtes. *AJA* v (1901) 287ff., 294ff. (Geom. chamber tombs, *tholoi*).

Lagou. *JHS* lvii (1937) 141 (Geom. *tholos*).

Ligortino. *ADelt* xvii (1961–2) B. 284f. (Geom. chamber tomb).

Piskokephalo. *PAE* 1953, 292f. (PG, Geom. chamber tomb).

Praisos. *BSA* viii (1901–2) 245ff. (Geom. chamber tombs).

Rotassi Embasos. *Kret. Chr.* 1955, 567; 1958, 468 (Geom. *tholos*).

Vrokastro. E. H. Hall, *Excavations in East Crete, Vrokastro* (1914).

EAST GREECE

Belevi. G. Perrot and C. Chipiez, *Histoire d l'Art* v (1890) 281f. (tumulus); *ÖJh* xxix (1934) Beibl. 116ff. (chamber tomb) and C. Praschniker, *Berlin VI. Kongr. Arch.* (1939) 405f. (its sculpture).

Chios. *ADelt* i (1915) 67ff. (town); *PAE* 1952, 520ff. (town, Rizari, sarcophagi); *BSA* xlix (1954) 126, 159ff. (town); xli (1940/5) 31ff. (various).

Clazomenae. *PAE* 1921, 16ff.

Cnidus, Lion Tomb. *Röm. Mitt.* lix (1944) 173ff.; *BSA* xlvii (1952) 181; Lawrence, *Greek Architecture* 196f.

Dardanos. *Anatolia* v (1960) 9ff. (chamber tomb).

Didyma. *AM* lxxi (1956) 145ff. (lion).

Ephesus. *Festschrift Eichler* (1967) 103ff.

Halicarnassus, Mausoleum. Dinsmoor, *Architecture of Ancient Greece*, 257ff.; K. Jeppesen, *Paradeigmata* (1958).

Ikaria. *ADelt* xviii (1963) B. 273ff.; *PAE* 1939, 141ff.

Kos. *Boll. d'Arte* xxxv (1950) 320ff.; *JdI* xlix (1934) 110ff. (Charmyleion).

'Larisa'. J. Boehlau and K. Schefold, *Larisa am Hermos* i (1940) 109ff.

Lesbos, Antissa. *BSA* xxxi (1930–1) 174ff.; xxxii (1931–2) 63ff.

Lesbos, other. *PAE* 1925–6, 150ff. (sarcophagus); *ADelt* xx (1965) B. 490 (Skala Loutron).

Melie. G. Kleiner, *Panionion und Melie* (1967) 161ff.

Miletus. G. Kleiner, *Ruinen von Milet* (1968) 124ff. (statuary), 127f. (*heroa*).

Mylasa. *Belleten* xvi 367ff. (chamber tomb).

Myrina. E. Pottier and S. Reinach, *La Nécropole de Myrina* (1888); *JdI* xxv (1910) 3ff. (chamber tomb near by).

Neandria. R. Koldewey, *Neandria* (1891).

Nisyros. *Clara Rhodos* vi/vii (1932–3) 471ff.

Pergamon. G. E. Bean, *Aegean Turkey* (1966) 91 (Asklepieion); *AA* 1966, 477f. (Mac. tomb, Elaia); Lawrence, *Greek Architecture* 229f. (crossed vault). Tumuli—*AA* 1906, 327; *AM* xxxii (1907) 240; xxxiii (1908) 428ff.; xxxv (1910) 388f.

Phocaea. *AA* 1914, 173; E. Akurgal, *Ruins of Turkey* (1969) 118 (chamber tombs).

Pitane. *AJA* lxv (1961) 51 (*kouros*); *Fasti Archeologici* xx (1965) 1984.

Priene. T. Wiegand, *Priene* (1904) 54f. (chamber tomb).

Rhodes town. *Clara Rhodos* i (1928) 53ff. (rock-cut); vi/vii (1932–3) 445ff.; *ADelt* xviii (1963) B. 324ff. (Classical); E. Dyggve, *Lindos* iii (1960) 498f. (Rhodine).

Rhodes, Exochi. K. F. Johansen, *Exochi, ein frührhodisches Gräberfeld* (1958 = *Acta Archaeologica* xxviii).

Rhodes, Ialysos. *Clara Rhodos* iii (1929); viii (1936) 7ff.; *Annuario* vi/vii (1923–4) 257ff.

Rhodes, Kameiros. *Clara Rhodos* iv (1931); vi/vii (1932–3) 1ff.

Rhodes, Lindos. *Lindos* iii (1960) 479ff.

Rhodes, Pontamo. *Clara Rhodos* ii (1932) 118ff.

Rhodes, Vroulia. K. F. Kinch, *Fouilles de Vroulia* (1914).

Samos. J. Boehlau, *Aus ionischen und italischen Nekropolen* (1898); *Antiquaries Journal* xxxix (1959) 202 (*stelai* overthrown); *Ath. Annals* ii (1969) 202ff. (pyre).

Smyrna (Bayrakli). *ÖJh* xxvii (1931) Beibl. 157f.; E. Akurgal, *Bayrakli, erster vorläufiger Bericht* (1950) 79ff.; *BSA* liii/liv (1958–9) 44ff., 49, 126; *Fasti Archeologici* vii (1952) 1593.

Smyrna, Tomb of Tantalus. *ÖJh* xxvii (1931) Beibl. 150ff.

CYCLADES ISLANDS

Andros. T. Sauciuc, *Andros* (1914).

Delos. *BCH* lxxxv (1961) 913ff.; lxxxviii (1964) 900f.; *Rev. Arch.* xli (1953) 10ff. (Archegesion); *ADelt* xii (1929) 181ff. (Rheneia); *Guide de Délos* (1965) 168f.

Kimolos. *BCH* lxxviii (1954) 146; *ADelt* xx (1965) B. 514; xxi (1966) B. 388ff.; N. M. Kontoleon in *Theoria* (Festschrift Schuchhardt) 129ff. (*stele*).

Melos. L. Ross, *Inselreisen* iii (1913) 10ff. (chamber tombs); *BSA* ii (1895–6) 71f., 75; iii (1896–7) 6.

Naxos. *AA* 1936, 159; *PAE* 1937, 117ff. Tsikalario—*ADelt* xviii (1963) B. 279ff.; xx (1965) B. 515ff.; xxi (1966) B. 391ff.

Paros. *AE* 1925–6, 114ff. (Classical); *ADelt* xviii (1963) B. 273 (Archaic); *AA* 1900, 23 and *JdI* l (1945) 66f. (raised sarcophagi).

Siphnos. *BSA* xliv (1949) 81ff.

Tenos. *Annuario* viii/ix (1935–6) 203ff.

Thera. H. von Gaertringen, *Thera* ii (1903) passim; 291ff. for Schiff's grave; *AM* xxviii (1903) 241ff.; *PAE* 1961, 201ff. (inscribed vases); 1965, 183ff. (*kouros* in situ, inscribed urn); 1966, 135ff. (*lebetes gamikoi*); *ADelt* xvii (1962) B. 269 (relief block); xix (1964) B. 409 (*phallos*); *Ergon* 1966, 115ff. (*lebetes gamikoi*); 1968, 93ff.; 1969, 164ff.

THE PELOPONNESE

Aegina. G. Welter, *Aigina* (1938) 52ff.; *AE* 1913, 88ff.; *AA* 1938, 30f. (*stele* crown), 510ff.; *ADelt* xviii (1963) B. 51; xix (1964) 74 (painted inscr. on sarcophagus); xxi (1966) B. 100ff.; xxii (1967) B. 146f.; Jeffery, 111.

Alipheira (Arcadia). A. K. Orlandos, *Arkadike Alipheira* (1967–8).

Argos. Mainly Geometric—*BCH* lxxvii-lxxxiii (1953–9) in Chronique des Fouilles; lxxxi (1957) 332ff. (warrior grave); *ADelt* xvii (1961–2) B. 55ff.; *AAA* ii (1969) 159ff.; iii (1970) 180ff. Classical—*ADelt* xv (1933–5) 16ff.

Asine. *Opusc. Ath.* vi (1965) 117ff.

Corinth. *Corinth* iii.2, 297ff.; vii.1; xiii (North Cemetery); *AJA* xl (1936) 43; (1937) 543ff. (linked tombs); *Hesperia* xi (1942) 143ff. (*heroon*); xvii (1948) 204; xxxi (1962) 133 (*kline*); xxxiii (1964) 89ff.; xxxvii (1968) 345ff. (Lechaion); xxxviii (1969) 5f. (stone markers); xxxix (1970) 12ff.

Diolkos. *AM* lxxi (1956) 57ff.

Kalamata. *ADelt* xx (1965) B. 207.

Karpophora (Messenia). *AAA* i (1968) 205ff. (PG *tholos*).

Kythera. C. Blümel, *Antike Kunstwerke* (1953) no. 7 (lion).

Lerna. *Hesperia* xxiii (1954) 7; xxv (1956) 171f.

Megalopolis. E. A. Gardner, *Megalopolis* (1893) 9f.

Mycenae. *AE* 1912, 127ff.; *BSA* xlix (1954) 259ff.; l (1955) 239ff.; li (1956) 128ff.

Myloi. *AE* 1955, Chronika 1ff.

Nauplion. *PAE* 1953, 191ff.; 1954, 232ff.; 1955, 234.

Navarino. *ADelt* xxi (1966) B. 164f.; *AAA* i (1968) 191ff.

Perachora. H. Payne, *Perachora* i (1940) 7.

Pharai (Achaia). *PAE* 1956, 196ff.; 1957, 11.

Pylos. *AJA* lxiii (1959) 127 (PG *tholos*).

Sicyon. *PAE* 1951, 189 (vase inscribed *heroos*); *ADelt* xxii (1967) B. 164ff.

Sparta. *BSA* xii (1905–6) 281; xiii (1906–7) 155f.; *ADelt* xix (1964) A. 123ff., 283–5 (Archaic); Jeffery, 201f. (Peloponnesian War *stelai*).

Stymphalos. *PAE* 1928, 120ff. (chamber tomb).

Theisoa (Arcadia). *AAA* i (1968) 189ff.

Tiryns. W. Müller and F. Oelmann, *Tiryns* i (1912) 127ff.; *AM* lxxviii (1963) 1ff.; *ADelt* xxii (1967) B. 180.

Troizen. G. Welter, *Troizen und Kalaureia* (1941) 39ff.; *Tiryns* i, 134.

Tsopani Rachi (Messenia). *ADelt* xviii (1963) B. 91ff. (tumulus, stone astragal).

Zygouries. C. W. Blegen, *Zygouries* (1928) 67f.

CENTRAL GREECE

Abai (Phocis). *PAE* 1906, 144.

Alyzia (Acarnania). *PAE* 1930, 141ff. (altar *heroon*).

Anaktorion. *ADelt* ii (1916) B. 50; *AE* 1953/4, 3; 1955, Chronika 16ff. (Hellenistic enclosure).

Anthedon. *AM* iii (1878) 389 (lion).

Corcyra. C. Rodenwaldt, *Korkyra* ii (1939) 176ff. (lions); J. F. Crome in *Mnemosyne* T. *Wiegand* (1938) 52 (Menekrates); *ADelt* xvii (1962) B. 204ff.; xix (1964) B. 315; xx (1965) B. 395.

Chaeronea. *AM* xxviii (1903) 301ff.; *Klio* xxxi (1938) 216f.; *AJA* lxii (1958) 311; A. S. F. Gow and D. L. Page, *The Garland of Meleager* (1968) ii, 295.

Delphi. P. le Bas, *Voyage Archéologique* (1847/58) pl. 40.1 (tomb door); *Fouilles de Delphes* v (1908) 163, 174f.; *BCH* lxi (1937) 44ff. (PG chamber tomb); *ADelt* xix (1964) B. 218; xx (1965) B. 299ff. (chamber); xxii (1967) B. 291 (pit).

Dritsa (Boeotia). *PAE* 1911, 140.

Euboea, general. G. A. Papabasileios, *Peri ton en Euboia archaion taphon* (1910); *BSA* lxi (1966) 33ff.

Euboea, Chalcis. *PAE* 1900, 63; 1902, 61ff.

Euboea, Eretria. *AE* 1886, 31ff.; 1903, 1ff.; *AM* xxvi (1901) 334ff. (chamber tomb); xxxviii (1913) 289ff.; *BSA* xlvii (1952) 1ff. (grave vases); *ADelt* xx (1965) 270f.; xxii (1967) B. 273ff. (*heroon*); xxiii (1968) B. 230f.; *Antike Kunst* ix (1966) 120ff.; xii (1969) 74ff. (*heroon*); C. Bérard, *Eretria* iii (1970).

Euboea, Lefkandi. *Arch. Reports 1967/8* 12; *AAA* ii (1969) 98ff.

Euboea, Vathia. *AM* xxvi (1901) 366ff. (Mac. tomb).

Halai. *Hesperia* xi (1942) 365ff.

Haliartos. *AE* 1967, Chronika 20ff.

Ithaca. *BSA* xlvii (1952) 227ff.

Kalydon. E. Dyggve, *Das Heroon von Kalydon* (1934).

Kephallenia. *AE* 1932, 3ff.; 1933, 68ff.

Leukas. W. Dörpfeld, *Alt-Ithaka* (1927) 250ff.; *AAA* iii (1970) 70f. (Hellenistic enclosure).

Medeon (Phocis). *ADelt* xix (1964) B. 224; C. Vatin, *Médéon de Phocide* (1969).

Megara. *AE* 1933, 120f.; *AAA* ii (1969) 339ff.

Myonia (Ozolian Locris). *AE* 1927–8, 106ff. (warrior grave).

Oineona (Locris). *PAE* 1906, 131ff. (chamber tomb).

Plataea. *PAE* 1899, 46f.

Rhitsona. *JHS* lxxxvii (1967) 128ff. (review of contents); *BSA* xiv (1907–8) 226ff.; *JHS* xxix (1909) 308ff.; xxx (1910) 336ff.; *AE* 1912, 102ff.; P. N. Ure, *Black Glaze Pottery* (1913), *Aryballoi and Figurines* (1934), *Sixth and Fifth Century Pottery* (1927).

Tanagra. B. Haussoullier, *Quomodo sepulchra Tanagraei decoraverunt* (1884); *PAE* 1887, 64; 1911, 132ff.; *AA* 1912, 240 (chamber tomb); *AM* x (1885) 159ff. (painted slabs).

Thebes. *ADelt* iii (1917) 25f. (painted *stele*), 211f.; xx (1965) B. pl. 284a (reused *stelai*); xxi (1966) B. 196f.; xxii (1967) 231ff.; xxiii (1968) B. 223 and *AE* 1967, Chronika 15f. (chamber tomb).

Thermopylae. *PAE* 1899, 82; Y. Béquignon, *La Vallée du Spercheios* (1937) 240f.; *AJA* lxii (1958) 212.

Thespiae. *PAE* 1882, 67ff.; 1911, 153ff.; Jeffery, 93f.

Trichonion (Aetolia). *AE* 1906, 69ff. (chamber tomb).

Vranesi. *PAE* 1904, 39ff.; *AM* xxx (1905) 132f.

NORTH GREECE

GENERAL

S. Casson, *Macedonia, Thrace and Illyria* (1926); N. G. L. Hammond, *Epirus* (1967).

MACEDONIA AND CHALCIDICE

Aivasil. *BSA* xxiii (1916–17) 18f.

Amphipolis. O. Broneer, *The Lion Monument at Amphipolis* (1941); *Ergon* 1959, 37ff.; 1960, 67ff., 76 (*stelai*); *Actes Congr. Arch. Class.* viii (1965) pl. 52.2 (siren). Mac. tombs—*BCH* xxii (1898) 335ff.; *Ergon* 1957, 36ff.; 1958, 71ff.; 1961, 66f.; 1965, 32.

Angisti. *AAA* i (1968) 249f. (Mac. tomb).

Chauchitsa. *BSA* xxiv (1919–21) 6ff.; xxvi (1923–5) 1ff.; *Opusc. Ath.* ix (1969) 21ff.

Derveni. *ADelt* xviii (1963) 193ff.

Dion. *ADelt* xxi (1966) B. pl. 369 (*trapeza*). Mac. tombs—*PAE* 1930, 36ff. (cf. *Antiquity* 1970, 143f.); 1956, 131ff.

Edessa. *ADelt* xxi (1966) B. 343ff. (chamber tomb).

Karytsa. *PAE* 1955, 151ff. (Mac. tomb).

Kastas (Amphipolis). *Ergon* 1960, 69ff. (Mac. tomb); 1965, 33ff. (tumulus).

Kilkis. *BCH* lxxviii (1954) 140 (Mac. tomb).

Kozani. *AE* 1948–9, 85ff.; *PAE* 1950, 281ff. (crossed graves); 1958, 96f.; 1960, 107.

Laïna. *BSA* xxiii (1918–19) 14f. (Mac. tomb).

Lakkoma. *BCH* lxxxv (1961) 812ff. (Mac. tomb).

Langaza. Mac. tombs—*JdI* xxvi (1911) 193ff.; *Balkan Studies* iii (1962) 449.

Lefkadia (Naoussa). Mac. tombs—P. Petsas, *O Taphos ton Lefkadion* (1966); *Atti VII Congr. Arch. Class.* i (1961) 401ff.; *Makedonika* ii (1953) 634ff.; *AA* 1943, 325ff.

Naoussa. *BCH* lxxviii (1954) 140 (Mac. tombs).

Niausta. K. F. Kinch, *Le tombeau de Niausta* (1920, Mac. tomb).

Nigrita. *ADelt* xxi (1966) B. 365ff. (Mac. tomb).

Nikesiani (Amphipolis). Tumulus—*Actes Congr. Arch. Class.* viii (1965) 297f.; *Ergon* 1959, 44ff.

Olynthus. D. M. Robinson, *Excavations at Olynthus* xi (1942); ii (1930) 60ff. (House of the Tombstone Carver).

Palatitsa. L. Heuzey and H. Daumet, *Mission archéologique de Macédoine* (1876) pl. 15 (Mac. tomb).

Pella. *ADelt* xx (1965) B. 416ff.; *Balkan Studies* i, 113ff. (Mac. tomb).

Philippi. *ADelt* xix (1964) B. 372ff. (Mac. tomb).

Potidaia. *ADelt* xxi (1966) B. 342 (chamber tomb).

Pydna. Heuzey-Daumet, *op. cit.*, pl. 17 (Mac. tomb; the *klinai* in the Louvre).

Salonika. *BSA* xxiii (1918–19) 38f.; *Makedonika* ii (1953) 599ff. Mac. tombs— *BSA* xxiii (1918–19) 40 (Monastir Road); *AA* 1943, 321ff.; *ADelt* xxii (1967) B. 399ff.; *Makedonika* ix (1969) 167ff. (A. Athanasios).

Sedes (Salonika). *AE* 1937. iii, 866ff. (chamber tombs).

Sermyle. *ADelt* ix (1924–5) B. 36ff.

Serrai (Aedonochori). *Heroon—AAA* i (1968) 248; *ADelt* xxii (1967) B. 423f.; xxiii (1968) B. 358.

Siderokastro. *ADelt* xxii (1967) B. 427 (Mac. tomb).

Stravroupolis. *PAE* 1953, 133ff. (Mac. tomb).

Syllata. *ADelt* xix (1964) A. 84ff.

Toumba. Petsas in *Charisterion . . . Orlandos* iii, 233ff.

Vergina. M. Andronikos, *Vergina* i (1969); *Atti VI Congr. preist. protost.* iii (1966) 3ff.; *PAE* 1953, 148ff. (chamber tomb); *ADelt* xvii (1961–2) A. 218ff.; xviii (1963) B. 217ff.; K. Romaios, *Makedonikos taphos tes Verginas* (1951); *Balkan Studies* v (1964) 301f. (painted *stele*); *Makedonika* ix (1969) 225ff.

Verroia. *AE* 1955, 22ff.; *ADelt* xviii (1963) B. 212; xix (1964) 351 (chamber tombs); xxii (1967) B. pl. 309e (*loutrophoros*), 407ff. (Mac. tomb); xxiii (1968) B. 345.

THRACE

Abdera. *ADelt* xx (1965) B. 460ff.; *Ergon* 1966, 61ff.
Elaeus. *BCH* xxxix (1915) 155ff.
Kazanlik. *AJA* xlix (1945) 402ff.
Kirkkilise. *BSA* xvii (1910–11) 76ff.; A. Mansel, *Kubbeli Mezarlari* (1943).
Maltepe. *AA* 1931, 418f.
Oisyme. *ADelt* xx (1965) 447ff.; *AAA* ii (1969) 198ff.

EPIRUS AND THE NORTH-WEST

Arta (Ambracia). *ADelt* xx (1965) B. 355ff.; *ADelt* x (1926) 63ff. (Hellenistic enclosure); *PAE* 1957, 85ff.
Corcyra. *ADelt* xvii (1961–2) B. 204; xviii (1963) B. 159; xix (1964) B. 315; xx (1965) B. 395; *AAA* iii (1970) 68ff.
Kassope. *PAE* 1952, 326ff. (Mac. tomb).
Preveza (Michalitsa). *ADelt* xvii (1962) B. 189f.; xix (1964) B. 306ff.; *AAA* iii (1970) 41ff. (enclosure with statues).
Vitsa Zagoriou. *ADelt* xxii (1967) B. 346ff.; xxiii (1968) B. 287ff.

THESSALY

Chyretiai. *PAE* 1914, 168.
Gonnokondylon. *PAE* 1911, 324ff. (*heroa?*).
Gremnos. *AA* 1956, 171ff. (tumulus).
Halos. *BSA* xviii (1911–12) 3ff.
Iolkos. *PAE* 1911, 303; 1960, 53ff.
Krannon. *ADelt* xvi (1960) B. 177ff.; *AA* 1960, 176f.; *Thessalika* iii (1960) 29ff.
Lamia. *AA* 1936, 131 (chamber tomb).
Larisa. F. Stählin, *Das hellenische Thessalien* (1924) 99; *AE* 1909, 27ff. (Mac. tomb).
Marmariani. *BSA* xxxi (1930–1) 1ff.
Omolion. *ADelt* xvii (1961–2) 175ff.
Pagasai–Demetrias. F. Stählin, *Pagasai und Demetrias* (1934) 132ff.
Paspalia. *PAE* 1909, 159ff. (man and dog).
Pelinna. *AAA* iii (1970) 208ff.
Pharsalos. *AE* 1950–1, 80ff. (Orphic band); *PAE* 1951, 155ff.; 1952, 199ff.; 1955, 140ff. (enclosures, *tholoi*).
Pherai. *PAE* 1907, 153ff. (*heroon*).
Pilaf-tepe. *JHS* xx (1900) 20ff. (tumulus).
Theotokou. *BSA* xiii (1906–7) 321f.

ISLANDS

Lemnos. *Annuario* xv/xvi (1932–3).
Samothrace. K. Lehmann, *Guide to Samothrace* (1966); *Archaeology* xvii (1964) 185ff.

Tenedos. *AJA* lxvii (1963) 189f. (chamber tomb).

Thasos. Jeffery, 300f. (*mnema* of Glaukos).

WESTERN GREEK COLONIES

Acragas. *NSc* 1925, 420ff.; *Fasti Archeologici* i (1946) 722 (mass grave); *Quaderni di arch. Agrigento* iii, 29ff.; Lawrence, *Greek Architecture* 221 (Tomb of Theron, etc.); P. Marconi, *Agrigento* (1929) 102 (triglyph sarcophagus).

Brindisi. *Atti e Mem. Soc. Magna Grecia* v (1964) 111ff.

Camarina. *Mon. Ant.* ix (1899) 201ff. (*cippi, loutrophoros*); xiv (1904) 783ff.; B. Pace, *Camarina* (1927) 111f. (stone tumuli).

Catania. *NSc* 1918, 68ff.

Caulonia. *Mon. Ant.* xxiii (1914) 906ff.

Croton. *NSc* 1932, 364ff.

Cumae. *Mon. Ant.* xiii (1903) 225ff.; xxii (1913).

Gela. *Mon. Ant.* xvii (1906) 232ff. (*cippi*); *NSc* 1932, 137ff. (killed strigil); 1956, 281ff.; 1960, 137ff.; *AA* 1954, 630 (Butera).

Gioia del Colle. *Mon. Ant.* xlv (1961) 144ff.

Himera. *Arch. Reports 1966–7* 41.

Ischia. *Röm. Mitt.* lx/lxi (1953–4) 37ff.; *Atti e Mem. Soc. Magna Grecia* i (1954) 11ff.; *Expedition* viii (1966) 4ff.; *JdI* lxxxi (1966) 1ff.

Leontinoi. *NSc.* 1941, 120ff.; 1955, 289ff.

Locri. *NSc* 1911 Suppl. 3ff.; 1913 Suppl. 4ff. (cenotaph?); 1917, 101ff. (*cippi*); *AA* 1966, 337.

Megara Hyblaea. *Mon. Ant.* i (1889) 766ff. (*cippi, kouros*); xxvii (1921) 180ff.; *NSc* 1949, 193f.; 1954, 80ff. (goddess with twins, *kouros*, horsemen), 390ff.; 1956, 168f.; *AA* 1964, 713ff. (rider relief); G. Vallet and F. Villard, *Megara Hyblaea* iv (1966) 55 (*naiskos* with *kouros*).

Metapontum. *NSc* 1940, 54ff.; 1966, 186ff.; *Arch. Reports 1966–7* 34.

Mylai. *AA* 1954, 545f.

Naxos. *NSc* 1903, 67.

Paestum. *NSc* 1948, 185ff. (*cippus*); 1951, 135ff.; *AA* 1956, 405ff. Painted tombs—P. Sestieri, in *Riv. Ist. Arch.* N. S. v/vi (1956–7) 65ff. (summary in *Arch. Reports 1957* 36ff.); *Atti e Mem.* ix/x (1968–9). Cenotaph— *Boll. d'Arte* xl, 53ff.; B. Neutsch, *Tes numphas emi hiaron* (1957).

Palermo. *Kokalos* xii (1966) 234ff.; *NSc* 1969, 277ff.

Rhegion. *NSc* 1942, 166ff.; 1957, 381ff.

Selinus. *AA* 1964, 782ff.; *NSc* 1966, 298ff.; 1968, 293ff.

Spina. *Spina e l'Etruria padana* (1959) 25ff.

Syracuse. *NSc* 1895, 109ff. (CXLII contracted); 1897, 471ff. (*cippi*); 1905, 381ff. (painted *cippus*); 1907, 743; 1925, 176ff., 296ff.; 1943, 33ff.; 1961, 405; *AJA* lxii (1966) 259ff. (early).

Tarentum. *NSc* 1906, 468ff.; 1936, 109ff.; 1940, 426ff.; 1964, 257ff. (Satyrion); *AA* 1966, 284ff.; *Atti e Mem.* viii (1967) 31ff. (athletes' tombs); *Annuario* xxxvii/viii (1959–60) 7ff.

Thapsos. *BCH* lxxvi (1952) 337.

Zancle. *NSc* 1954, 51ff.

BLACK SEA COLONIES

All early sources are well reviewed in E. Minns, *Scythians and Greeks* (1913). We add selected references to some later works.

Apollonia. *Sov. Arch.* 1969, 75 (painted *stele*).

Istros. *Dacia* iii (1959) 143ff.; *Histria* (ed. Condurachi) ii, 409ff.

Kallatis. *Dacia* v (1961) 275ff.

Kerch. *Materials and Researches* lxix (1959) 108ff.

Mesembria. *AM* xxxvi (1911) 308ff.

Nymphaeum. *Materials and Researches* lxix (1959) 5ff.

Sinope. E. Akurgal and L. Budde, *Vorläuf. Bericht* (1956) 33 ff.

CYRENAICA

Cyrene. J. Cassels, *BSR* xxiii (1955) 1ff.; A. Rowe, *Cyrenaican Expeditions of the University of Manchester* (1956, 1959); *BSA* lxii (1967) 241ff. (false façades). Aniconic and other busts—Cassels, *op. cit.*, 5; F. Chamoux, *Cyrène sous les Battiades* 293ff.; E. Rosenbaum, *Catalogue of Cyrenaican Portrait Sculpture* (1960) 14.

Messa. *Libya Antiqua* i (1964) 127ff.

Tolmeita Mausoleum. *Quaderni di archeologia della Libia* iii (1954) 33ff.